# Philippine
COOKING     IN     AMERICA

**MRS. MARILYN RANADA DONATO, B.S., R.D.**
Registered Dietitian of the American Dietetic Association
Nutrition Counselor - Diet Therapy Consultant
B.S. Foods and Nutrition, Holy Spirit College, Manila, Philippines

## SEVENTH REVISED EDITION

| | |
|---|---|
| First Printing, | 1972 |
| Second Printing, | 1973 |
| Third Printing, | 1975 |

Fourth Printing, Revised Edition, 1977

Fifth Printing,        1979

Sixth Printing, Second Revised Edition, 1980

Seventh Printing, Third Revised Edition, 1982

Eighth Printing, Fourth Revised Edition, 1985

Ninth Printing, Fifth Revised Edition, 1987

Tenth Printing, Sixth Revised Edition, 1991

Eleventh Printing, Seventh Revised Edition, 1995

Copyright, 1972, 1977, 1980, 1982, 1985, 1987, 1991, 1995 by **Marilyn Ranada Donato**

All rights reserved. This book, or parts thereof, must not be reproduced in any form without permission.

Library of Congress Catalog Card Number A-451287

Printed in the United States of America

**Copyright 1968-1995 by CIRCULATION SERVICE, INC., P.O. Box 7306, Leawood, Kansas 66207
World's Largest Publisher of Personalized Cook Books
Fund Raising Programs and Programs of Service
For Church, School and Civic Organizations
Printed in the United States of America**

## INTRODUCTION

For the many Filipinos in America, Canada and other countries, Philippine cooking is an inherent must.

A Filipino who leaves the Philippines to go to other countries for study, for permanent residence or for a visit, will long for his homeland's dishes, aggravated by his inexperience at cooking. It is with this situation in mind that this book is written. May this book be of help to the beginners, thus making them feel less homesick and to the "expert" ones may it serve as a good reference for everyday menu planning and preparation.

The recipes compiled have been kitchen-tested and adjusted to availability, practicality and acceptance to American environs. Substitutions may be made to certain food ingredients; and variations in measurements and seasonings may be made to suit the individual's taste and preference. Flexibility makes cooking more fun. Experience is the best teacher. Try and try again is a good motto to have.

To all those who want adventure in their taste for foreign dishes, this book offers an exciting one. Philippine cooking is an exotic blending of Spanish, Chinese, Japanese, Malayan and American cultural influences.

## PREFACE TO THE SEVENTH REVISED EDITION
## ELEVENTH PRINTING, 1995

Since 1972, easier Philippine recipes have evolved. Of note is the availability of new products, such as packaged mixes for sinigang, palabok or luglug, Oriental sauces, powdered or frozen coconut milk, powdered achuete, fried garlic granules, flaked smoked fish, to name a few. All of these make cooking easier and more fun.

Keep checking the food stores for new products. Times are exciting! Experiment with the new products, this way you can find out how, when and where to use the ingredient best. Also, try substituting the more convenient product for the traditional. Microwave cooking of Philippine recipes is another exciting experiment to try.

Let us eat, drink and be merry, for tomorrow we diet! And diet we must. In the event there is interest and commitment in trying A DIET TO LIVE WITH, 1200 - 1500 CALORIE CONTROLLED DAILY DIET GUIDELINES found within Basic Kitchen Information, Thumb Index, which are un-numbered pages immediately after Page 8, I have designed meal plans which to me is the most important of this newest cookbook revision. It would please me no end, even if only you take a peek at it. Thank you!

## CONTENTS

| | |
|---|---:|
| Introduction .................................................................. | 3 |
| Preface to the Seventh Revised Edition, | |
|     Eleventh Printing, 1995 ........................................ | 4 |
| Acknowledgement ......................................................... | 6 |
| Tips and Notes from the Author ................................. | 7 |
| Basic Kitchen Information : A Diet to Live With | |
|     1200 - 1500 Calorie Controlled Daily Diet Guidelines | 8a |
|     Desirable Weight to Aim For | 8c |
| Recipe Section - | |
|     Appetizers, Pickles, Relishes ............................ | 9 |
|     Soups, Salads ....................................................... | 13 |
|     Meat, Fish, Poultry .............................................. | 25 |
|     Eggs, Cheese, Casserole ..................................... | 69 |
|     Vegetables ............................................................ | 83 |
|     Breads, Rolls, Pies, Pastry ................................. | 89 |
|     Cakes, Cookies, Icing .......................................... | 99 |
|     Desserts ................................................................. | 107 |
|     Candy, Jelly, Jam, Preserves ............................ | 119 |
|     Beverages and Miscellaneous ........................... | 123 |
| Substitutions for Philippine Items ............................. | 125 |
| How to Extract Fresh Coconut Milk .......................... | 126 |
| How to Bone a Chicken ............................................... | 127 |
| How to Cook a Husband (Spouse?) ........................... | 127 |
| Dinner Menus ............................................................... | 129 |
| Party Menus ................................................................. | 130 |
| Illustrations of  1.) Ingredients ................................. | 131 |
|                     2.) Cutting Method ........................ | 135 |
| Glossary ......................................................................... | 137 |
| Index ............................................................................... | 143 |
| About the Author ......................................................... | 151 |
| Book Order ................................................................... | 152 |

## ACKNOWLEDGMENT OF APPRECIATION

I want to express my appreciation to those who gave unsparingly of their time and help in the completion of this cookbook.

Special acknowledgment to:

Amparo Tuason Donato

Virginia Escobar Leffel

Dr. and Mrs. Florencio A. Hipona

Antonio T. Donato, M.D., my husband

*Marilyn R. Donato, R.D.*

Marilyn R. Donato, R.D.

## TIPS AND NOTES FROM THE AUTHOR

Before using any recipe:
1. Read and understand every word of the recipe from beginning to end. Know what you are going to do and how.
2. Have ingredients and equipment on hand.
3. Measure all ingredients carefully.
4. Follow directions for cooking. The experienced cook may take liberties with or make changes in a recipe.

Abbreviations Used:
   Tbsp. - tablespoon
   tsp. - teaspoon
   lb. - pound
   oz. - ounce
   MSG - monosodium glutamate

About MSG (monosodium glutamate), I must say that I find MSG to greatly improve the taste of the many dishes contained herein. Use MSG when you have it, but it is not an indispensable ingredient in the recipes which call for it.

Rice is a staple Philippine food. Check that the rice you buy is enriched. Plain boiled rice is served with almost all of the main dishes. An electric rice cooker becomes a most useful piece of equipment, for a family or an individual, assuring one of rice being cooked automatically, to perfection.

Vinegar used in the recipes is white distilled. With so many types of vinegar available here, use any with discretion according to one's taste.

The use of vegetable oil, preferably the polyunsaturates (corn oil, sesame oil, cottonseed oil, soybean oil, sunflower oil and safflower oil), is endorsed to lower cholesterol intake. Lard and animal fat have a high cholesterol content. Trim off visible fat in meat and skim off fat in cooked dishes.

As you know recipes for dishes can have several variations. What may be a recipe of "Adobo" to one may be done a different way by another, with the addition or omission of one or more ingredient. Be creative and do your own thing, yet not losing the characteristic of a particular dish.

Perhaps the name of an ingredient is unfamiliar (check the Glossary), but you will find that all ingredients are easily come by today in any American city. They can be obtained from local supermarkets and Oriental food stores near your area. Canvass.

A typical Philippine table serves 5 - 6 dishes (including plain boiled rice and dessert). The servings in the recipes have been portioned in such that 2 or more dishes are served. Use the servings specified in the recipes as a guide.

I have included information on basic nutrition with the hope that you will follow nutritional food eating habits.

To each and everyone good health and happy eating!

# The Basic Kitchen Information Pages™

**THUMB INDEX**

- REMOVE STAINS
- PARTY PLANNING
- 6 STEPS TO THE PERFECT PIE
- TIME TABLE for MEAT COOKERY
- FREEZING PREPARED FOODS
- EVERYDAY HERB GUIDE
- A DIET TO LIVE WITH
- QUANTITIES TO SERVE 100 PEOPLE
- BURNING UP CALORIES
- FIRST AID for HOUSEHOLD EMERGENCIES, HOW TO CONVERT TO METRIC SYSTEM
- STEAK COOKING CHART, PARENTS' GLOSSARY, MISCELLANEOUS INFORMATION

## Expression of Appreciation

For their help and cooperation in providing this indexed, up-to-date, authentic information of basic value to our book, our organization and the sponsors wish to thank the helpful institutions, businesses, Governmental agencies and the home economists who worked on it.

National Live Stock and Meat Board.

U.S. Department of Agriculture.

Armour and Co.

Wheat Flour Institute.

Copyright 1968-1994 by CIRCULATION SERVICE, INC.
P.O. Box 7306, Leawood, Kansas 66207

## EQUIVALENTS

| | |
|---|---|
| 3 tsps. | 1 tbsp. |
| 4 tbsps. | ¼ cup |
| 5⅓ tbsps. | ⅓ cup |
| 8 tbsps. | ½ cup |
| 10⅔ tbsps. | ⅔ cup |
| 12 tbsps. | ¾ cup |
| 16 tbsps. | 1 cup |
| ½ cup | 1 gill |
| 2 cups | 1 pt. |
| 4 cups | 1 qt. |
| 4 qts. | 1 gal. |
| 8 qts. | 1 peck |
| 4 pecks | 1 bu. |
| 16 ozs. | 1 lb. |
| 32 ozs. | 1 qt. |
| 8 ozs. liquid | 1 cup |
| 1 oz. liquid | 2 tbsps. |

(For liquid and dry measurements use standard measuring spoons and cups. All measurements are level.)

## WEIGHTS AND MEASURES

**Baking powder**
  1 cup = 5½ ozs.

**Cheese, American**
  1 lb. = 2⅔ cups cubed

**Cocoa**
  1 lb. = 4 cups ground

**Coffee**
  1 lb. = 5 cups ground

**Corn meal**
  1 lb. = 3 cups

**Cornstarch**
  1 lb. = 3 cups

**Cracker crumbs**
  23 soda crackers = 1 cup
  15 graham crackers = 1 cup

**Eggs**
  1 egg = 4 tbsps. liquid
  4 to 5 whole = 1 cup
  7 to 9 whites = 1 cup
  12 to 14 yolks = 1 cup

**Flour**
  1 lb. all-purpose = 4 cups
  1 lb. cake = 4½ cups
  1 lb. graham = 3½ cups

**Lemons, juice**
  1 medium = 2 to 3 tbsps.
  5 to 8 medium = 1 cup

**Lemons, rind**
  1 lemon = 1 tbsp. grated

**Oranges, juice**
  1 medium = 2 to 3 tbsps.
  3 to 4 medium = 1 cup

**Oranges, rind**
  1 = 2 tbsps. grated

**Gelatin**
  3¼ oz. pkg. flavored = ½ cup
  ¼ oz. pkg. unflavored = 1 tbsp.

**Shortening or Butter**
  1 lb. = 2 cups

**Sugar**
  1 lb. brown = 2½ cups
  1 lb. cube = 96 to 160 cubes
  1 lb. granulated = 2 cups
  1 lb. powdered = 3½ cups

# To Remove STAINS From Washables

## ALCOHOLIC BEVERAGES
Pre-soak or sponge fresh stains immediately with cold water, then with cold water and glycerine. Rinse with vinegar for a few seconds if stain remains. These stains may turn brown with age. If wine stain remains, rub with concentrated detergent; wait 15 min.; rinse. Repeat if necessary. Wash with detergent in hottest water safe for fabric.

## BLOOD
Pre-soak in cold or warm water at least 30 minutes. If stain remains, soak in lukewarm ammonia water (3 tablespoons ammonia per gallon water). Rinse. If stain remains, work in detergent, and wash, using bleach safe for fabric.

## CANDLE WAX
Use a dull knife to scrape off as much wax as possible. Place fabric between two blotters or facial tissues and press with warm iron. Remove color stain with non-flammable dry cleaning solvent. Wash with detergent in the hottest water safe for fabric.

## CHEWING GUM
Rub area with ice, then scrape off with dull blade. Sponge with dry cleaning solvent; allow to air dry. Wash in detergent and hottest water safe for fabric.

## CHOCOLATE AND COCOA
Pre-soak stain in cold or warm water. Wash in hot water with detergent. Remove any grease stains with dry cleaning solvent. If color remains, sponge with hydrogen peroxide, wash again.

## COFFEE
Sponge or soak with cold water as soon as possible. Wash, using detergent and bleach safe for fabric. Remove cream grease stain with non-flammable dry cleaning solvent. Wash again.

## CRAYON
Scrape with dull blade. Wash in hottest water safe for fabric, with detergent and 1-2 cups of baking soda.
**NOTE:** If full load is crayon stained, take to cleaners or coin-op dry cleaning machines.

## DEODORANTS
Sponge area with white vinegar. If stain remains, soak with denatured alcohol. Wash with detergent in hottest water safe for fabric.

## DYE
If dye transfers from a non-colorfast item during washing, immediately bleach discolored items. Repeat as necessary BEFORE drying. On whites use color remover.
**CAUTION:** Do not use color remover in washer, or around washer and dryer as it may damage the finish.

# To Remove STAINS From Washables

## EGG
Scrape with dull blade. Pre-soak in cold or warm water for at least 30 minutes. Remove grease with dry cleaning solvent. Wash in hottest water safe for fabric, with detergent.

## FRUIT AND FRUIT JUICES
Sponge with cold water. Pre-soak in cold or warm water for at least 30 minutes. Wash with detergent and bleach safe for fabric.

## GRASS
Pre-soak in cold water for at least 30 minutes. Rinse. Pre-treat with detergent. Wash, using detergent, hot water, and bleach safe for fabric. On acetate and colored fabrics, use 1 part of alcohol to 2 parts water.

## GREASE, OIL, TAR
Method 1: Use powder or chalk absorbents to remove as much grease as possible. Pre-treat with detergent or non-flammable dry cleaning solvent, or liquid shampoo. Wash in hottest water safe for fabric, using plenty of detergent.
Method 2: Rub spot with lard and sponge with a non-flammable dry cleaning solvent. Wash in hottest water and detergent safe for fabric.

## INK--BALL-POINT PEN
Pour denatured alcohol through stain. Rub in petroleum jelly. Sponge with non-flammable dry cleaning solvent. Soak in detergent solution. Wash with detergent and bleach safe for fabric.

## INK--FOUNTAIN PEN
Run cold water through stain until no more color will come out. Rub in lemon juice and detergent. Let stand 5 minutes. Wash.
If a yellow stain remains, use a commercial rust remover or oxalic acid, as for rust stains.
**CAUTION:** HANDLE POISONOUS RUST REMOVERS CAREFULLY. KEEP OUT OF REACH OF CHILDREN. NEVER USE OXALIC ACID OR ANY RUST REMOVER AROUND WASHER AND DRYER AS IT CAN DAMAGE THE FINISH. SUCH CHEMICALS MAY ALSO REMOVE PERMANENT PRESS FABRIC FINISHES.

## LIPSTICK
Loosen stain with a non-flammable dry cleaning solvent. Rub detergent in until stain outline is gone. Wash in hottest water and detergent safe for fabric.

## MEAT JUICES
Scrape with dull blade. Pre-soak in cold or warm water for 30 minutes. Wash with detergent and bleach safe for fabric.

## MILDEW
Pre-treat as soon as possible with detergent. Wash. If any stain remains, sponge with lemon juice and salt. Dry in sun. Wash, using hottest water, detergent and bleach safe for fabric.
**NOTE:** Mildew is very hard to remove; treat promptly.

# To Remove STAINS From Washables

## MILK, CREAM, ICE CREAM
Pre-soak in cold or warm water for 30 minutes. Wash. Sponge any grease spots with non-flammable dry cleaning solvent. Wash again.

## NAIL POLISH
Sponge with polish remover or banana oil. Wash. If stain remains, sponge with denatured alcohol to which a few drops of ammonia have been added. Wash again. Do not use polish remover on acetate or triacetate fabrics.

## PAINT
-oil base
Sponge stains with turpentine, cleaning fluid or paint remover. Pre-treat and wash in hot water. For old stains, sponge with banana oil and then with non-flammable dry cleaning solvent. Wash again.
-water base
Scrape off paint with dull blade. Wash with detergent in water as hot as is safe for fabric.

## PERSPIRATION
Sponge fresh stain with ammonia; old stain with vinegar. Pre-soak in cold or warm water. Rinse. Wash in hottest water safe for fabric. If fabric is yellowed, use bleach. If stain still remains, dampen and sprinkle with meat tenderizer, or pepsin. Let stand 1 hour. Brush off and wash. For persistent odor, sponge with colorless mouthwash.

## RUST
Soak in lemon juice and salt or oxalic solution (3 tablespoons oxalic acid to 1 pint warm water). A commercial rust remover may be used.
**CAUTION:** HANDLE POISONOUS RUST REMOVERS CAREFULLY. KEEP OUT OF REACH OF CHILDREN. NEVER USE OXALIC ACID OR ANY RUST REMOVER AROUND WASHER OR DRYER AS IT CAN DAMAGE THE FINISH. SUCH CHEMICALS MAY ALSO REMOVE PERMANENT PRESS FABRIC FINISHES.

## SCORCH
Wash with detergent and bleach safe for fabric. On heavier scorching, cover stain with cloth dampened with hydrogen peroxide. Cover this with dry cloth and press with hot iron. Rinse well.
**CAUTION:** Severe scorching cannot be removed because of fabric damage.

## SOFT DRINKS
Sponge immediately with cold water and alcohol. Heat and detergent may set stain.

## TEA
Sponge or soak with cold water as soon as possible. Wash using detergent and bleach safe for fabric.

# PARTY PLANNING

## Buffet Setting

A buffet makes it easy to serve a large group in a small dining area. This setting can be used for any meal by just placing the food in the order of your menu, plates first and eating utensils last.

1. Plates; 2. Main dish;
3. Gravy boat on liner plate;
4. Vegetable dish;
5. Other side dish;
6. Salad bowl; 7. Relish tray; 8. Basket of rolls;
9. Napkins with knives, fork and spoons;
10. Salt and pepper;
11. Centerpiece and candles.

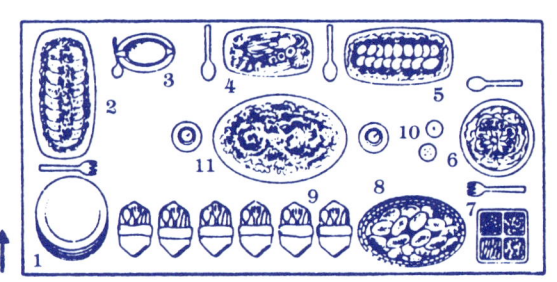

## Luncheon

A luncheon can be great fun no matter what size the crowd. An optional fruit or soup first course could be followed by:
1. Hot casserole or omelet, bread and a light dessert.
2. Cold combination salad, bread and a rich dessert.
3. Small salad, hot main dish and dessert.

1. Bread and butter plate and knife; 2. Water glass; 3. Optional drink glass; 4. Napkin; 5. Luncheon fork; 6. Dessert fork; 7. First course bowl and liner plate; 8. Luncheon plate; 9. Knife; 10. Teaspoon; 11. Soup spoon.

## Dinner

You don't have to wait for a special occasion to have a formal dinner party. Sunday dinners with family and friends is a wonderful reason to celebrate by serving a formal dinner and it will almost guarantee help with the extra dishes!

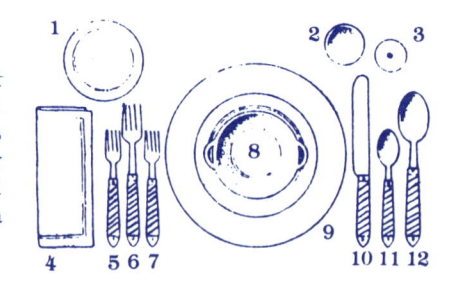

1. Salad plate; 2. Water glass; 3. Optional drink glass; 4. Napkin;
5. Salad fork; 6. Dinner fork; 7. Dessert fork; 8. First-course bowl and liner plate; 9. Dinner plate; 10. Dinner knife; 11. Teaspoon; 12. Soup spoon.

# PARTY PLANNING

## Napkin Folding

Add a final decorative touch to your dinner table by folding napkins into any of the shapes below. Napkins may also be placed on the dinner plates.

### BUTTERFLY

Form a triangle from an open napkin. Fold the right corner to the center.

Take the left corner up to center, making a diamond. Keeping the loose points at the top, turn the napkin over, then fold upward, to form a triangle.

Tuck the left corner into the right. Stand up napkin; turn it round, then turn the petals down; it's now a butterfly.

### ARTICHOKE

Place all 4 points to the center of an opened napkin.

Fold the 4 points to the center of the napkin once more.

Repeat a third time; turn napkin over and fold points to the center once more.

Holding finger firmly at center, unfold 1 petal first from underneath each corner.

Pull out 4 more from between the petals. Then pull out the next 4 under the petals.

The artichoke now has 12 points.

### SILVER BUFFET

Fold the napkin over twice to form a square. Hold the square in a diamond shape.

Take the top 2 flaps and roll them halfway down the napkin.

Fold under the right and left points at the sides. There is now a pocket into which you can place the knife, fork and spoon.

# 6 Easy Steps
## TO THE

**1** The ingredients for the perfect pie crust: 1 teaspoon salt, 2/3 cup vegetable shortening, 2 cups flour, and cold water.

**2** Cut shortening into flour and salt mixture with a fork or pastry blender until crumbs are coarse and granular.

**3** Add 3 to 6 tablespoons cold water, a little at a time. Mix quickly and evenly through the flour until the dough just holds together.

# Perfect Pie

**4** Roll half the dough to about one-eighth inch thickness. Lift edge of pastry cloth and roll crust onto rolling pin. Line pie pan, allowing one-half inch crust to extend over edge.

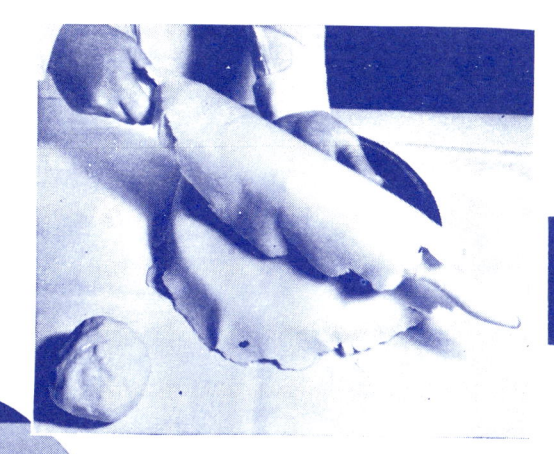

**5** Add filling. Roll out top crust, making several gashes to allow escape of steam. Place over filling. Allow top crust to overlap lower crust. Fold top crust under the lower and crimp edges.

**6** And here is the perfect pie, baked in a moderately hot oven (425° F.) for thirty-five minutes.

# TIME TABLE FOR MEAT COOKERY

## Broiling

| CUT | THICKNESS | WEIGHT RANGE | APPROXIMATE TOTAL TIME (MINUTES) | | |
|---|---|---|---|---|---|
| | | | RARE | MEDIUM | WELL DONE |
| **BEEF** | | | | | |
| Rib Steak | 1 inch | 1-1½ lb. | 8-10 | 12-14 | 18-20 |
| Club Steak | 1 inch | 1-1½ lb. | 8-10 | 12-14 | 18-20 |
| Porterhouse | 1 inch | 1½-2 lbs. | 10-12 | 14-16 | 20-25 |
| | 1½ inch | 2½-3 lbs. | 14-16 | 18-20 | 25-30 |
| | 2 inch | 3-3½ lbs. | 20-25 | 30-35 | 40-45 |
| Sirloin | 1 inch | 2½-3½ lbs. | 10-12 | 14-16 | 20-25 |
| | 1½ inch | 3½-4½ lbs. | 14-16 | 18-20 | 25-30 |
| | 2 inch | 5-5½ lbs. | 20-25 | 30-35 | 40-45 |
| Ground Beef Patties | ¾ inch | 4 oz. each | 8 | 12 | 15 |
| Tenderloin | 1 inch | | 8-10 | 12-14 | 18-20 |
| **LAMB** | | | | | |
| Rib or Loin Chops (1 rib) | ¾ inch | 2-3 oz. each | — | — | 14-15 |
| Double Rib | 1½ inch | 4-5 oz. each | — | — | 22-25 |
| Lamb Shoulder Chops | ¾ inch | 3-4 oz. each | — | — | 14-15 |
| | 1½ inch | 5-6 oz. each | — | — | 22-25 |
| Lamb Patties | ¾ inch | 4 oz. each | — | — | 14-15 |
| **HAM, BACON & SAUSAGE** | | | | | |
| Ham Slices | ½ inch | 9-12 oz. each | — | — | 10-12 |
| | ¾ inch | 1-1¼ lb. | — | — | 13-14 |
| | 1 inch | 1¼-1¾ lbs. | — | — | 18-20 |
| Bacon | | | | | 4-5 |
| Pork Sausage Links | | 12-16 to the lb. | — | — | 12-15 |
| Broiling Chickens (drawn) halves | | 1-1½ lbs. | — | — | 30-35 |

## Stewing

| CUT | WEIGHT RANGE | APPROXIMATE TIME |
|---|---|---|
| Beef—1-1½ inch cubes from neck, chuck, plate or heel of round | 2 lbs. | 2½-3 hours |
| Veal or Lamb 1-1½ inch cubes from shoulder or breast | 2 lbs. | 1½-2 hours |
| Chicken | 3½-4 lbs. | 2-2½ hours |

## Simmering in Water

| CUT | WEIGHT RANGE | APPROXIMATE TIME |
|---|---|---|
| Fresh Beef Brisket or Plate | 8 lbs. | 4-5 hours total |
| Corned Beef Brisket half or whole | 4-8 lbs. | 4-6 hours total |
| Cross Cut Shanks of Beef | 4 lbs. | 3-4 hours total |
| Fresh or Smoked Beef Tongue | 3-4 lbs. | 3-4 hours total |
| Pork Hocks | 3/4 lbs. | 3 hours total |
| Whole Ham | 12-16 lbs. | 18-20 min. per lb. |
| Ham Shanks | 5-6 lbs. | 25-30 min. per lb. |
| Smoked Pork Butt (boneless) | 2-3 lbs. | 40 min. per lb. |
| Picnic | 7-8 lbs. | 35-40 min. per lb. |
| Chicken | 3½-4 lbs. | 2-2½ hours total |

# TIME TABLE FOR MEAT COOKERY

## Roasting

| CUT | WEIGHT RANGE | COOKING TEMP. | INTERNAL MEAT TEMP. | APPROXIMATE TIME |
|---|---|---|---|---|
| **BEEF** | | | | |
| Standing Ribs (3) | 6-8 lbs. | 325° F. | | |
|   Rare | | | 140° F. | 16-18 min. per lb. |
|   Medium | | | 160° F. | 20-22 min. per lb. |
|   Well Done | | | 170° F. | 25-30 min. per lb. |
| Rolled Rib | 5-7 lbs. | 325° F. | | Add 10-12 min. per lb. to above time |
| Rump-boneless | 5-7 lbs. | 325° F. | 170° F. | 30 min. per lb. |
| **VEAL** | | | | |
| Leg (center cut) | 7-8 lbs. | 325° F. | 170° F. | 25 min. per lb. |
| Loin | 4½-5 lbs. | 325° F. | 170° F. | 30-35 min. per lb. |
| Rack 4-6 ribs | 2½-3 lbs. | 325° F. | 170° F. | 30-35 min. per lb. |
| Shoulder-bone-in | 6-7 lbs. | 325° F. | 170° F. | 25 min. per lb. |
| Shoulder Boneless Roll | 5-6 lbs. | 325° F. | 170° F. | 35-40 min. per lb. |
| **LAMB** | | | | |
| Leg | 6-7 lbs. | 325° F. | 175-180° F. | 30-35 min. per lb. |
| Shoulder Bone-in | 5-7 lbs. | 325° F. | 175-180° F. | 30-35 min. per lb. |
| Shoulder Boneless Roll | 4-6 lbs. | 325° F. | 175-180° F. | 40-45 min. per lb. |
| **FRESH PORK** | | | | |
| Loin | 4-5 lbs. | 350° F. | 185° F. | 30-35 min. per lb. |
| Cushion Shoulder | 4-6 lbs. | 350° F. | 185° F. | 35-40 min. per lb. |
| Shoulder Boned & Rolled | 4-6 lbs. | 350° F. | 185° F. | 40-45 min. per lb. |
| Shoulder Butt | 4-6 lbs. | 350° F. | 185° F. | 45-50 min. per lb. |
| Fresh Ham | 10-14 lbs. | 350° F. | 185° F. | 30-35 min. per lb. |
| Spare Ribs (1 side) | 1½-2½ lbs. | 350° F. | 185° F. | 1-1½ hrs. total |
| **SMOKED PORK** | | | | |
| Ham—whole | 10-12 lbs. | 325° F. | 150-155° F. | 18-20 min. per lb. |
| | 14-16 lbs. | 325° F. | 150-155° F. | 16-18 min. per lb. |
| Ham-half | 6-8 lbs. | 325° F. | 150-155° F. | 25-27 min. per lb. |
| Ham—2 inch slice | 2½-3 lbs. | 325° F. | 170° F. | 1½ hrs. total |
| Picnic | 5-8 lbs. | 325° F. | 170° F. | 33-35 min. per lb. |
| **POULTRY** | | | | |
| Chickens stuffed weight | 4-5 lbs. | 325° F. | 185° F. | 35-40 min. per lb. |
| Chickens over 5 lbs. | | 325° F. | 185° F. | 20-25 min. per lb. |
| Turkeys stuffed weight | 6-10 lbs. | 325° F. | 185° F. | 20-25 min. per lb. |
| Turkey | 10-16 lbs. | 325° F. | 185° F. | 18-20 min. per lb. |
| Turkey | 18-25 lb | 325° F. | 185° F. | 15-18 min. per lb. |

Geese—Same as turkey of similar weight.
Duck—Same as heavy chicken of similar weight.

## Braising

| CUT | WEIGHT RANGE | APPROXIMATE TIME |
|---|---|---|
| Beef Pot Roast, Chuck, Rump or Heel of Round | 3-5 lbs. | Brown then simmer 3½-4 hours |
| Swiss Steak (round) 1 in. thick | 2 lbs. | Brown then simmer 1½-2 hours |
| Flank Steak | 1½-2 lbs. | Brown then simmer 1½ hours |
| Beef Short Ribs | 2-2½ lbs. | Brown then simmer 2-2½ hours |
| Ox Tails | 1-1½ lbs. | Brown then simmer 3-4 hours |
| Rolled Lamb Shoulder Pot Roast | 3-5 lbs. | Brown then simmer 2-2½ hours |
| Lamb Shoulder Chops | 4-5 oz. each | Brown then simmer 35-40 min. |
| Lamb Neck Slices | ½ lb. each | Brown then simmer 1-1½ hours |
| Lamb Shanks | 1 lb. each | Brown then simmer 1½ hours |
| Pork Rib or Loin Chops | 4-5 oz. each (¾-1 inch) | Brown then simmer 35-40 min. |
| Pork Shoulder Steaks | 5-6 oz. each | Brown then simmer 35-40 min. |
| Veal Rolled Shoulder Pot Roast | 4-5½ lbs. | Brown then simmer 2-2½ hours |
| Cutlets or Round | 2 lbs. | Brown then simmer 45-50 min. |
| Loin or Rib Chops | 3-5 oz. each | Brown then simmer 45-50 min. |

# Freezing Prepared Foods

## PACKAGING MATERIALS

Materials used for packaging foods for freezing should keep the air out and the moisture in so select containers that are moisture-vapor resistant or the food will dry out.

Waxed papers, household aluminum foil, and cartons for cottage cheese and ice cream are *not suitable*, because they are *not* moisture-vapor-resistant.

Select a *size* that will hold enough vegetable or fruit for a meal for your family.

Select containers that pack easily into a little space.

Consider cost of containers and if they are re-useable, or not. If they are reuseable, a high initial cost may be justified.

- *Rigid* containers are made of aluminum, glass, plastic, tin or heavily waxed cardboard. They can be used for vegetables, fruits, cooked foods or liquids.
- *Non-Rigid* containers-as sheets and bags of cellophane, heavy aluminum foil, plastic film, polyethylene, or laminated paper are used for foods that are firm but irregularly shaped, like poultry, meat, and baked goods.
- *Bags* are generally used inside cartons as moisture resistant liners.

There is no economy in using poor quality packaging materials.

Fill packages carefully, allowing for the necessary head space for the particular kind of food.

Force or draw out as much air as possible, seal tightly, label, freeze immediately, and store at 0° F or lower.

Foods should be frozen in amounts which will ordinarily be eaten in one meal. To treat light colored fruits to prevent darkening, use ascorbic acid. When freezing fruit in sugar syrup, add ½ teaspoon ascorbic acid for each quart syrup. When freezing fruit in dry sugar, sprinkle ascorbic acid dissolved in water over fruit before adding sugar. Use ¼ teaspoon ascorbic acid in ¼ cup cold water to each quart of fruit.

*Freezing Prepared Foods May Not Save Time. It May Allow Time To Be Used To Better Advantage.*

## GENERAL INFORMATION

Prepare the dish as if it were to be served right away, but do not cook quite done. Reheating for serving will finish the cooking.

Cheese or crumb toppings are best added when the food is reheated for serving.

Pastry crumbs frozen unbaked are more tender, and flaky, and have a fresher flavor than those baked and then frozen.

Cool the cooked food quickly. Pour out in shallow pans or place the uncovered pan of food in iced or very cold water; change water to keep it cold.

As soon as the food is cool-60°F or less, pack promptly into moisture-vapor-resistant containers or packaging material. Pack tightly to force out as much air as possible.

To have the food in desired amounts for serving and for quicker defrosting, separate servings with 2 pieces freezer paper.

Since many main dishes are semi-liquid it is desirable to pack them in rigid containers. Foods frozen in containers with wide-mouthed openings do not have to be thawed completely to remove from container.

Some main dishes may be frozen in the containers in which they were baked.

Freezer weight foil (.0015 gauge) may be used to line the baking dish or pan. After the main dish is frozen (unwrapped) in this container, remove from the baking dish and package. The food may be reheated by slipping it and the foil into the baking pan.

Allow head space for freezing liquid and semi-liquid foods. Seal; label; freeze quickly and store at 0° F or lower.

Most precooked, frozen, main dishes are reheated, either in the oven or on top of the range. Reheating in the oven takes little attention and usually preserves the texture of the food better. Reheating on top of the range in a double boiler or a sauce pan is faster. When using a double boiler, start with warm, not hot, water in the lower pan so the food won't stick. Food reheated over direct heat needs to be stirred. This stirring may give a less desirable texture.

If partial thawing is necessary, before the food can be removed from the package, place in luke warm water for a few minutes. Complete thawing should be done in the refrigerator. If it takes more than 3 or 4 hours, thawing at room temperature may cause dangerous spoilage.

It is best to freeze meat pies and turnovers unbaked.

You can use any good meat loaf recipe for freezing. Just make enough for several meals instead of one and freeze the extra loaves.

Nuts are likely to discolor and become bitter when frozen in a salad mixture.

# Suggested Maximum Home-Storage periods To Maintain Good Quality in Purchased Frozen Foods

| Food | Approximate holding period at 0° F. | Food | Approximate holding period at 0° F. |
|---|---|---|---|
| **Fruits and vegetables** | | **Meat - Continued** | |
| Fruits: | Months | Cooked meat: | Months |
| Cherries | 12 | Meat dinners | 3 |
| Peaches | 12 | Meat pie | 3 |
| Raspberries | 12 | Swiss steak | 3 |
| Strawberries | 12 | **Poultry** | |
| Fruit juice concentrates: | | Chicken: | |
| Apple | 12 | Cut-up | 9 |
| Grape | 12 | Livers | 3 |
| Orange | 12 | Whole | 12 |
| Vegetables: | | Duck, whole | 6 |
| Asparagus | 8 | Goose, whole | 6 |
| Beans | 8 | Turkey: | |
| Cauliflower | 8 | Cut-up | 6 |
| Corn | 8 | Whole | 12 |
| Peas | 8 | Cooked chicken and turkey: | |
| Spinach | 8 | Chicken or turkey dinners | |
| **Baked goods** | | (sliced meat and gravy) | 6 |
| Bread and yeast rolls: | | Chicken or turkey pies | 6 |
| White bread | 3 | Fried chicken | 4 |
| Cinnamon rolls | 2 | Fried chicken dinners | 4 |
| Plain rolls | 3 | **Fish and shellfish** | |
| Cakes: | | Fish: | |
| Angel | 2 | Fillets: | |
| Chiffon | 2 | Cod, flounder, haddock, | |
| Chocolate layer | 4 | halibut, pollack | 6 |
| Fruit | 12 | Mullet, ocean perch, sea | |
| Pound | 6 | trout, striped bass | 3 |
| Yellow | 6 | Pacific Ocean perch | 2 |
| Danish pastry | 3 | Salmon steaks | 2 |
| Doughnuts: | | Sea trout, dressed | 3 |
| Cake type | 3 | Striped bass, dressed | 3 |
| Yeast raised | 3 | Whiting, drawn | 4 |
| Pies (unbaked): | | Shellfish: | |
| Apple | 8 | Clams, shucked | 3 |
| Boysenberry | 8 | Crabmeat: | |
| Cherry | 8 | Dungeness | 3 |
| Peach | 8 | King | 10 |
| **Meat** | | Oysters, shucked | 4 |
| Beef: | | Shrimp | 12 |
| Hamburger or chipped | | Cooked fish and shellfish: | |
| (thin) steaks | 4 | Fish with cheese sauce | 3 |
| Roasts | 12 | Fish with lemon butter sauce | 3 |
| Steaks | 12 | Fried fish dinner | 3 |
| Lamb: | | Fried fish sticks, scallops, | |
| Patties (ground meat) | 4 | or shrimp | 3 |
| Roasts | 9 | Shrimp creole | 3 |
| Pork, cured | 2 | Tuna pie | 3 |
| Pork, fresh: | | **Frozen desserts** | |
| Chops | 4 | | |
| Roasts | 8 | Ice cream | 1 |
| Sausage | 2 | Sherbet | 1 |
| Veal: | | | |
| Cutlets, chops | 9 | | |
| Roasts | 9 | | |

# EVERY DAY HERB GUIDE

| | ANISE SEED | BASIL | BAY LEAVES | CARAWAY SEED | DILL SEED | OREGANO | ROSEMARY | SAGE | SESAME SEED | TARRAGON | THYME | TURMERIC |
|---|---|---|---|---|---|---|---|---|---|---|---|---|
| **APPETIZERS & BEVERAGES** | Adds licorice flavor to Milk or Tea | Pizza, Stuffed Celery, Butter Spreads, Tomato Juice | Tomato and Vegetable Juices | Add whole to Popcorn Balls, Cheese Spreads, Dips, Tea | Use ½ tsp. in Spreads, Avocado Dip, a dash in Tomato Juice | Pizza, Guacamole, Sharp Cheese Spread, Vegetable & Tomato Juice | Gin Punch | Sharp Cheese Spreads, Tea | Add to Dips and Spreads. Sprinkle toasted seed over Canapes | Avocado Dip, Liver Pate, Vegetable & Tomato Juices | Fish Spreads, Clam & Tomato Juices | |
| **BREADS & ROLLS** | Use as garnish or add to dough for Coffeecake and Sweet Rolls | | | Biscuits, Waffles, Rye Bread, Rolls | Rye and Dark Breads | Herb Bread | Biscuits, Corn Bread | Biscuits, Corn Bread, Waffles | Use generously in Biscuits, Buns, Coffeecake, Waffles Breads | | Biscuits | |
| **CAKES & COOKIES** | Add whole or crushed to Spongecake, Spicecake, Cupcakes | | | Delightful addition to Poundcake, Spicecake | Use crushed in Poundcake | | | | Cheesecake | | | |
| **CASSEROLES** | An unusual touch in Stew | Crush leaves just before adding to Goulash, Stews, Veal Scaloppine, Meat Pies, Spanish Rice, Stuffing | All Stews, Chicken Casseroles & Rice Dishes | Meat Pie Crusts, Stews, Noodle Dishes | Lamb Stew, Macaroni, Chicken Dishes. Use ¼ to ½ tsp. per 4 servings | Use ½ tsp. for 6 servings, crushed, in Chili Con Carne, Tamale Pie, Beef & Veal Stew | Use ¼ tsp. per 4 servings, crushed, in Corned Beef & Cabbage, Ham Loaf, Chicken Stew, Beef Stew, Dumplings | Use ¼ tsp. per 4 servings in Stews, Cheese Casseroles, Stuffings & Dumplings | Dumplings, Crumb Toppings, Rice Dishes | Use ¼ tsp. per 4 servings in Chicken A La King, Cheese Casseroles | Use ½ tsp. for 4 servings, crushed in Stews, Chipped Beef, Creamed Chicken, Croquettes, Fricassees | Macaroni & Noodle Dishes, Rice Dishes where Saffron is not used, Curried Dishes |
| **DESSERTS** | Springerle, Butter Cookies, Candies, All Fruit Pies, Compotes, Applesauce, Stewed Apples | | Use crushed or whole in Rolled Cookies & Candies, Baked & Stewed Apples | Rolled "Dilly" Cookies, Apple Pie | | | | Rolled Cookies, Pastries, Pecan Pie, Piecrusts | | | Rolled Cookies | |
| **EGGS & CHEESE** | Cottage & Cream Cheese | Scrambled Eggs, Souffles, Rarebits, Cream & Cottage Cheese | | Cottage Cheese, Rarebits | Omelets, Egg Dishes, Cottage & Cream Cheese | Scrambled Eggs, Omelets | Omelets, Deviled & Scrambled Eggs | Creamed Eggs, Cheddar & Cottage Cheese | Soft Cheeses | Omelets, Eggs Benedict, All Egg Dishes, Cottage Cheese | Shirred Eggs, Cottage Cheese | Sprinkle on Souffles, Creamed, Deviled & Scrambled Eggs |

| | | | | | | | | | | | | |
|---|---|---|---|---|---|---|---|---|---|---|---|---|
| **FISH** | Hard Shelled Crab, Shrimp, Steamed Cod | Shrimp, Lobster, Halibut | Cod, Boiled or Steamed Shrimp, Crab & Lobster, Poached Halibut & Salmon | Clams, Oysters, Shrimp | Halibut, Shrimp, Sole, Lobster | Shrimp, Clams, Lobster, Stuffed Fish | Salmon, Crab, Shrimp, Halibut, Creamed Seafood | Baked Halibut, Salmon, Cod | Sprinkle on Fish before broiling or add to breading | Crab, Lobster, Salmon, Tuna | Sprinkle lightly on Tuna, Scallops, Crab, Sole, Clams | Creamed Salmon, Lobster, Shrimp |
| **MEAT & POULTRY** | Use ¼ tsp. for 4 servings of Veal, Chicken, Duck, Sausage | Veal Roast, Lamb Chops, Liver, Barbecued Chicken, Duck, Sausage | Pot Roast, Oxtails, Shish Kebab, Sauerbraten, Boiled Pork or Chicken | Spareribs, Roast Pork, Liver, Kidneys, Goose | Beef, Veal, Pork Chops, Lamb Chops | Meatloaf, Meat balls, Pork, Veal, Swiss Steak, Duck, Lamb, Sausage Stuffings | Beef, Pork, Veal, Lamb, Poultry, Game | All Pork Dishes, Duck, Hamburgers, Sausage, Meat Loaf | Pork Chops, Chicken Cutlets, Lamb, add 2 tsp. to 1 lb. ground beef for hamburgers | Broiled Chicken, Squab, Duck, Steaks, Veal | All Meats, Meatloaf, Liver, Chicken, Turkey | Add ½ tsp. to Curried Lamb or Beef, Broiled Chicken |
| **PRESERVES & PICKLES** | Add whole to Sweet Pickles | Mustard Sauce | Beets, Mixed & Sour Pickles | Beets, Sour & Mixed Pickles | Dill Pickles, of course! | Mustard Sauce | 🌿 | Mustard Sauce | Mustard Sauce | Mustard Sauce, Sour Pickles | Mustard Sauce | Chow Chow, Chutney, Mixed Pickles, Relishes |
| **SALADS & DRESSINGS** | Use whole or crushed in Waldorf Fruit and Vegetable Salads | Aspics, Tossed, Chicken, Seafood & Cucumber Salads, French & Russian Dressings | Aspics, Tomato Salad, French Dressing | Add whole to Potato, Vegetable, Tomato & Cucumber Salads, Cole Slaw, Dressings | Potato, Macaroni, Cucumber & Vegetable Salads, French & Sour Cream Dressings | Egg, Bean, Tomato, Vegetable, Seafood Salads | Fruit or Meat Salads | Salad Greens & French Dressing | Vegetable Salads & Dressings | Tossed, Chicken, Fruit, Seafood, Egg Salads, Dressings & Vinegars | Tossed, Beet & Tomato Salads, Tomato Aspic | Use ½ tsp. per cup in French & Mayonnaise Dressings, or ¼ tsp. for color |
| **SAUCES & GRAVIES** | 🌿 | Seafood, Butter, Spaghetti, Tomato & Pizza Sauces | Bordelaise & Marinades | Marinades, Seasoned Butters | Crush and add to Cream Sauce, Spiced Vinegar, Drawn Butter | Spaghetti, Tomato, Cream, Butter Sauces, Marinades & Gravies | Cheese, A La King, Barbecue, Spaghetti & Tomato Sauces, Brown Gravy | Add a dash to Brown & Cream Gravies, Barbecue Sauce | 🌿 | Bearnaise, Butter, Mustard, Tartar, Sweet-Sour Sauces, Marinades | Bordelaise, Creole, Butter & Barbecue Sauces | Add ¼ tsp. to Butter, Cheese, Cream & Mustard Sauces |
| **SOUPS & CHOWDERS** | 🌿 | Bean, Beef, Pea, Tomato, Potato, Turtle, Manhattan Clam Chowder | Vegetable, Bean, Fish Chowders | Creamed, Fish Bisques | Chicken, Cream of Tomato, Split Pea, Navy Bean | Bean, Beef, Minestrone, Tomato Soups & Fish Chowder | Chicken, Minestrone, Split Pea, Vegetable | Creamed, Fish, Chicken, Chowder, Consomme | Creamed Soups | Chicken, Consomme, Mushroom, Fish, Pea, Tomato | Gumbo, Fish & Clam, Pea, Vegetable | Add a dash to Creamed Soups and Chowders |
| **VEGETABLES** | Eggplant, Peas, Squash, String Beans, Zucchini; perfect for all Tomatoes | Asparagus, Beets, Beans, Carrots, Artichokes, Boiled Potatoes, Tomatoes | Asparagus, Cauliflower, French Fried Potatoes, Cabbage, Sauerkraut | Add ¼ tsp. to Beets, Cabbage, Peas, Carrots, Turnips, Cauliflower, Sauerkraut, Tomatoes | Onions, Potatoes, Peas, Spinach, String Beans, Tomatoes, Zucchini | Eggplant, Beans, Peas, Squash, Spinach, Boiled Potatoes, Sauteed Mushrooms | Green Beans, Eggplant, Brussels Sprouts, Onions, Lima Beans, Peas, Tomatoes | Use toasted as garnish for Asparagus, Boiled Potatoes, Green Beans, Tomatoes, Spinach | Asparagus, Beans, Broccoli, Cabbage, Cauliflower, Mushrooms, Potatoes, Tomatoes | Artichokes, Beans, Beets, Carrots, Mushrooms, Onions, Tomatoes, Potatoes | Sprinkle on Creamed Potatoes |

# A DIET TO LIVE WITH

Good nutrition is important whether you are dieting to lose weight or to maintain your ideal weight. A good low-calorie diet meets your daily nutritional needs, subtracting calories without sacrificing the minerals, vitamins and other food requirements. With the lists below you can keep your diet varied and exciting. It is imperative that you combine choices from each of the groups daily.

## GROUP I: DARK GREEN AND YELLOW VEGETABLES

These vegetables are high in essential minerals- iron, calcium and phosphorus - and in vitamins A and C. A one cup serving of the starred (*) vegetables will supply all the vitamin A you need daily. Using two or more of the other vegetables listed will round out your daily nutritional needs. This does not include butter or margarine. Those calories are counted from Group IX.

**35 calories per ½ cup serving:**

\* Carrots   \* Pumpkin   \* Winter squash (butternut, acorn or hubbard)

**20 calories per ½ cup serving:**

| | | | |
|---|---|---|---|
| Asparagus (6 spears) | Broccoli | * Spinach | Green Beans |
| Green Peppers | * Kale | * Dandelion Greens | Tomatoes |
| Turnip Greens | * Collards | * Mustard Greens | |

\* Escarole and Lettuce equal 15 calories in a one cup serving.

## GROUP II: OTHER VEGETABLES

These vegetables are also important for daily nutritional needs. Plan one or more servings per day and do not substitute with vegetables in Group I. These vegetables do not include butter or margarine. Those calories are counted from Group IX.

**50 calories for ½ cup serving:**

Beets   Onions   Parsnips   Turnips (¾ cup)

**15 calories or less per ½ cup serving:**

| | | | |
|---|---|---|---|
| Bean Sprouts | Brussel Sprouts | Cabbage | Cauliflower |
| Celery | Chard | Cucumbers | Endive |
| Radishes | Kohlrabi | Mushrooms | Okra |
| | Sauerkraut | Zucchini | Yellow Squash |

## GROUP III: HIGH VITAMIN C FRUITS

One serving of any fruit listed here will meet your daily need for vitamin C.

1 cup of fresh strawberries is 50 calories.

**70 calories per serving:**

1 cup unsweetened grapefruit sections, (fresh or canned)
6 oz. grapefruit juice
1 medium size orange
6 oz. orange juice
1 cup papaya cubes

## GROUP IV: MEDIUM-HIGH VITAMIN C FRUITS

Serve two portions of these each day, or one portion plus one of the starred vegetables listed in Group I. These fruits are 40 calories per serving.

| | | |
|---|---|---|
| ¼ cantaloupe | ½ grapefruit, fresh | ½ cup red raspberries |
| 1 tangerine | 1 cup tomato juice | |

## GROUP V: OTHER FRUITS

| | |
|---|---|
| 1 small apple | ½ cup unsweetened applesauce |
| 2 fresh apricots | Dried apricots, 4 halves |
| ½ small banana | ½ cup fresh blackberries |
| ½ cup fresh blueberries | 10 dark, sweet cherries |
| 2 figs, fresh or dried | 2 dates, fresh or dried |
| ½ cup Tokay, Malaga or seedless grapes | ¼ cup grape juice |
| 1 cup cubed watermelon | 1 wedge honeydew 7 x 2 |
| ⅓ medium papaya | ½ Mango |
| 1 small pear | 1 medium peach |
| ⅓ cup unsweetened pineapple juice | ½ cup cubed pineapple |
| 1 Tbsp. seedless raisins | 2 medium plums |

## GROUP VI: MILK

With any diet, a pint of low fat milk a day is a must for adults and this counts as 180 calories. Milk may be incorporated into dishes in the meal or as a beverage with meals or as a snack inbetween meals.

## GROUP VII: MEATS

This group includes beef, veal, lamb, pork, ham and poultry, fish, cheese and eggs. We require 375 calories of cooked lean meat or their equivalent every day.

**For a 225 calorie serving:**

| | |
|---|---|
| 1 slice prime rib roast, 5 x 3½ x ½ in. | 1 broiled veal chop |
| 1 slice sirloin or round roast, 5 x 4 x ¼ in. | 1 broiled ground beef patty (4oz. raw) |
| 1 slice roast lamb, 4 x 4 x ¼ in. | 3 slices roast turkey 3 x 3 x¼ in. |
| 1 slice baked ham, 5½ x 3½ x ¼ in. | 3 slices of roast chicken 3 x 3 x ¼ in. |
| 2 slices roast pork, 3 x 1½ x ½ in. | 1 fried breast from 2 lb. chicken |
| 3 slices roast veal, 3 x 2 x ½ in. | ½ cup boned, canned chicken |
| 1 broiled loin lamb chop | 1 piece broiled halibut, 4 x 3 x ½ in. |
| 1 broiled pork chop | 1 piece broiled or baked salmon, 4 x 3 x½ in. |
| 1 cup low-fat cottage cheese | |

**For 150 calorie serving:**

½ of 2 lb. chicken, broiled
3 medium size chicken livers, broiled
1 piece liver, 3½ x 2½ x ½ in.
2½ slices canned corned beef, 3 x 2¼ x ¼ in.
2 slices bologna
3 slices boiled tongue, 5 x 3 x ⅛ in.
1 frankfurter, boiled
2 slices packaged boiled ham
9 shrimp (20 to the lb.) boiled
12 med. oysters
⅔ cup crab meat

¾ cup low-fat cottage cheese
1 cube cheddar cheese, 1½ in.
2 eggs, boiled or poached
⅓ cup canned salmon
½ cup water packed tuna
1 piece boiled haddock, 4½ x 4 x ½ in.
1 piece boiled mackerel, 4 x 2 x ½ in.
1 fishcake, 2½ in. in diameter
4 small, Atlantic-type sardines
2 large California type sardines
12 cherrystone clams

## GROUP VIII: HIGH STARCH FOODS

70 calories without butter or margarine

1 slice bread (16 slices to a lb.)
2 graham crackers
5 square saltines
3 rectangular wafers
½ cup whole wheat cereal
⅓ cup cooked rice
1 small baked or broiled potato
½ medium baked sweet potato
⅓ cup cooked noodles or macaroni
¼ cup baked beans without pork
1 cup popped corn

1 two inch dinner roll
20 oyster crackers
3 square soda crackers
½ cup oatmeal
¾ cup dry cereal flakes or puffs
½ cup cooked grits
½ cup mashed potato (milk added only)
½ cup cooked spaghetti
⅓ cup cooked beans
½ cup corn

## GROUP IX: BUTTER, MARGARINE, FATS OR OILS

55 calories per serving

1 pat butter or margarine (1/16 of a stick)
2 Tbsp. light cream
2 Tbsp. dairy sour cream
1 Tbsp. cream cheese
6 small nuts

1½ tsp. vegetable or olive oil
1 Tbsp. heavy cream
1½ tsp. mayo or salad dressing
1 Tbsp. seasoned salad dressing

# Quantities to Serve 100 People

| | |
|---|---|
| COFFEE | - 3 LBS. |
| LOAF SUGAR | - 3 LBS. |
| CREAM | - 3 QUARTS |
| WHIPPING CREAM | - 4 PTS. |
| MILK | - 6 GALLONS |
| FRUIT COCKTAIL | - 2½ GALLONS |
| FRUIT JUICE | - 4 NO. 10 CANS (26 LBS.) |
| TOMATO JUICE | - 4 NO. 10 CANS (26 LBS.) |
| SOUP | - 5 GALLONS |
| OYSTERS | - 18 QUARTS |
| WEINERS | - 25 LBS. |
| MEAT LOAF | - 24 LBS. |
| HAM | - 40 LBS. |
| BEEF | - 40 LBS. |
| ROAST PORK | - 40 LBS. |
| HAMBURGER | - 30-36 LBS. |
| CHICKEN FOR CHICKEN PIE | - 40 LBS. |
| POTATOES | - 35 LBS. |
| SCALLOPED POTATOES | - 5 GALLON |
| VEGETABLES | - 4 NO. 10 CANS (26 LBS.) |
| BAKED BEANS | - 5 GALLON |
| BEETS | - 30 LBS. |
| CAULIFLOWER | - 18 LBS. |
| CABBAGE FOR SLAW | - 20 LBS. |
| CARROTS | - 33 LBS. |
| BREAD | - 10 LOAVES |
| ROLLS | - 200 |
| BUTTER | - 3 LBS. |
| POTATO SALAD | - 12 QUARTS |
| FRUIT SALAD | - 20 QUARTS |
| VEGETABLE SALAD | - 20 QUARTS |
| LETTUCE | - 20 HEADS |
| SALAD DRESSING | - 3 QUARTS |
| PIES | - 18 |
| CAKES | - 8 |
| ICE CREAM | - 4 GALLONS |
| CHEESE | - 3 LBS. |
| OLIVES | - 1¾ LBS. |
| PICKLES | - 2 QUARTS |
| NUTS | - 3 LBS. SORTED |

To serve 50 people, divide by 2
To serve 25 people, divide by 4

# CALORIES BURNED UP DURING TEN MINUTES OF CONTINUOUS ACTIVITY

| According to Body Weight ⇨ | Body Wt.# | 150# | 175# | 200# | 225# | 250# | 275# | 300# |
|---|---|---|---|---|---|---|---|---|
| **PERSONAL ACTIVITIES** | | | | | | | | |
| Sleeping | | 12 | 14 | 16 | 18 | 20 | 22 | 24 |
| Sitting (TV or reading) | | 12 | 14 | 16 | 18 | 20 | 22 | 24 |
| Sitting (Conversing) | | 18 | 21 | 24 | 28 | 30 | 34 | 37 |
| Washing/Dressing | | 32 | 38 | 42 | 47 | 53 | 58 | 63 |
| Standing quietly | | 14 | 17 | 19 | 21 | 24 | 26 | 28 |
| **SEDENTARY OCCUPATION** | | | | | | | | |
| Sitting/Writing | | 18 | 21 | 24 | 28 | 30 | 34 | 37 |
| Light Office Work | | 30 | 35 | 39 | 45 | 50 | 55 | 60 |
| Standing (Light activity) | | 24 | 28 | 32 | 37 | 40 | 45 | 50 |
| **HOUSEWORK** | | | | | | | | |
| General Housework | | 41 | 48 | 53 | 60 | 68 | 74 | 81 |
| Washing Windows | | 42 | 49 | 54 | 61 | 69 | 76 | 83 |
| Making Beds | | 39 | 46 | 52 | 58 | 65 | 75 | 85 |
| Mopping Floors | | 46 | 54 | 60 | 68 | 75 | 83 | 91 |
| Light Gardening | | 36 | 42 | 47 | 53 | 59 | 66 | 73 |
| Weeding Garden | | 59 | 69 | 78 | 88 | 98 | 109 | 120 |
| Mowing Grass (power) | | 41 | 48 | 53 | 60 | 67 | 74 | 81 |
| Mowing Grass (manual) | | 45 | 53 | 58 | 66 | 74 | 81 | 88 |
| Shoveling Snow | | 78 | 92 | 100 | 117 | 130 | 144 | 160 |
| **LIGHT WORK** | | | | | | | | |
| Factory Assembly | | 24 | 28 | 32 | 37 | 40 | 45 | 50 |
| Truck-Auto Repair | | 42 | 49 | 54 | 61 | 69 | 76 | 83 |
| Carpentry/Farm Work | | 38 | 45 | 51 | 58 | 64 | 71 | 78 |
| Brick Laying | | 34 | 40 | 45 | 51 | 57 | 62 | 67 |
| **HEAVY WORK** | | | | | | | | |
| Chopping Wood | | | 86 | 96 | 109 | 121 | 134 | 156 |
| Pick & Shovel Work | | | 79 | 88 | 100 | 110 | 120 | 130 |

( # = lb.)

# CALORIES BURNED UP DURING TEN MINUTES OF CONTINUOUS ACTIVITY (Continued)

| According to Body Weight ⇨ | Body Wt.# | 150# | 175# | 200# | 225# | 250# | 275# | 300# |
|---|---|---|---|---|---|---|---|---|
| **LOCOMOTION** | | | | | | | | |
| Walking - 2 mph | | 35 | 40 | 46 | 53 | 58 | 64 | 69 |
| One mile - @ 2 mph | | 105 | 120 | 140 | 157 | 175 | 193 | 210 |
| Walking - 4½ mph | | 67 | 78 | 87 | 98 | 110 | 120 | 131 |
| One mile - 4½ mph | | 89 | 103 | 115 | 130 | 147 | 160 | 173 |
| Walking Upstairs | | 175 | 201 | 229 | 259 | 288 | 318 | 350 |
| Walking Downstairs | | 67 | 78 | 88 | 100 | 111 | 122 | 134 |
| Jogging - 5½ mph | | 108 | 127 | 142 | 160 | 178 | 197 | 215 |
| Running - 7 mph | | 141 | 164 | 187 | 208 | 232 | 256 | 280 |
| Running - 12 mph (sprint) | | 197 | 230 | 258 | 295 | 326 | 360 | 395 |
| Running in place (140 count) | | 242 | 284 | 325 | 363 | 405 | 447 | 490 |
| Bicycle - 5½ mph | | 50 | 58 | 67 | 75 | 83 | 92 | 101 |
| Bicycle - 13 mph | | 107 | 125 | 142 | 160 | 178 | 197 | 216 |
| **RECREATION** | | | | | | | | |
| Badminton or Volleyball | | 52 | 67 | 75 | 85 | 94 | 104 | 115 |
| Baseball (except pitcher) | | 47 | 54 | 62 | 70 | 78 | 86 | 94 |
| Basketball | | 70 | 82 | 93 | 105 | 117 | 128 | 140 |
| Bowling (nonstop) | | 67 | 82 | 90 | 100 | 111 | 122 | 133 |
| Dancing - moderate | | 42 | 49 | 55 | 62 | 69 | 77 | 86 |
| Dancing - vigorous | | 57 | 67 | 75 | 86 | 94 | 104 | 115 |
| Square Dancing | | 68 | 80 | 90 | 103 | 113 | 124 | 135 |
| Football | | 83 | 97 | 110 | 123 | 137 | 152 | 167 |
| Golf - foursome | | 40 | 47 | 55 | 62 | 68 | 75 | 83 |
| Horseback Riding (trot) | | 67 | 78 | 90 | 102 | 112 | 123 | 134 |
| Ping Pong | | 38 | 43 | 52 | 58 | 64 | 71 | 78 |
| Skiing - (alpine) | | 96 | 113 | 128 | 145 | 160 | 177 | 195 |
| Skiing - (cross country) | | 117 | 137 | 158 | 174 | 194 | 214 | 235 |
| Skiing - (water) | | 73 | 92 | 104 | 117 | 130 | 142 | 165 |
| Swimming - (backstroke) 20 yd/min | | 38 | 43 | 52 | 58 | 64 | 71 | 79 |
| Swimming - (breaststroke) 20 yd/min | | 48 | 55 | 63 | 72 | 80 | 88 | 96 |
| Swimming - crawl 20 yd/min | | 48 | 55 | 63 | 72 | 80 | 88 | 96 |
| Tennis | | 67 | 80 | 92 | 103 | 115 | 125 | 135 |
| Wrestling, Judo or Karate | | 129 | 150 | 175 | 192 | 213 | 235 | 257 |

( # = lb.)

# FIRST AID IN HOUSEHOLD EMERGENCIES

**POISONING:** When a poison has been taken internally, start first aid at once. Call doctor immediately.

- *Dilute* poison with large amounts of liquids — milk, or water.
- Wash out by inducing vomiting, when not a strong acid, strong alkali or petroleum.
- For acid poisons do not induce vomiting, but neutralize with milk of magnesia. Then give milk, olive oil or egg white. Keep victim warm and lying down.
- For alkali poisons such as lye or ammonia, do not induce vomiting.
- Give lemon juice or vinegar. Then give milk and keep victim warm and lying down.
- If poison is a sleeping drug, induce vomiting and then give strong black coffee frequently. Victim must be kept awake.
- If breathing stops, give artificial respiration.

**SHOCK:** Shock is brought on by a sudden or severe physical injury or emotional disturbance. In shock, the balance between the nervous system and the blood vessels is upset. The result is faintness, nausea, and a pale and clammy skin. Call ambulance immediately. If not treated the victim may become unconscious and eventually lapse into a coma.

- Keep victim lying down, preferably with head lower than body.
- Don't give fluids unless delayed in getting to doctor, then give only water. (Hot tea, coffee, milk or broth may be tried if water is not tolerated.)
- Never give liquid to an unconscious person. Patient must be alert.
- Cover victim both under and around his body.
- Do not permit victim to become abnormally hot.
- Reassure victim and avoid letting him see other victims, or his own injury.
- Fainting is most common and last form of shock. Patient will respond in 30-60 seconds by merely allowing patient to lie head down if possible on floor.

**FRACTURES:** Pain, deformity or swelling of injured part usually means a fracture. If fracture is suspected, don't move person unless absolutely necessary, and then only if the suspected area is splinted. Give small amounts of lukewarm fluids and treat for shock.

**BURNS:** Apply or submerge the burned area in cold water. Apply a protective dry sterile cloth or gauze dry dressing if necessary. Do not apply grease or an antiseptic ointment or spray. Call doctor and keep patient warm (not hot) with severe burns.

- If burn case must be transported any distance, cover burns with clean cloth.
- Don't dress extensive facial burns. (It may hinder early plastic surgery.)

**WOUNDS: Minor Cuts**—Apply pressure with sterile gauze until bleeding stops. Use antiseptic recommended by your doctor. Bandage with sterile gauze. See your doctor. **Puncture Wounds**—Cover with sterile gauze and consult doctor immediately. Serious infection can arise unless properly treated.

**ANIMAL BITES:** Wash wounds freely with soap and water. Hold under running tap for several minutes if possible. Apply an antiseptic approved by your doctor and cover with sterile gauze compress. Always see your doctor immediately. So that animal may be held in quarantine, obtain name and address of owner.

**HEAT EXHAUSTION:** Caused by exposure to heat or sun. Symptoms: Pale face, moist and clammy skin, weak pulse, subnormal temperature, victim usually conscious.

Treatment: Keep victim lying down, legs elevated, victim wrapped in blanket. Give salt water to drink (1 tsp. salt to 1 glass water) ½ glass every 15 minutes. Call doctor.

## GENERAL DIRECTIONS FOR FIRST AID

1. Effect a prompt rescue.
2. Maintain an open airway.
3. Control severe bleeding by direct pressure over bleeding site. No tourniquet.
4. Give First Aid for poisoning.
5. Do not move victim unless it is necessary for safety reasons.
6. Protect the victim from unnecessary manipulation and disturbance.
7. Avoid or overcome chilling by using blankets or covers, if available.
8. Determine the injuries or cause for sudden illness.
9. Examine the victim methodically but be guided by the kind of accident or sudden illness and the need of the situation.
10. Carry out the indicated First Aid.

# How To Convert To Metric System

## Length

| When You Know: | Multiply by: | To Find: |
|---|---|---|
| millimeters | 0.04 | inches |
| centimeters | 0.4 | inches |
| meters | 3.3 | feet |
| kilometers | 0.6 | miles |
| inches | 2.54 | centimeters |
| feet | 30 | centimeters |
| yards | 0.9 | meters |
| miles | 1.6 | kilometers |

## Weight

| When You Know: | Multiply by: | To Find: |
|---|---|---|
| grams | 0.035 | ounces |
| kilograms | 2.2 | pounds |
| ounces | 28 | grams |
| pounds | 0.45 | kilograms |

## Volume

| When You Know: | Multiply by: | To Find: |
|---|---|---|
| milliliters | 0.2 | teaspoons |
| milliliters | 0.07 | tablespoons |
| milliliters | 0.03 | fluid ounces |
| liters | 4.23 | cups |
| liters | 2.1 | pints |
| liters | 1.06 | quarts |
| liters | 0.26 | gallons |
| teaspoons | 5 | milliliters |
| tablespoons | 15 | milliliters |
| fluid ounces | 30 | milliliters |
| cups | 0.24 | liters |
| pints | 0.47 | liters |
| quarts | 0.95 | liters |
| gallons | 3.8 | liters |

## Temperature

| When You Know: | Multiply by: | To Find: |
|---|---|---|
| degrees Celsius | 9/5, and add 32 | degrees Fahrenheit |
| degrees Fahrenheit | 5/9 (after subtracting 32) | degrees Celsius |

# STEAK COOKING CHART

### -To Prepare Your Steaks-

Thaw in refrigerator, bring meat to room temperature before cooking. You can successfully cook frozen steaks. Start by searing both sides to seal in juices. Then reduce heat for slow cooking to allow the inside to thaw. Follow the chart below, but allow about twice the cooking time for frozen steaks.

For juicier and more flavorful steaks, tongs should be used when handling or turning. Cooking units vary of course and it is always advisable to run your own tests when cooking steaks. The chart below is a guide.

### The cooking times below are for fully thawed steaks.
Filet Mignons take one to two minutes less total time to cook.

| Cooking Instructions | | Red-Hot Charcoal 2¾" from heat source | | Pre-heated oven broiler 2" from heat source | |
|---|---|---|---|---|---|
| Thickness | Doneness | First side | After turning | First side | After turning |
| ¾" | Rare | 4 Minutes | 2 Minutes | 5 Minutes | 4 Minutes |
| | Medium | 5 Minutes | 3 Minutes | 7 Minutes | 5 Minutes |
| | Well | 7 Minutes | 5 Minutes | 10 Minutes | 8 Minutes |
| 1" | Rare | 5 Minutes | 3 Minutes | 6 Minutes | 5 Minutes |
| | Medium | 6 Minutes | 4 Minutes | 8 Minutes | 6 Minutes |
| | Well | 8 Minutes | 6 Minutes | 11 Minutes | 9 Minutes |
| 1¼" | Rare | 5 Minutes | 4 Minutes | 7 Minutes | 5 Minutes |
| | Medium | 7 Minutes | 5 Minutes | 8 Minutes | 7 Minutes |
| | Well | 9 Minutes | 7 Minutes | 12 Minutes | 10 Minutes |
| 1½" | Rare | 6 Minutes | 4 Minutes | 7 Minutes | 6 Minutes |
| | Medium | 7 Minutes | 6 Minutes | 9 Minutes | 7 Minutes |
| | Well | 10 Minutes | 8 Minutes | 13 Minutes | 11 Minutes |
| 1¾" | Rare | 7 Minutes | 5 Minutes | 8 Minutes | 7 Minutes |
| | Medium | 8 Minutes | 7 Minutes | 9 Minutes | 8 Minutes |
| | Well | 11 Minutes | 9 Minutes | 14 Minutes | 12 Minutes |

If you prefer to cook your steaks in your conventional oven, do not thaw, and preheat oven to 450°. As a guide for medium-rare steaks allow approximately:
10-11 minutes per side for an 8 oz. Filet of Prime Rib
12-13 minutes per side for an 8 oz. Top Sirloin
9 minutes per side for an 11 or 12 oz. Boneless Strip Sirloin
10-11 minutes per side for a 6 oz. Filet Mignon

Because ovens may vary in the amount of heat produced and the best distance to place the meat from the burners, tests on your equipment are valuable.

# PARENTS' GLOSSARY OF KIDS' KITCHEN TERMS

**Appetizing :** Anything advertised on TV.
**Boil :** The point a parent reaches upon hearing the automatic "yuk" before a food is even tasted.
**Casserole :** Combination of favorite foods that go uneaten because they are mixed together.
**Chair :** Spot left vacant by mid-meal bathroom visit.
**Cookie (Last One) :** Item that must be eaten in front of a sibling.
**Crust :** Part of a sandwich saved for the starving children of: China, India, Africa, or Europe (check one).
**Desserts :** The reason for eating a meal.
**Evaporate :** Magic trick performed by children when it comes time to clear the table or wash dishes.
**Fat :** Microscopic substance detected visually by children on pieces of meat they do not wish to eat.
**Floor :** Place for all food not found on lap or chair.
**Fork :** Eating utensil made obsolete by the discovery of fingers.
**Fried Foods :** Gourmet cooking.
**Frozen :** Condition of children's jaws when spinach is served.
**Fruit :** A natural sweet not to be confused with dessert.
**Germs :** The only thing kids will share freely.
**Kitchen :** The only room not used when eating crumbly snacks.
**Leftovers :** Commonly described as "gross".
**Liver :** A food that affects genes, creating a hereditary dislike.
**Lollipop :** A snack provided by people who don't have to pay dental bills.
**Macaroni :** Material for a collage.
**Measuring Cup :** A kitchen utensil that is stored in the sandbox.
**Metric :** A system of measurement that will be accepted only after forty years of wandering in the desert.
**Napkin :** Any worn cloth object, such as shirt or pants.
**Natural Food :** Food eaten with unwashed hands.
**Nutrition :** Secret war waged by parents using direct commands, camouflage, and constant guard duty.
**Plate :** A breakable Frisbee.
**Refrigerator :** A very expensive and inefficient room air conditioner.
**Saliva :** A medium for blowing bubbles.
**Soda Pop :** Shake 'N Spray.
**Table :** A place for storing gum.
**Table Leg :** Percussion instrument.
**Thirsty :** How your child feels after you've said your final "good night".
**Vegetable :** A basic food known to satisfy kid's hunger - but only by sight.
**Water :** Popular beverage in underdeveloped countries.

# Try saying "Good Morning" as though you really meant it

Then (tomorrow, say) try treating some teen-ager like an adult.

Find someone to praise for doing a good job — waitress, bus driver, newsboy, store clerk, anyone.

Show respect for an older person's experience (or fortitude).

Be patient with someone who doesn't understand as quickly as you do.

Write or phone someone having a difficult time. Say you know it's rough, but you have faith in him.

*Look* pleasant.

Do your job a little better. Maybe you'll get some praise, but certainly you'll get more satisfaction.

Help someone — a handicapped across a street, a young man or woman looking for a job (whether you can give it or not, give him hope) or an older one, discouraged in his.

Contribute to some church or charity — money if you can, time if you can't.

It just could be that this sort of *understanding* is what this country needs right now.

Try it tomorrow — all day tomorrow. You might be surprised!

Courtesy THE WARNER & SWASEY COMPANY

## 1200 - 1500 CALORIE CONTROLLED DIET
## USING "A DIET TO LIVE WITH"

AMOUNTS TO EAT DAILY:  LIMIT TO:

Group I: Dark green and yellow vegetables — 3 servings

Group II: Other vegetables — 2 servings

Group III, IV, IV: Fruits — 1 serving from each fruit group totalling 3 servings

Group V: Milk — 1 serving or 2 cups

Group VII: Meats — 2 servings
 1 from 225 calories and 1 from 150 calories

Group VII: High starch foods — 6 servings

Group IX: Butter, margarine, fats or oils — 5 servings
(Be sure to include those used in cooking or added to food)

### BREAKDOWN OF AMOUNTS TO EAT DAILY (EXAMPLE)

Breakfast:  From:

  1 egg or 2 small sardines — Group VII Meats, 1/2 serving

  1/3 cup cooked rice or

  1 slice bread — Group VII, 1 serving

  6 oz. orange juice or

  1 cup fresh strawberries — Group III, 1 serving

  1 cup low-fat milk — Group VI, 1/2 serving

  Coffee or tea (with artificial sweetener

  or little milk) — 0 calories

  Water — 0 calories

Lunch:

  2 oz. chicken adobo sandwich — Group VII, 1/2 serving

  with lettuce, tomato, carrots — Group I, 2 servings

  2/3 cup cooked rice (instead of

  2 bread slices with sandwich) — Group VII, 2 servings

  1/2 small banana — Group V, 1 serving

  Low calorie beverage or water — 0 calories

Supper:

    3 oz. lean pork or fish sinigang

| | |
|---|---|
| sinigang | Group VII, 1 (225 calorie) serving |
| With green beans, spinach, tomato | Group I, 2 servings |
| 2/3 cup cooked rice | Group VII, 2 servings |
| 1/2 cup fresh grapes | Group V, 1 serving |
| Low calorie beverage or water | 0 calories |

Bedtime Nourishment:

| | |
|---|---|
| 1 cup low-fat milk | Group VI, 1/2 serving |

USE ABOVE INFORMATION AS A FREQUENT GUIDELINE ONLY. DO NOT BE TOO RIGID.

NOTE: A number of adult Filipinos are overweight or are becoming overweight, compounded with problems of high blood pressure, stroke and diabetes. I have been asked to address these problems by offering sound information on healthy Filipino diet in America and elsewhere. The <u>amounts</u> of any food or drink consumed is a number one consideration making sure to include all the Food Groups to ensure balanced nutrition. Use salt, patis, soy sauce, and MSG (see Glossary) sparingly or cut down on your usual usage; otherwise avoid these seasonings. Daily exercise appropriate for the person is a <u>MUST</u>. See Page 129 for more Philippine menu ideas.

There is no substitute for individual nutrition counseling with a Filipino registered dietitian for your lifetime of healthy eating of Filipino-American foods and drinks. Let me know if I can be of help by calling 1-540-345-2033.

## DESIRABLE WEIGHT TO AIM FOR

| Women Height | Weight in lbs.* From - To | Men Height | Weight in lbs.* From - To |
|---|---|---|---|
| 4'9"  | 106 - 118 | 5'1"  | 126 - 136 |
| 4'10" | 108 - 120 | 5'2"  | 128 - 138 |
| 4'11" | 110 - 123 | 5'3"  | 130 - 140 |
| 5'0"  | 112 - 126 | 5'4"  | 132 - 143 |
| 5'1"  | 115 - 129 | 5'5"  | 134 - 146 |
| 5'2"  | 118 - 132 | 5'6"  | 137 - 149 |
| 5'3"  | 121 - 135 | 5'7"  | 140 - 152 |
| 5'4"  | 124 - 138 | 5'8"  | 143 - 155 |
| 5'5"  | 127 - 141 | 5'9"  | 146 - 158 |
| 5'6"  | 130 - 144 | 5'10" | 149 - 161 |
| 5'7"  | 133 - 147 | 5'11" | 152 - 165 |
| 5'8"  | 136 - 150 | 6'0"  | 155 - 169 |
| 5'9"  | 139 - 153 | 6'1"  | 159 - 173 |
| 5'10" | 142 - 156 | 6'2"  | 162 - 177 |
|       |           | 6'3"  | 166 - 182 |

*Medium build, without clothing
Source: Metropolitan Life Insurance Co.

For more information, please see "A DIET TO LIVE WITH" and "CALORIES BURNED UP DURING TEN MINUTES of CONTINUOUS ACTIVITY" found in the Basic Kitchen Information Pages.

# Appetizers
# Pickles
# Relishes

# New Hints

Use paper cups as handy containers for your "drippings" in the refrigerator as they take up little room and can be thrown away when empty.

To remove burned-on starch from your iron, sprinkle salt on a sheet of waxed paper and slide iron back and forth several times. Then polish it with silver polish until roughness or stain is removed.

Spray garbage sacks with ammonia to prevent dogs from tearing the bags before picked up.

You can clean darkened aluminum pans easily by boiling in them two teaspoons of cream of tartar mixed in a quart of water. Ten minutes will do it.

To dry drip-dry garments faster and with fewer wrinkles, hang garment over the top of a dry cleaner's plastic bag.

When food is too salty add a cut raw potato, then discard the potato once it is boiled.

If the dish is too sweet, add salt. On a main dish you can add a teaspoon of vinegar.

If the food is too sharp, a teaspoon of sugar will soften the taste.

If a main dish or vegetable is too sweet add a teaspoon or two of vinegar.

To pick up slivers of glass, it helps to use a dampened paper towel.

If zippers stick, just run some bar soap over the zipper and the zipper will work fine.

To draw a straighter line, use a knife instead of a pencil.

To prevent your salt shaker from clogging up, keep a few grains of rice inside the shaker.

To remove your child's crayon marks from linoleum or tile, use silver polish.

Most times very hot water will revive your wilted flowers.

Cheese will not dry out if it is wrapped in a cloth dampened with vinegar.

Your new white tennis shoes will last longer if sprayed heavily with starch when you first get them.

To get the corn silk off of corn on the cob, brush downward with a paper towel.

To cut a pie into five equal pieces, first cut a Y in the pie and then two large pieces can be cut in half.

## APPETIZERS, PICKLES AND RELISH

### ACHARA  (Pickles)

6 cups sauerkraut (2 lb. pkg.)
1 cup seedless raisins
2 cups coarsely grated carrots (3 large)
10 small pickling onions
1 green pepper, sliced thin
3 cloves garlic, sliced thin, (optional)
1 tsp. fresh ginger, sliced thin (optional)
2 c. vinegar
1 c. water
2 c. sugar
3 Tbsp. salt

Jars with tight covers, sterilized.
Wash sauerkraut in cold water. Press and drain out water. Mix sauerkraut, raisins, carrots, onions, green pepper, garlic and ginger. Fill clean jars with the mixture. Meanwhile, boil vinegar, water, sugar and salt. When boiling, pour into filled jars. Let cool before putting covers. Store in refrigerator.
Yields: about 10 to 12 cups.
NOTE: Sauerkraut is used as a substitute for grated green papaya. Share some achara with friends after you make this. Good for gift-giving during holidays.

### KIMCHI (Oriental Pickled Cabbage)

1 head Chinese cabbage
4 Tbsp. salt
1 carrot, grated
1 red pepper, finely sliced
2 cloves garlic, crushed
1 tsp. fresh ginger, minced
1 Tbsp. sugar

Cut cabbage leaves into 2 lengthwise then cut into 1-inch pieces. Sprinkle on salt, cover and let stand 4 to 5 hours. Wash cabbage under cold water and drain well, pressing out extra water from cabbage. Add carrot, red pepper, garlic, ginger and sugar. Mix well.
Store, covered, in the refrigerator for 2 days before using.
Makes about 2 cups.
NOTE: Kimchi is a good accompaniment or relish for baked, broiled or fried main dishes.

## RELISH PHILIPPINE

| | |
|---|---|
| 1 c. fresh radish, thinly sliced | 1 clove garlic, minced |
| 1/2 c. green pepper, diced | 1/4 c. vinegar |
| 2 Tbsp. onion, diced | 2 Tbsp. sugar |
| pinch of powdered ginger or minced fresh ginger | 1 tsp. salt |

Combine all ingredients in a bowl and mix well. Chill overnight, if desired. Chopped fresh broccoli, 1 cup may be additional ingredient. Also chopped fresh tomato added before serving. Good with roast pork, fried chicken and other fried dishes.
Serves 4.

## BAGOONG ALAMANG GUISADO (Sauteed Salted Shrimp Fry)

| | |
|---|---|
| 3 Tbsp. cooking oil | 1/2 c. pork, sliced fine |
| 3 garlic cloves, crushed | 1 jar (12 oz.) bagoong alamang |
| 2 Tbsp. onions, minced | (see Glossary) |
| 1/4 c. tomatoes, minced | |

In hot oil, brown garlic, add onions and tomatoes and cook for 3 minutes. Add pork, stir and cook for 15 minutes or until pork is cooked. Add alamang and simmer for 7 minutes. Store in refrigerator.
NOTE: Have very good ventilation when cooking this. Check that clothes closets are closed tightly.
Sugar (2 teaspoons) and vinegar (3 tablespoons) may be added when adding bagoong.

## BURONG ISDA (Fermented Fish)
## OR - BURONG KANIN (Fermented Rice)

| | |
|---|---|
| 1 lb. fresh fish fillet, preferably catfish | 2 tsp. salt |
| 1 c. uncooked rice, preferably short gain | sterilized jars with covers |

Wash fish and thoroughly dry with paper towels. Slice fish in small pieces. Meantime, cook rice in about 3 cups of water until rice is done and very soft. Remove from heat and mix fish and salt in very hot rice, mixing well until mixture cools. When cool, transfer to dry sterilized jars packing mixture firmly down with spoon to remove air spaces. When completely cool to touch, cover jars tightly. Store inside kitchen cabinet, at room temperature, for 3 to 4 days for fermentation. Mixture will be bubbly.

In 1/4 cup cooking oil, saute' 6 crushed garlic cloves and 1 medium onion, finely sliced, for 3 minutes. Add fermented rice and continue sauteeing for 5 minutes.

If desired, 2 tablespoons vinegar may be added for a more sour taste. Let mixture cool completely. Transfer to clean and dry sterilized jars, cover tightly and store in refrigerator where it can keep for 3 months. Serve as a side dish with steamed or boiled eggplant, bitter melon, mustard greens or lettuce.

NOTE: Excellent as appetizer. Zeny Calilung says that the fermented rice smells like the dickens while sauteeing so it is best to have ventilation fans going. Zeny calls this dish "balao-balao" or "Tagilo" in Pampango.

### CHICKEN CHITCHARON

2 cups chicken skin with fat    1 tsp. salt

Simmer chicken skin and salt in covered pan until oil comes out. Fry chicken skins in its own oil until crisp and golden brown, turning as needed.

Serve as appetizer for 3.

### DILIS CRISPS  (Anchovy Crisps)

1/3 c. sugar    1 pkg. (8 oz.) dried "dilis"
1/3 c. vinegar    (see Glossary)
1 tsp. Tabasco red hot sauce    2 c. flour
1/2 tsp. salt

In a bowl mix sugar, vinegar, Tabasco and salt. Toss "dilis" in this mixture until "dilis" are well coated. Dredge "dilis" in flour. Fry in medium hot oil, separating "dilis" until golden brown and crispy. Good for snacking or as appetizer.

Serves 6.

### FRIED BEAN CURD   (Tokwa)

4 bean curds

Cut bean curds into half-inch strips. Deep-fry to a golden brown. Drain on paper towel. Dip in a mixture of 2 tablespoons soy sauce, 3 tablespoons vinegar, 1 garlic clove (crushed), pepper and salt to taste. This is used as an appetizer.

## FRIED SQUID STRIPS/RINGS

2 lb. fresh or frozen squid, cleaned, cut into strips or rings
1 tsp. salt
1 tsp. MSG
1 cup all-purpose flour
1/2 cup cooking oil

Drain squid strips very well. Pat dry with paper towel. Sprinkle salt and MSG evenly on squid. Put flour in a small paper bag and shake several strips of squid in it.

In hot oil, fry coated squid until golden brown, dropping one strip at a time. Drain on paper towel. Fried squid strips should be crispy. Very good as appetizer or snack.

Serves 5.

## KILAWIN (Pig Ears)

6 pieces pig ears, cleaned
1 tsp. salt
1/3 c. soy sauce
1/4 c. vinegar
2 garlic cloves, crushed
dash of pepper

Boil ears in about 4 cups of water with salt for 1 hour or until ears are tender. Remove ears from stock and slice into 1/4-inch strips. Mix soy sauce, vinegar, garlic and pepper and pour over strips. Mix thoroughly. Very good as appetizer.

Makes 4 servings.

## PATA

6 pig's feet, cleaned and split, if desired
1 tsp. salt
enough oil for deep-fat frying

In a covered pot, boil pig's feet and salt in about 5 cups of water, until pig's feet are tender, about 1 hour. Better still, pressure cook for 30 minutes. Drain very well.

Deep-fat fry in enough hot oil to cover, until crispy and golden brown. Serve with a dipping mixture of 1/4 cup vinegar, 1/4 cup soy sauce and clove of crushed garlic. Used as appetizer.

# Soups, Salads, Dressings & Sauces

## THE SOUP POT

* Steak, roast or poultry bones can be frozen until needed for soup stock.

* If the soup or stew is too salty, add cut raw potatoes and discard them once they have cooked and absorbed the salt.

* Instant soup stock will always be on hand if you save the pan juice from cooking meats. Pour liquid into ice cube trays and freeze. Place solid cubes in freezer bags or foil.

* To prevent curdling of the milk or cream in soup add the soup to the milk rather than vice versa. Or add a bit of flour to the milk and beat well before combining.

* Always start cooking bones and meat in cold, salted water.

* The easiest way to skim off fat from soup is to chill until the fat hardens on top of the liquid. If time will not permit this, wrap ice in paper toweling and skim over the top.

## THE SALAD BOWL

* To remove the core from a head of lettuce, hit the core end sharply against the counter top or side of sink. Then the core will twist out easily.

* Put salad greens or cole slaw in a metal bowl and place in the freezer for a few minutes.

* Rubbing waxed paper over the inside and outside of a wooden salad bowl will prevent it from becoming sticky.

* If you cut the root end off the onion last you'll shed less tears.

* To prevent soggy salads, place an inverted saucer in the bottom of the salad bowl. The excess dressing will drain under the saucer and keep the greens crisp.

* Lettuce and celery will crisp up faster if you add a few raw slices of potato to the cold water you use to soak them.

## SAUCE SUGGESTIONS

* Make sure that flour is well browned before adding it to liquid for gravy. This will prevent lumpy gravy and also assure a rich brown gravy.

* Placing flour in a custard cup in the oven next to the roast will assure nice brown flour for gravy when the meat is done.

## SOUPS, SALADS

### PANCIT MOLO (Philippine Wanton Soup)

#### Stuffed Wrappers:

| | |
|---|---|
| 1 c. ground pork | 1 scallion, chopped |
| 1/4 c. water chestnuts, chopped | 1 Tbsp. soy sauce |
| 1 garlic clove, minced | 1/8 tsp. pepper |
| 1/2 tsp. MSG | 20 wanton wrappers, 3-inch squares (see Glossary) |
| 1 egg | |
| 1/2 c. shrimps, shelled, chopped | |

#### Soup:

| | |
|---|---|
| 8 c. water or broth | 1/2 of mixture for stuffed wrappers |
| 1 garlic clove, minced | |
| 1 tsp. MSG | 1 Tbsp. patis (see Glossary) |

In a bowl, thoroughly mix first 9 ingredients for stuffed wrappers. Save half of mixture for soup. On the center of each wanton wrapper, place a teaspoon of remaining mixture, moisten edges, bring and press corners together. Set aside. In a large covered pot, boil soup ingredients 3 minutes. Season to taste. Drop stuffed wanton wrappers, simmer covered 20 minutes. Serve hot garnished with chopped scallions. Serves 8 to 10.

NOTE: For a short-cut variation, prepare soup using all of mixture for stuffed wrappers. Instead of stuffed wanton wrappers, use egg noodles (miki). Stuffed wanton wrappers can be made ahead of time, kept in a box and stored in the freezer for several weeks. Thaw before cooking. For PINSEC: Deep-fat fry stuffed wanton wrappers until golden brown. Drain on paper towel. Serve with Sweet and Sour Sauce (see recipe).

## CHICKEN WITH MISUA SOUP

3 Tbsp. vegetable oil
2 garlic cloves, crushed
1 medium onion, sliced
1 chicken (about 2 lb.), cut
   to serving pieces
2 Tbsp. patis (see Glossary)

1 tsp. salt
1/2 tsp. MSG
1/4 tsp. pepper
6 c. water
4 oz. misua (see Glossary)

In a pot, lightly brown garlic in hot oil, add onions and chicken. Season with patis, salt, MSG and pepper. Cover and let simmer for 10 minutes. Add water and gently boil for 30 minutes, or until chicken is tender. Stir in misua. Serve at once. Serves 6.

## MISUA SOUP (Thread-Like Noodle Soup)

2 Tbsp. vegetable oil
2 garlic cloves, crushed
3 Tbsp. onion, minced
1 c. ground pork or ham
5 c. chicken, beef or any
   other meat broth or water

1 tsp. salt
1 tsp. MSG
2 oz. misua (see Glossary)
1 scallion, chopped

Brown garlic in hot oil, stir in onions, then pork. Cook 15 minutes. Add broth, salt and MSG. Cover and let simmer for 10 minutes. Just before serving, stir in misua and scallions and boil a minute. Serve hot. Serves 6.

NOTE: If desired, crack an egg for each serving in boiling soup, right after adding misua. Egg should be whole and cooked a minute, undisturbed.

## MAMI CHICKEN SOUP (Chinese Style)

1/4 lb. egg noodles, cooked
   according to pkg. directions
1 c. cooked chicken, shredded
   or diced
6 c. chicken broth, fat skimmed

1 hard cooked egg, shelled,
   coarsely chopped
3 Tbsp. green scallions,
   chopped
2 Tbsp. fried garlic chips

Prepare 6 soup bowls and equally portion drained cooked noodles, chicken, eggs, green scallions, into each bowl. Pour boiling broth in each bowl. Garnish with garlic chips. Serve hot with patis (fish sauce). Serves 6.

NOTE: Cooked lean pork may be used in place of chicken.

## VEGETABLE SOUP

1/2 lb. lean pork, sliced into thin strips
1 tsp. soy sauce
1 tsp. cornstarch
1/2 tsp. sherry
1/4 tsp. sugar
6 c. water
1/8 tsp. powdered ginger
1/4 tsp. vegetable oil
2/3 to 1 lb. Chinese cabbage, cut crosswise into 1-inch pieces
2 tsp. salt
1/2 tsp. MSG

Thoroughly mix pork, soy sauce, cornstarch, sherry and sugar; set aside. In rapidly boiling water, add ginger powder, oil and Chinese cabbage. Cook uncovered for 2 minutes. Stir in pork mixture, cook uncovered 3 minutes. Season with salt and MSG. Serve hot. Serves 6.

NOTE: Recipe may be varied by using beef or chicken in place of pork and spinach, pechay (see Glossary) or mustard greens instead of Chinese cabbage.

## EGG NOODLE SOUP

4 oz. dry egg noodles, (about 1 1/2 c.)
1/2 lb. lean pork, sliced into thin strips
1 tsp. soy sauce
1/2 tsp. sugar
1 tsp. cornstarch
1/2 tsp. sherry
1 tsp. vegetable oil
2 tsp. salt
1/2 tsp. MSG

Cook egg noodles in 5 cups boiling water. Stir frequently and cook, uncovered, for 7 to 10 minutes, or until noodles are cooked to desired doneness. Test doneness by biting a piece. Drain and set aside.

Thoroughly mix pork, soy sauce, sugar, cornstarch and sherry. In 5 cups rapidly boiling water, stir in pork mixture and cook covered 3 minutes. Add cooked noodles, oil, salt and MSG. Stir and let boil once. Serve hot. Serves 6.

## EGG DROP SOUP

1/2 lb. lean pork, sliced into thin strips
1/2 tsp. sherry
1/2 tsp. cornstarch
1/2 tsp. cornstarch dissolved in 2 Tbsp. water
1/2 tsp. sesame oil (optional)
1/2 tsp. MSG
1 tsp. soy sauce
1/4 tsp. sugar
6 c. water
2 tsp. salt or patis (see Glossary)
2 eggs, well beaten

Thoroughly mix pork with soy sauce, sherry, sugar and 1/2
(Cont.)

teaspoon cornstarch. In rapidly boiling water stir in pork mixture for 3 minutes. Add dissolved cornstarch, sesame oil, salt or patis and MSG. Stir in eggs. Turn off heat. Serve hot. Serves 6.

NOTE: This recipe can be as varied as using chicken or beef instead of pork and adding leafy vegetables, if desired.

## HOT AND SOUR SOUP

1/2 lb. lean pork, sliced into thin strips
3 pieces dried mushrooms, softened, sliced
1 tsp. sherry
1/4 tsp. powdered ginger
1/2 tsp. MSG

2 tsp. cornstarch dissolved in 4 Tbsp. water
1/2 tsp. salt
1 Tbsp. soy sauce
1/2 tsp. pepper
1 Tbsp. vinegar

Stir pork strips into rapidly boiling water. After 2 minutes, add mushrooms, sherry, pepper, ginger and vinegar. Simmer 4 minutes. Stir in dissolved cornstarch, add salt, MSG and soy sauce. Stir 1 minute and serve hot. Serves 6.

NOTE: The quantity of seasonings can be varied to one's taste. A few drops of Tabasco red hot sauce may be added.

## BASIC PHILIPPINE MARINADE FOR SALADS

1/2 c. vinegar
2 Tbsp. sugar (optional)
2 1/2 tsp. salt
1/8 tsp. pepper, more or less

1 1/2 Tbsp. sesame oil (optional), or salad oil
3 Tbsp. chopped green onions or any raw onion

Mix ingredients thoroughly. Correct seasonings to taste. Pour over any bite-sized raw vegetables desired or canned and drained green beans, wax beans, red kidney beans, mustard greens, etc. Marinate for a few hours or a day in refrigerator.

Marinade is enough for about 6 servings of salad.

NOTE: This marinade, when sugar and sesame oil are deleted, and a teaspoon of finely sliced ginger root is added, becomes an excellent marinade for fresh raw oysters cocktail or for "Kilawin" (see Glossary).

## BEAN SALAD DELUXE

1 c. canned cut green beans, drained
1 c. canned cut wax beans, drained
1 c. canned red kidney beans, drained

1/2 c. ready-to-eat pepperoni or salami, finely cut
1 c. olives, black or green, drained
2 Tbsp. anchovies (optional), mixed with marinade below

1 c. canned garbanzos (chick peas), drained

Basic Philippine Marinade for Salads (see recipe above)

Toss first 6 ingredients together until mixed. Pour over Basic Philippine Marinade with anchovies. Marinate for several hours or overnight in refrigerator.

Great as appetizer, salad or as a cold vegetable dish.

Serves 4 to 6.

NOTE: Other favorite salad dressings may be used in place of Marinade above.

## MONGO BEAN SPROUTING

1 c. dried mongo beans (see Glossary)

Sprouting one's fresh bean sprouts is easy. Here's how to: Wash beans. Soak overnight in water. Line a cookie sheet pan with very wet old, clean bath towel. Spread soaked beans, cover with wet bath towel. Wrap with dark plastic bag, i.e., garbage bag. Leave in a dark place at room temperature. Will sprout in 5 days.

Check in-between days that towel is moist, otherwise sprinkle a little water on young sprouts. When sprouts are ready (before leaves form), wash, drained and store in refrigerator. Use within 2 to 3 days.

Yields 8 to 10 cups bean sprouts.

NOTE: Sprouts can be eaten raw in salads like Bean Sprouts Salad (see recipe). Can be used in recipes like Lumpia, Guisado and Chop Suey (see recipes).

## BEAN SPROUTS (Togue) SALAD

1 lb. bean sprouts, fresh or canned
1 Tbsp. rice wine or vodka
1 Tbsp. chopped scallions

2 Tbsp. soy sauce
2 Tbsp. sesame oil
1/2 tsp. MSG

Wash fresh bean sprouts. Boil about 4 cups water, add fresh bean sprouts, shut off heat and let bean sprouts stand in hot water for 3 minutes. Drain very well. When using canned bean sprouts, drain and proceed as follows. Mix other ingredients. Pour on drained bean sprouts and mix well. Refrigerate for at least an hour or longer.

Serves 4 to 6.

## BURONG MUSTASA  (Salt-Preserved Mustard Greens)

| | |
|---|---|
| 1 lb. fresh mustard greens, cleaned, free from dirt and grime | 1 to 2 c. water or second rice washing |
| 1 1/2 Tbsp. salt | 1 qt. size jar with cover, cleaned, sterilized, or any suitable container |
| 1/4 c. vinegar | |

Soak greens in tub of cold water. Shake off water from each leaf, discarding wilted ones and hard stems.

In a big pot boil about 4 cups of water until rapidly boiling. Remove from heat; stir in greens just to blanch and quickly drain off hot water into strainer to hold greens.

Pour cold running water over blanched greens to cool. With clean hands squeeze out water from greens and transfer greens to clean containers. Sprinkle on salt. Add vinegar. Let stand maybe an hour, if desired. Add about 1 to 2 cups water or second rice washing until greens are immersed. Cover tightly and store in refrigerator. Ready to eat in a day or so.

Serves 6.

NOTE: Greens may be stored in refrigerator indefinitely.

Serve as is or serve with fresh tomato slices and chopped onions. Greens may be chopped and added to scrambed eggs before cooking.

When greens float, press down or turn over as greens must be immersed in solution.

Two tablespoons of sugar may be added for a Chinese-style recipe.

Radish or white turnip, sliced or grated, may be used instead of greens.

## CAMOTE TOPS SALAD  (Sweet Potato Green Buds)

Ask to harvest only the tender green leaf buds of your American friend's sweet potato garden. It won't hurt the garden and I know of no American who uses the leaves. Your American friend will probably be so amazed and delighted to know that those leaf buds are edible. If only they knew how nutritionally rich those tender sweet potato leaf tops are and how deliciously they could be cooked ——.

Anyway, wash those green tops with lots of cold water to remove grime or dirt. For about 3 cups of tops, stir into 1 cup rapidly boiling water. Cook, covered, for 3 minutes or until greens are tender. Do not overcook. Drain.

Meanwhile, mix:

1 large sliced tomato  
2 Tbsp. chopped raw onion  
1/2 tsp. minced fresh ginger  

2 Tbsp. fish sauce (patis or bagoong - see Glossary)

    Add to drained greens; mix well. Salt, if needed, or squeeze on fresh lemon juice, if desired.
    The best!
    NOTE:  Salt may be used in place of fish sauce.

## CHICKEN SALAD

2 c. chicken, cooked, diced  
1 c. carrots, cooked, diced  
1/2 c. beets, cooked or canned, diced  
1/2 c. sweet relish  
1 1/2 c. mayonnaise  
1/8 tsp. pepper  
3 c. potatoes, cooked, diced  
2 c. apples, pared, diced  
1 tsp. salt  

    In a large bowl toss chicken with the rest of the ingredients to mix well.  Refrigerate until well chilled.
    Serves 8 to 10.

## CUCUMBER SALAD WITH PEANUTS

1 cucumber, pared  
1 Tbsp. sugar  
1/2 tsp. salt  
dash of pepper  
3 Tbsp. chopped peanuts  
1 Tbsp. vinegar  
2 Tbsp. chopped Chinese parsley  

    Cut cucumber lengthwise into 4, then slice 1/4-inch thick. Combine with the rest of the ingredients and mix well. Chill.
    Serves 3.

## FRUIT SALAD

1 can (14 oz.) condensed milk  
3 cans (1 lb. 14 oz. size) fruit cocktail, drained  
1 can (1 lb. 4 oz size) pineapple tidbits, drained  
1 can (11 oz.) Mandarin oranges, drained  
4 large apples, pared, diced  
1 pkg. (8 oz.) cream cheese, softened at room temperature  

    Beat condensed milk and cream cheese to a smooth consistency. Pour into a large bowl container drained fruit cocktail, pineapple tidbits, Mandarin orange and diced apple. Blend thoroughly. Chill or freeze an hour before serving.
    Serves 15.
    NOTE:  To avoid discoloration of apples, prepare it last and
    (Cont.)

mix right away with the salad mixture or marinate diced apple in fruit syrup.

Save drained syrup from canned fruits and use it for cooking Ham Smoked Pork Shoulder (see recipe) or for making Sweet and Sour Sauce (see recipe).

A cup of preserved macapuno and/or preserved Kaong (see Glossary) may be added.

## FRESH SPINACH SALAD

1 pkg. fresh spinach (about 3/4 lb.), cleaned
2 hard-boiled eggs, chopped
3 Tbsp. fried bacon crumbs or bits

### Special Dressing:

1 c. catsup
1/2 c. vinegar
1/2 c. oil
1/2 c. sugar
1 small onion, chopped
1 Tbsp. Worcestershire sauce
salt and pepper to taste

Put prepared spinach in salad bowl, removing hard stems and wilted leaves. Sprinkle on eggs and bacon. Set aside.

Mix or blend dressing ingredients and toss with spinach mixture or let individuals put on their own dressing.

NOTE: The special dressing is excellent with spinach. Fresh sliced mushrooms, cherry tomatoes and other raw bite-sized vegetables may be used.

## SPINACH SALAD

1 lb. spinach, fresh or frozen
2 ripe tomatoes, fresh
1 scallion, finely sliced
2 Tbsp. patis or anchovy sauce (see Glossary)
1/2 tsp. fresh ginger, minced (optional)

In a covered pot, cook spinach in very little amount of water (2 tablespoons when using fresh spinach and practically no added water for frozen spinach) for about 3 minutes or until spinach is just cooked. Cool. Mix rest of ingredients with spinach. Garnish with lemon wedges.

Serves 4.

NOTE: This recipe is a substitute for kangkong salad.

## MANGO SALAD

1 green mango, peeled, cubed or sliced
1 raw carrot, peeled, cubed or sliced
12 red radishes, cubed or sliced

5 Tbsp. vinegar
1 Tbsp. sugar
1 tsp. salt
2 tsp. sesame oil (optional)
1/8 tsp. pepper, more or less

Prepare vegetables; set aside. Mix remaining ingredients and pour over vegetables, coating vegetables well. Marinate for at least an hour or overnight in refrigerator. Good as appetizer or accompaniment for fried or greasy foods.
Serves 4.
NOTE: Additional ingredients, such as red cherry tomatoes, cauliflowerettes, chopped raw onions or green onions, may be used. Makes a colorful salad.

## SOTANGHON SALAD

### Salad:

2 oz. bean threads (sotanghon)
1 big carrot, pared, cut into 2-inch long thin strips
2 celery stems, cut into 2-inch long thin strips, exclude leaves

1 medium cucumber, unpared, seeds removed, cut into thin strips
3 eggs, well beaten with 1/4 tsp. salt
2 Tbsp. vegetable oil

### Salad Dressing:

1 Tbsp. soy sauce
3 Tbsp. vinegar
3 Tbsp. vegetable oil

1/4 MSG
1/2 tsp. sugar
1 1/2 tsp. salt

Prepare salad ingredients. Soak bean threads in hot water for 10 minutes or until soft. Soak carrots, celery and cucumber in separate bowls of ice water. Set aside in refrigerator.
Heat fry pan and coat with just enough vegetable oil. Pour just enough beaten egg to cover pan. Cook until egg is slightly brown on both sides. Cook rest of the beaten egg this way. Cut fried egg into long thin strips. Set aside.
Drain separately carrots, celery, cucumber and softened bean threads. Arrange carrot strips around large serving platter, arrange egg strips over carrots, celery strips over egg strips, half of bean threads over celery, cucumber over bean threads and
(Cont.)

top with remaining bean threads. Set aside.

Mix salad dressing ingredients thoroughly. When ready to serve, pour over arranged salad platter.

Serves 8 to 10.

## BARBECUE SAUCE

1/4 c. soy sauce
3 Tbsp. catsup
1 Tbsp. garlic salt or 1 garlic clove, crushed and 2 tsp. salt
1/4 tsp. pepper

3 Tbsp. Hoisin sauce, (see Glossary)
2-3 Tbsp. sugar
2 tsp. sherry
1 tsp. MSG

Mix ingredients thoroughly. Marinate meat in this mixture for at least 2 hours, or even overnight. Sauce is enough to marinate 2 to 3 pounds of pork chops or chicken, cut into serving pieces. Oven or charcoal broil marinated meat.

NOTE: A cup of ginger ale or Seven-Up may be added, especially for chicken barbecue.

## SWEET AND SOUR SAUCE

1/2 c. vinegar
1/4 c. water
1/3 c. sugar
1 tsp. salt
1/4 tsp. MSG

2 Tbsp. catsup
1/2 tsp. red hot sauce, if desired
1 1/2 Tbsp. cornstarch dissolved in 2 Tbsp. water

Mix first 7 ingredients to produce a sweet and sour taste, varying measurement of ingredients if necessary to suit one's taste. Bring to a boil, reduce heat to low, add dissolved cornstarch while stirring continuously. Simmer 2 minutes or until sauce is thickened. Use sauce for Lumpia Macao, Camaron Rebosado, Lechon or Fried Chicken (see recipes).

Yields: about 1 cup.

## LIVER SAUCE

1 small can (4 3/4 oz.) liver pate (Sell's) or liver spread
1/3 c. vinegar
1 c. water
1/3 c. sugar
1/3 c. bread crumbs

1/3 tsp. powdered black pepper
1 tsp. salt
2 Tbsp. vegetable oil
1 Tbsp. finely chopped garlic
2 Tbsp. finely chopped onion

Mix first 7 ingredients. Season to taste. In hot oil, saute' garlic until brown, then add onions and saute' until transparent. Add liver mixture. Reduce heat to low and cook, stirring constantly, until mixture boils and thickens.

Yields almost 2 cups.

Good for Lechon or Roast Pork.

## SATE SAUCE

| | |
|---|---|
| 1/4 c. soy sauce | 1 1/2 tsp. hot pepper sauce |
| 1/2 c. water | 1/4 tsp. garlic powder |
| 5 Tbsp. peanut butter | 1/4 tsp. onion powder |
| 1 Tbsp. vinegar or lemon juice | 1 tsp. cornstarch |
| 3-4 Tbsp. sugar | |

Blend all ingredients to a smooth consistency. Taste and season to individual preference. Boil slowly for 3 minutes while stirring until thick. Makes less than a cup of sauce for Sate Babi (see recipe).

Write your extra recipes here:

Write your extra recipes here:

# Main Dishes
## Meat, Fish, Poultry

# MEAT, FISH AND POULTRY NOTES

* Baking fish on a bed of celery and onions will add to the taste as well as keep the fish from sticking.

* Coating will adhere to chicken better if it has been chilled for an hour before cooking.

* Sprinkle salt in the frying pan before adding meat and there will be less grease splattered.

* For a juicier burger rub both sides with cold water before grilling.

* Place cold water and cornstarch or flour in a jar with tight lid. Shake the jar until liquid is well mixed and lumps are gone. Then slowly add this mixture to pan drippings and stir while bringing gravy to a boil.

* Always roast poultry breast side down so the white meat will not dry out. Turn the bird for the last portion of cooking so that it will brown well.

* Rubbing poultry with salt and lemon juice will lessen any unpleasant odor.

* Unwaxed dental floss is good for trussing poultry because it will not burn.

* If gravy is too greasy, a bit of baking soda can be added without affecting the taste of the gravy.

* Pour pan drippings into a tall jar. The grease will rise to the top in minutes and can be removed for grease free gravy.

* Meat loaf won't crack when baking if it's rubbed with cold water before going in the oven.

* Adding cold water to the bottom of the broiling pan before cooking meat helps absorb smoke and grease and makes clean up easier.

* To speed up hamburger cooking, poke a hole in their centers when shaping. This causes the center to cook quickly and the holes are gone when the hamburgers are finished cooking.

* A large roast can be carved more easily after it stands for about 30 minutes.

* Meat or chicken may be floured easily by placing in a bag with flour and shaking well.

* Add a little lemon juice to water while boiling to make fish firm and white.

* To avoid odors while cooking fish, cover with browned butter and lemon juice.

## MEAT, FISH, POULTRY

### BEEF ORIENTAL

2 1/2 Tbsp. sugar
2 Tbsp. sesame oil
1/2 tsp. minced fresh ginger
   or powdered ginger
1 Tbsp. garlic powder or
   1 clove, minced
1/4 tsp. pepper
1/2 c. chopped scallions
5 Tbsp. soy sauce
2 Tbsp. sesame seeds
1 Tbsp. MSG
1/4 c. vegetable oil
1 1/2 lb. beef sirloin or flank,
   thinly sliced into strips

   Mix first 9 ingredients very well, then pour on beef strips. Mix well and marinate for at least 3 hours. In hot oil (about 3 tablespoons), saute' just enough marinated beef strips to cover the pan, for 5 minutes.
   Transfer to a covered serving dish. Cook the rest of the meat this way, adding more vegetable oil as needed. Serve hot with Bean Sprouts Salad (see recipe).
   Serves 6.
   NOTE: When using less tender cuts of beef, sprinkle about a teaspoon of meat tenderizer half an hour before cooking.

### BEEF STEAK PHILIPPINE

2 lb. boneless beef, sliced
   into 1/4-inch thick (sirloin,
   top or bottom may be used)
1/4 c. soy sauce
1 tsp. MSG
1/2 c. sliced onion rings
1 1/2 Tbsp. lemon juice
1/4 tsp. pepper
3 Tbsp. vegetable oil

   When purchasing beef ask butcher to slice beef for you. Combine soy sauce, lemon juice, pepper and MSG. Pour over beef slices. Mix well. Marinate several hours, if time permits. Saute' onion in hot oil until transparent. Transfer to platter. Increase heat to medium-high and pan-fry beef slices a few at a time until browned on both sides. Serve hot with sauteed onions and French fries, if desired.
   Serves 6.
   NOTE: Meat tenderizer may be lightly sprinkled on beef slices a few minutes before cooking. If sauce is desired with the beef steak, double recipe for marinade and save remaining marinade after browning beef. Add about 1/2 to 3/4 cup of water to marinade and bring to boil. Thicken with 2 teaspoons of corn-
   (Cont.)

starch dissolved in 2 tablespoons water. Add browned beef slices and simmer for 5 minutes. Serve hot with sauteed onions.

## BEEF TONGUE ESTOFADO

1 fresh beef tongue (about 4 to 5 lb.)
3 garlic cloves, crushed
3 ripe medium-sized tomatoes or 1 small can tomato paste
1 tsp. whole peppercorns
1 bay leaf
3 Tbsp. soy sauce
2 tsp. salt
2 medium potatoes, peeled and quartered
3 Tbsp. vegetable oil
1/4 c. sliced onion
3 Tbsp. vinegar or cooking wine
3 Tbsp. sugar
2 tsp. MSG
6 baby carrots

Immerse tongue in a large pot of boiling water for 15 minutes. Drain, peel off outer skin or scrape with a knife, and trim the root ends. Wash tongue. In large pot, heat cooking oil and tongue. Saute' in garlic, onion and tomatoes. Add 1 cup of water, peppercorns, bay leaf, vinegar or wine, soy sauce, sugar, salt and MSG. Cover and cook over low heat for 2 1/2 hours, adding more water as needed and pricking tongue to let sauce penetrate. Pressure cooking takes about 1 hour only. Season to taste. When tongue is tender, cook in potatoes and carrots until soft. Slice tongue; pour sauce over when ready to serve. Makes 8 servings.

NOTE: Tongue may be marinated in the seasonings for several hours before browning. Save marinade to simmer tongue in. Stuffed olives and mushrooms may be added during last 15 minutes of cooking.

## CALDERETTA

2 lb. beef or lamb, cut into 1 1/2-inch chunks
4 Tbsp. soy sauce
1/2 tsp. salt
2 garlic cloves, crushed
1 (8 oz.) tomato sauce
2 medium potatoes, peeled and quartered
1 tsp. MSG
1/2 c. stuffed olives
3 Tbsp. sherry or vinegar
2 Tbsp. vegetable oil
1 medium onion, sliced
1/2 lb. (about 6 inches long) pepperoni, sliced 1/4-inch thick, diagonally
1/2 tsp. pepper
1 medium green pepper, seeds removed, cut into 1-inch squares

Season meat with soy sauce, sherry or vinegar, and salt. Set aside. In hot oil brown garlic, add onions and cook until transparent. Add tomato sauce and beef, stir 2 minutes; reduce heat to low and simmer covered for 15 minutes. Add about 2 cups water, simmer covered for 45 minutes or until meat is tender. Add pepperoni, potatoes, MSG and pepper. Simmer 7 minutes, or until potatoes are soft. Taste. Add olives and green pepper;

cook 3 minutes more.

Serves 6 to 8.

NOTE: In the Philippines goat's meat is the popular main ingredient.

## CALLOS  (Beef Tripe)

3 Tbsp. vegetable oil
1 small onion, sliced
2 lb. beef tripe, cleaned and cut into 1 1/2-inch squares
1/2 tsp. salt
1/2 c. sliced pepperoni
1 carrot, cut into 1/2-inch cubes
1 c. canned chick peas, (garbanzos) drained

1 medium green pepper, sliced
2 garlic cloves, crushed
1 can (8 oz.) tomato sauce
1/4 tsp. pepper
1 medium potato, cut into 1/2-inch cubes
1 tsp. MSG

Brown garlic in hot oil, then add onion. Stir until transparent. Add tomato sauce, tripe, salt and pepper. Stir for 5 minutes. Add 5 cups water, simmer covered for 1 1/2 hours or until tripe is tender.

Add pepperoni, potato, carrots and MSG. Simmer covered for 5 minutes. Season to taste. Add chick peas and green pepper. Simmer, covered, for 7 minutes more.

Serves 6.

## CHARCOAL BROILED STEAK

2 lb. steak
1 small onion, minced or 1/2 tsp. powdered
1 tsp. MSG
1/4 tsp. pepper
2 Tbsp. sherry or wine

1 garlic clove, crushed, or 1/2 tsp. powdered
1 tsp. salt
2-3 Tbsp. sugar
4 Tbsp. soy sauce
2 Tbsp. vegetable oil

Trim off visible fat on steak, if necessary. Mix next 8 ingredients and marinate steak in it for an hour or more. Steak should be at room temperature and brushed or coated with oil before starting to broil. Make several cuts around the fat edges so that steak will stay flat during broiling.

Broil steak over red hot coals no longer smoking or flaming. Cook on one side to desired doneness, turn and cook the other side. To test, cut meat and see if meat is done to suit you. Don't overcook. Serve hot.

(Cont.)

Serves 4.

NOTE: Allow 1/2 pound boneless steak for 1 person and 3/4 to 1 pound steak bone in. Broil meat, 2 to 4 inches above coals. For an inch-thick steak, broil for a total of 10 to 12 minutes for rare; 14 minutes for medium.

## EMPANADA (Meat Turnover)

| | |
|---|---|
| 1 lb. ground beef | 1/2 c. raisins, seedless |
| 1 small onion, minced or | 1 garlic clove, minced or |
| 1/2 tsp. onion powder | 1/2 tsp. garlic powder |
| 1 c. diced potato (1 medium) | 1 tsp. salt |
| dash of pepper | 1/2 tsp. MSG |

Brown ground beef in uncovered pan. When oil comes out, push meat to one side and saute' garlic until brown, then add onion. Mix in meat. Add potato and cook, while stirring, until potatoes are tender. Season with salt, pepper and MSG. Mix in raisins, taste; let cool. Meanwhile, prepare pastry.

Pastry:

pie crust, ready-made, enough for 2 (9-inch) pie crusts

Follow directions on package of pie-crust mix. Instead of rolling out dough to the shape of a pie pan, form 1-inch balls. Sprinkle flour on rolling pin and rolling surface. Roll out ball 1/8-inch thick and about 6 inches circumference. Put a spoon of meat mixture on one side of dough and fold in half-moon shape. Press edges with fork prongs. Trim irregular edges. Arrange empanadas on greased baking sheet. Bake at 425° for 12 to 15 minutes, or until golden brown.

Makes 20 empanadas.

Empanada Pastry (Another recipe):

| | |
|---|---|
| 3 c. all-purpose flour | 1/2 c. water |
| 4 Tbsp. sugar | 1/3 c. oil |
| 1/2 tsp. MSG | 3 egg yolks, save egg whites |
| 1/2 tsp. salt | for sealing empanadas |

Mix and knead all ingredients until dough is soft. On floured board, roll to 1/8-inch thick. Cut into 4 or 5-inch diameter circles. Use wide-mouthed jar, can or cup for cutting circles. Put a spoonful of meat filling (see Empanada recipe) on center of each circle, fold to half-moon shape, wet edges with enough egg white and press and seal edges. Deep fat fry in hot oil, until golden brown on both sides. Drain on paper towels.

Makes about 2 dozen.

NOTE: Reroll dough remnants to cut more circles.

One can put any meat filling desired. Flaked cooked chicken may be used instead of beef. Peas or diced carrots are other items which can be added. Children and adults enjoy empanadas as finger foods. Good for "baon" (lunch bag) as well. Buttermilk biscuit dough or Country Style biscuit dough which comes in tube packages of 10 biscuits in each package, are very economical and labor-saving when used as pastry. Just flatten the biscuit with oiled fingers (no rolling required) and proceed to fill and shape empanadas as below.

**TRIMMING EMPANADA**  **TRIMMED EMPANADA**

## MECHADO

2 1/2 lb. boneless whole piece of beef (any roast)
1 can (8 oz.) tomato sauce
1/4 c. onions, sliced
2 Tbsp. vinegar
1 tsp. salt
1/4 tsp. cinnamon (optional)
2 tsp. MSG
1/4 c. soy sauce
3 cloves garlic, crushed
2 Tbsp. wine or cooking sherry
1/2 tsp. pepper
2 bay leaves

Mix all other ingredients in a pot, then marinate beef in mixture. Cover and simmer for 30 minutes. Add a cup of water and continue to simmer, covered, for 1 1/2 hours more, or until meat is tender. Taste and correct seasoning if needed. Slice crosswise against fibers when serving.

NOTE: A strip of pork fat may be inserted lengthwise in middle of beef, skim off extra fat after meat is cooked. Quartered potatoes and baby carrots may be added during last 10 minutes.

## MEAT LOAF

2 eggs  
1 c. bread crumbs  
1/2 c. sweet relish  
1 tsp. MSG  
1/2 tsp. pepper  
1 tsp. salt  

2 lb. ground beef (or combination of ground beef and ground pork)  
1 c. milk  
1 c. seedless raisins (optional)  
1 medium onion, minced  

    Preheat oven to 350°.
    In large bowl, beat eggs slightly with fork. Stir in milk and bread crumbs until bread crumbs are thoroughly moistened. Add the rest of the ingredients and mix very well. Transfer to an 8-cup capacity loaf pan or shape into a loaf on a baking dish. Bake 1 hour. Remove to platter.
    Serves 12.
    NOTE: Two hard-cooked eggs, cut into 8 wedges, may be arranged in the middle of the loaf before baking.


## MORCON (Beef Roll)

1 piece beef flank (about 2 lb.)  
1/4 c. soy sauce  
1 small can (4 oz.) Vienna sausage, drained  
2 hard-cooked eggs, halved lengthwise  
1 fresh carrot, quartered lengthwise  

1 small onion, chopped  
1 tsp. MSG  
1/4 c. vinegar  
1/4 tsp. pepper  
1/4 c. sweet pickles  
1/2 c. stuffed olives  
1 garlic clove, crushed  
1 can (8 oz.) tomato sauce  
1/2 bay leaf (optional)

Marinate beef flank in a mixture of vinegar, soy sauce and pepper for 10 minutes or more. Drain beef. Save marinade. Spread beef flank and arrange in rows Vienna sausage, sweet pickles, hard-cooked eggs, stuffed olives and carrot all over beef. Carefully roll with fibers lengthwise and secure with string. Simmer covered in a mixture of the marinade, garlic, onion, tomato sauce, MSG and bay leaf and 1 1/2 cups water for 1 hour or until meat is tender. Season to taste. Transfer meat roll to a platter, remove string and slice 1/2-inch thick crosswise. Pour sauce over meat. Garnish with parsley.
Serves 6.

## PINAPAITAN (Bitter-Flavored Meat)

- 1 lb. beef tripe, sliced fine or diced
- 1 lb. beef, boneless, sliced fine or diced
- 1/2 lb. beef liver, sliced fine or diced, soaked in 2 to 3 Tbsp. vinegar
- 1 Tbsp. salt
- 2 Tbsp. oil
- 4 cloves fresh garlic, minced
- 1 medium onion, sliced fine
- 2 Tbsp. fresh ginger root, sliced fine
- 1/4 tsp. beef bile

Prepare meats and sprinkle salt on them. Set aside.
In hot oil saute' garlic until fragrant; add onion, saute' a minute then add ginger root, sauteeing another 2 minutes. Keeping heat on high, add tripe and beef, constantly stirring until most of liquid evaporates.
Now, add about 4 cups water and let simmer, covered for 1 hour or until meats are tender. Season to taste with salt and pepper, if desired. Add liver, soaked in vinegar, and simmer, covered, for another 7 minutes or until liver is tender. Stir in beef bile; boil 1 minute.
Serve hot.
Serves 4.
NOTE: This dish is popular in the Ilocos region - beef bile being the unique ingredient. Ask your butcher or friends who kill their own cattle to save the beef bile for you. Bile can be frozen.

## POCHERO

- 3 beef shins, preferably center cut
- 1 small onion, sliced
- 1 ripe cooking banana (plantain), or green eating banana, sliced 1-inch thick
- 1/4 lb. green beans
- 1 tsp. MSG
- 1 Tbsp. salt
- 1/2 c. pepperoni, sliced (optional)

(Cont.)

| | |
|---|---|
| 1 small sweet potato, quartered | 1/2 small cabbage, halved
1 scallion |

Boil beef shins in 5 cups water with salt and onions for 1 1/2 hours or until meat is tender. Add pepperoni, sweet potato and bananas. Cook 5 minutes, then add rest of ingredients. Cook another 3 minutes, until vegetables are done. Salt to taste if necessary. Skim off fat. Broth may be served in individual soup bowls while meat and vegetables are arranged on a platter.
Serves 3.

NOTE: Other meats like chicken, pork or beef cubes, or combination of these, can be used, and may be sauteed first in garlic, onion and tomatoes before boiling in water. Canned, drained chick peas (garbanzos), may be included with the other vegetables.

## PICADILLO (Boiled Ground Beef)

| | |
|---|---|
| 1 1/2 Tbsp. vegetable oil | 3 garlic cloves, crushed |
| 1/4 c. onions, sliced | 1/3 c. tomatoes, sliced |
| 2 c. ground beef (1/2 lb.) | 1 tsp. salt |
| 1/4 tsp. pepper | 1/2 tsp. MSG |
| 2 c. water | 2 c. diced potato |

Brown garlic in hot oil, stir in onions, then tomatoes for 3 minutes. Add ground beef and cook until brown. Season with salt, pepper and MSG. Add water. Cover and let boil for 10 minutes. Taste and season if needed. Add potatoes and cook until potatoes are soft.
Serves 5.

NOTE: Ground beef may be browned first without added oil, then proceed to saute' garlic, onions and tomatoes. The sauteed ground beef mixture is a basis for ground Beef Tortilla (see recipe), or Empanada (see recipe). Cook in quantity and refrigerate or freeze, for various dishes. Sliced green beans or sliced cabbage may even be cooked in place of potatoes. Lovers of raisins, add it.

## SPICY BEEF WITH GREEN PEPPER

| | |
|---|---|
| 2 lb. lean boneless beef | 1 medium-size green pepper, seeds removed, then thinly sliced into strips |
| 2 Tbsp. sherry | |
| 2 Tbsp. soy sauce | |
| 1/4 tsp. sugar | 1/4 c. vegetable oil |
| 1/2 tsp. salt | 1/2 tsp. fresh ginger, minced |
| 1 Tbsp. cornstarch dissolved in 2 Tbsp. water | 1 tsp. red hot pepper or red hot sauce |
| | 1 Tbsp. soy sauce |

Slice beef into thin strips. Marinate in next 4 ingredients for at least 30 minutes or longer. Thoroughly mix beef with cornstarch dissolved in water just before cooking beef. In very hot oil, brown ginger; stir in beef, add red hot pepper or red hot sauce and stir. Cook 5 minutes on high heat.

Remove from heat and transfer beef to a dish. Set aside. In same pan heat a tablespoon of oil on high heat, add green pepper and stir-cook for a minute. Add 1 tablespoon soy sauce. Transfer cooked beef back to pan, stir-cook with green pepper for 1 minute. Serve hot.

Serves 6 to 8.

NOTE: Boneless chicken breast or boneless pork may be used in place of beef.

## ADOBO (Chicken and Pork)

1 chicken, about 2 lb., cut into serving pieces
1 lb. pork butt, cut into 1 1/2 cubes or pork chops
1/2 c. vinegar
3 garlic cloves, crushed
1/2 laurel leaf (optional)
1/2 c. soy sauce
1/2 tsp. whole peppercorns

Mix all ingredients in a pot. Let stand an hour or even overnight. Cook covered on medium-high heat until mixture boils. Reduce heat to medium, turn meat and cook, covered, for 1 hour or until meat is tender and only a small amount of liquid is left. Serve with plain boiled rice.

Serves 6.

NOTE: After meat is cooked, it may be browned by heating a tablespoon of oil until hot, then browning the drained meat. Pour over remaining liquid where meat was cooked, before serving. Chicken or pork may be used individually.

## AFRITADA PORK AND CHICKEN

1 lb. pork, cut into 1 1/2-inch cubes
1 tsp. salt
2 Tbsp. soy sauce or patis (see Glossary)
1 large green pepper, cut into strips
1 small chicken (about 2 lb.), cut to serving pieces
3 Tbsp. vegetable oil
1 medium onion, sliced
1 tsp. MSG
2 garlic cloves, crushed
1/2 c. sliced tomatoes
1/8 tsp. pepper
3 medium potatoes, peeled and quartered

Wash and pat dry pork and chicken and sprinkle salt on them.
(Cont.)

Set aside. In hot oil, saute' garlic until light brown. Add onion and cook until transparent. Stir in tomatoes and cook until mushy. Add pork and chicken, cover and cook until oil comes out, stirring occasionally. Add soy sauce or patis (see Glossary), pepper, MSG and about 1 1/2 cups of water. Cook covered until meat is tender, about 35 minutes, and half of broth has evaporated. Season to taste. Add potatoes and cook until soft, then add green pepper. Mix thoroughly. Simmer 3 more minutes.

Serves 6 to 8.

## BATCHOY

1 lb. each pork kidney,
  liver, pancreas, cleaned
1 lb. pork loin
1 tsp. salt
3 Tbsp. oil
3 garlic cloves, crushed

1 medium onion, sliced fine
1 Tbsp. fresh ginger, sliced
2 to 3 c. broth or water
1/2 tsp. MSG
1/2 tsp. pepper

Slice internal organs and pork loin in small pieces. Sprinkle on salt. In hot oil saute' garlic and onions, add nuts and ginger; saute' for 5 minutes. Simmer, covered, for 15 minutes. Add broth or water, MSG and pepper. Simmer, covered, for another 20 minutes. Correct seasonings.

Serves 6.

NOTE: Fresh chives and young onions, chopped fine, can be used to sprinkle on top just before serving.

Visoyans add 1 cup of misua (see Glossary) just before serving, while adding more broth. One-half cup of hog's or beef blood, clotted and diced, may be added at the last 5 minutes of simmering.

## BICOL HOT EXPRESS

2 lb. boneless pork, sliced
  into small pieces
4 garlic cloves, crushed
1 medium onion, sliced fine

3 Tbsp. bagoong (see Glossary),
  (optional)
1 1/2 c. coconut milk
10 or more pieces hot chili
  peppers, sliced

Mix all ingredients except peppers in a pot. Simmer, covered, for 30 minutes, stirring occasionally until oil oozes out and meat is cooked. Stir in hot peppers and cook for another 5 to 10 minutes.

Serves 6.

NOTE: Thanks to Sarah Loyola from the province of Bicol for this recipe. This is supposed to be a spicy hot dish appropriate as appetizer or chaser for drinks. Salt instead of bagoong may be used, according to taste.

## BINAGOONGAN  (Sauteed Pork in Salted Seafood Sauce)

| | |
|---|---|
| 2 lb. pork butt, cut in pieces | 1 tsp. MSG |
| 2 Tbsp. cooking oil | 1 tsp. salt |
| 2 Tbsp. sliced onion | 3 cloves garlic, crushed |
| 2 Tbsp. fish or shrimp bagoong or patis (see Glossary) | 1/4 c. sliced tomatoes |

Sprinkle salt on pork pieces. In hot oil saute' garlic until brown; stir in onions, then tomatoes. Cook for 2 minutes, increase heat to high and stir in pork, then bagoong. Cook, uncovered, until pork fat comes out. Add about 1/2 cup of water, season with MSG. Reduce to medium heat and cook, covered, for 20 minutes, or until water is almost evaporated.
    Serves 4.
    NOTE: Pork chops may also be used.

## BURONG BABI  (Cured Pork, Pampanga-style)

| | |
|---|---|
| 3 lb. boneless pork butt, sliced thinly (1/8 to 1/4-inch thick) | 1 c. sugar |
| | 1/2 c. salt |
| | 1 tsp. salt peter |

Press both sides of pork slices in the mixture of sugar, salt and salt peter. Transfer to a clay or glass bowl and cover; let cure for 3 days. Sun dry preferably. To serve, fry or broil.
    Serves 6.
    NOTE: For a Chinese-flavored meat, add 1 teaspoon 5 spice seasoning to curing mixture, and a few drops of red food coloring.

## CHINESE SAUSAGE

| | |
|---|---|
| 5 lb. boneless pork butter with fat (3 parts lean, 2 parts fat) | 1/4 tsp. red food color, (optional) |
| 2 Tbsp. soy sauce | 1 tsp. 5-spice powder (optional) |
| 1/2 c. sugar | 1/2 c. vodka or other cheap, strong grain alcohol |
| 1 Tbsp. salt | |
| 1 tsp. MSG (monosodium glutamate) | 4 yards sausage casing (see Longaniza recipe) |
| 1 tsp. saltpeter (optional - see Glossary) | |

Coarsely grind or finely dice pork. It must not be as finely ground as hamburger. Thoroughly mix remaining ingredients, except casing, and pour over pork. Mix vigorously by hand. Let marinate 1 hour or overnight. Insert pork mixture into casing.
                                                            (Cont.)

Form sausage links by tying every 6 inches of sausage. If possible, sun-dry for 3 days; if not, hang indoors for 3 to 5 days or until dry. Can be frozen or kept in refrigerator for several days. Sausage may be steamed, or sliced thinly and pan-fried with onion or garlic slivers. Chinese sausage adds interesting flavor to noodle (pancit) dishes, fried rice, meat and vegetable dishes.

## CHITCHARON

2 lb. boneless pork with skin, fat and meat layer, preferably belly portion
1 tsp. salt
oil for deep-fat frying

Cut pork in about 2 x 3-inch pieces, 1-inch thick. Boil in salted water for 15 to 20 minutes. Drain well. Chill. Deep-fat fry in medium-hot oil, covered, until skin is bubbly and golden brown. Drain on paper towel. Cut into bite-size pieces. If desired, serve with anchovy sauce or 'bagoong' (see Glossary) mixed with fresh sliced tomatoes, chopped scallions or onions, and a pinch of minced fresh ginger; or Liver Sauce or Sweet and Sour Sauce (see recipes).
NOTE: When frying, pork pieces should be immersed in oil. Chitcharon can be refrigerated or frozen and used as flavor enhancer in Pinakbet or Dinengdeng (see recipes).

## CHORIZO DE BILBAO (Spanish Sausage)

3 lb. boneless beef, coarsely ground
1 lb. boneless pork, coarsely ground
1 Tbsp. salt
2 tsp. sugar
5 Tbsp. paprika
1/2 tsp. pepper
1 Tbsp. dried minced garlic
1/8 tsp. saltpeter (optional), (see Glossary)
1 Tbsp. liquid smoke
3 yards sausage casing

Combine all ingredients, except casing, and mix very well by hand for 10 minutes. Cover; cur in refrigerator 2 days. Insert into casing. Form sausage links by tying with thread every 6 inches of sausage. Dry under full sun for 3 days or dry in warm oven (120°F.) for 1 day. (If desired, put dried sausage in dry, clean jars and pour boiling lard to preserve Chorizo de Bilbao.)
To Use: Slice diagonally and pan-fry or add uncooked sausage to casserole dishes, such as Chicken Pastel, Tongue Estofado and other Spanish dishes.
NOTE: Meat must be finely cut, but not as fine as hamburger. Pepperoni is a good substitute for Spanish sausage. Liquid Smoke can be found where the flavoring and spice section is at your supermarket. Ask the grocer.

## DINUGUAN

2 lb. pork butt or pork with skin, sliced into small pieces (1 x 1/2-inch)
1 1/2 tsp. salt
3 Tbsp. cooking oil
2 ripe tomatoes, chopped
1/2 c. hog's blood

4 pieces green hot pepper (if available, otherwise use 1/2 tsp. powdered pepper)
1 tsp. MSG
1/3 c. vinegar
2 cloves garlic, crushed
2 Tbsp. onions, sliced
1/2 bay leaf, if desired

Sprinkle salt over pork pieces and add vinegar. In a pot, saute' garlic, onion and tomatoes in hot oil. Add seasoned pork and bay leaf and cook covered until pork pinkness is gone and oil comes out.

Mix about 2 cups water with the hog's blood, then add to pork, little by little while stirring continuously. Simmer covered for 30 minutes. Add green hot pepper and MSG. Simmer 5 more minutes. Season to taste. Serve with puto (see Glossary) or boiled rice.

Makes 6 servings.

NOTE: Internal organs, like heart, liver, and pancreas may be used together with pork meat. One-half teaspoon of oregano added, gives a pungent aroma.

## EASY BARBECUE PORK CHOPS

1/4 c. Worcestershire sauce
2 lb. pork chops

2 Tbsp. soy sauce
1/4 c. sugar

Combine Worcestershire sauce and soy sauce. Dip each pork chop in sauce, then sprinkle half a teaspoon of sugar on each side of the pork chops. Marinate in sauce for 2 hours or overnight in the refrigerator. Bake in preheated 325° to 350° oven. After 30 minutes, turn pork chops and bake another 30 minutes.

Serves 6.

NOTE: This recipe is very good on spareribs as well.

## EMBUTIDO (Ground Meat Roll)

1 lb. ground pork
1 c. milk
3/4 c. seedless raisins (optional)

1/2 c. sweet relish
1/2 tsp. pepper
1 small onion, minced

(Cont.)

1 tsp. salt
1 tsp. MSG
2 eggs, beaten
1 c. bread crumbs

1 small can (4 oz.) Vienna
  sausages, drained, or 3 hot dogs,
  quartered lengthwise
2 hard-cooked eggs, quartered

Preheat oven to 350°.

Mix first 10 ingredients very well. Shape mixture to a 4 x 12-inch rectangular loaf on a 12 x 18-inch piece of aluminum foil. Arrange in alternate rows the hard cooked eggs and sausages on the loaf. Shape loaf into a 2-inch diameter roll, with eggs and sausages inside. Securely wrap the meat roll lengthwise with the aluminum foil and close both ends. Transfer wrapped roll on a pan and bake at 350° for 1 hour and 15 minutes. Before serving, remove wrapping and slice crosswise 1/2-inch thick. Serve hot or cold with catsup.

Serves 10.

## **FRIED PORK SLICES**

3 Tbsp. soy sauce
1 Tbsp. cooking wine
1/2 tsp. MSG
1/2 tsp. minced fresh ginger
  or powdered ginger
dash pepper
4 Tbsp. sugar

1/2 tsp. garlic salt
1 Tbsp. sesame oil
1/4 c. flour
1 lb. pork slices, 1/2-inch
  thick x 2 x 2-inch
vegetable oil for deep frying

Mix first 8 ingredients. Marinate pork slices in mixture for at least 2 hours or overnight in refrigerator. Drain pork slices. Put flour in a small bag and shake 2 or 3 pork slices at a time, completely coating them. Deep-fry in hot oil until crispy and golden brown on both sides, about 10 minutes in all. Drain on paper towels. Serve hot.

Serves 4.

## **GUISADO** (Basis for Sauteed Dishes)

1 lb. boneless pork, cut
  into small pieces
1/2 lb. medium shrimps,
  shelled, slit into 2
1 tsp. salt
1 garlic clove, crushed

1 medium tomato, ripe, finely
  sliced (omit for pancit and
  lumpia, see note)
1/2 tsp. MSG
2 Tbsp. vegetable oil
1 small onion, finely sliced
1/4 tsp. pepper

Prepare pork and shrimps. Sprinkle salt on them. Set aside. In hot oil, lightly brown garlic, add onions, stir-cook until transparent. Add tomatoes; stir-cook until mushy. With heat on high, add pork pieces, stir-cook for 5 minutes, or until pork pinkness is gone. Add about 1/4 cup water. Cover and cook over medium heat for 10 minutes or until pork is tender. Add shrimps, MSG, pepper and patis. Stir-cook for 5 to 7 minutes. Season to taste.

Yields about 3 cups of guisado.

NOTE: With this basic guisado recipe, one can cook various dishes like Pancit*, Lumpia*, practically all vegetable "guisado" recipes like Cabbage guisado*, and soups. Cook this in large quantities, increasing cooking time. Divide to meal-size portions, label and freeze for future use. This way labor, time and fuel are reduced when preparing a dish.

Guisado can be eaten as is. A teaspoon of patis (see Glossary) or soy sauce may be used as additional seasoning.

*See recipes.

## HAM SMOKED PORK SHOULDER

1 smoked pork shoulder, (about 4 lb.)
2 c. pineapple juice
1/2 c. brown sugar or 1/3 c. white sugar
1 Tbsp. vinegar

Wash smoked pork shoulder in cold water to remove excess smoky taste. Add pineapple juice, sugar and vinegar. Prick meat with fork or sharp pointed knife to let added ingredients penetrate. If time permits marinate overnight or several days in the refrigerator, turning meat occasionally for seasoning to penetrate better. Simmer, covered, with the marinade for 1 hour, turning meat once and basting with the sauce.

Drain ham, peel off skin and sprinkle more sugar on cooked ham. Bake, uncovered, in 350° oven for 1 hour or until golden brown. May be served hot or cold.

Serves 8.

NOTE: Fruit syrup saved from drained canned fruits may be used to marinate and simmer ham in.

## HIGADO

2 lb. boneless pork, diced 3/4-inch
1/ lb. pork or beef liver, diced
1/2 lb. heart, diced (optional)
1/2 lb. kidney, diced, (optional)
1/2 c. vinegar
1/2 c. soy sauce
1 tsp. salt
1/4 tsp. pepper
3 Tbsp. oil
5 garlic cloves, minced
1/2 c. onion, sliced
2 green peppers, seeds removed, diced
2 c. canned green peas, drained
1/2 tsp. MSG            (Cont.)

Season meats with vinegar, soy sauce, salt and pepper. Marinate 1/2 hour, lesser or longer.

In hot oil, brown garlic; add onion, saute' a minute then add seasoned meats. Saute' uncovered until most of liquid evaporates. Add about 1 1/2 cups of water. Simmer, covered, for 1/2 hour or until meat is tender, stirring occasionally. Liquid remaining should be a small amount. Add green pepper and monosodium glutamate. Cook, covered, 3 minutes, then add green peas. Cook just to heat peas, while stirring.

Serves 6.

## HUMBA  (Pork in Brown Sauce)

3 lb. pork hocks or pork shoulder, cut into serving pieces
3 garlic cloves, crushed
1/2 c. vinegar
1/4 c. sugar, preferably brown
1/4 c. soy sauce
1 bay leaf
1/2 tsp. MSG
1 c. water

Mix all ingredients in large pot, cover and simmer for 1 hour, or until pork is tender. Serve hot.

Serves 6.

NOTE: Other ingredients to use if desired are 1/4 teaspoon oregano, 1/2 teaspoon peppercorns, 3 tablespoons salted black beans, 1/2 cup peanuts, and 1 cup dried banana blossoms. The longer the seasonings marinate the pork, the more tasty the dish.

## LECHON DE LECHE  (Suckling Pig Roast)

1 whole suckling pig, 20 to 25 lb.
1/4 c. peppercorns, freshly ground or pounded
1 c. garlic salt

Order suckling pig in advance from meat store, butcher or piggery. Wash pig very well and pat dry with paper towels. Rub the inside and outside of the pig with sufficient garlic salt. Rub the inside with freshly ground peppercorns.

For outdoor charcoal roasting, ready 4 (20 pound) bags of charcoal briquets. With a pole (10 feet long, 3 inch diameter bamboo pole or unfinished bannister from a lumber shop), thrust pig from mouth through anus. Close or sew up abdomen. With wire tie front and hind legs tightly around the pole, so pig will not go around pole while pole is being rotated. Wrap a piece of aluminum foil around part of pole exposed to fire. Start fire with a bag of charcoal, adding more as needed during roasting period. Start to roast when charcoals are glowing. Pig should be roasted 2 feet above the fire.

Have two persons rotate pig continuously for about 6 hours. During roasting period baste the skin with water every 15 minutes. Sprinkle water on live coals whenever fire flares up. Skin should be crisp and golden brown when done. Cut to serving pieces. Serve with Liver Sauce (see recipe).

Serves 25.

For oven roasting: Preheat oven large enough for whole pig, to 350°. Instead of using pole, truss legs forward, close to the body. Keep mouth open with a standing piece of stick or wood put between upper and lower jaw. Put pig on oven wire rack and place a big pan lined with aluminum foil on the next lower oven rack to catch the meat drippings.

Brush pig skin with oil or melted lard. Loosely cover with a large piece of aluminum foil. Roast for about 7 hours (25 minutes roasting time to the pound), basting approximately every hour with the fat drippings.

During last hour, increase heat to 425°, basting every 15 minutes to make skin hard and crisp. Remove from oven, replace stick between the mouth with a red apple, garnish with parsley or scallions, and roasted chestnuts, if desired.

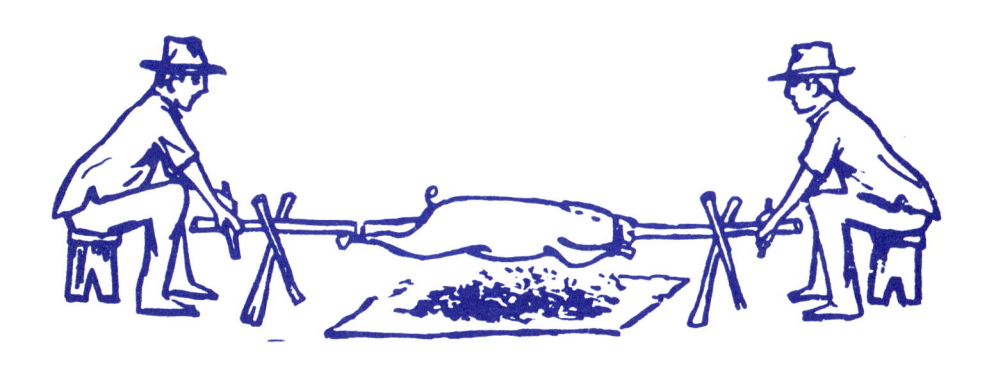

## LECHON   (Pork Roast)

| | |
|---|---|
| 1 fresh pork shoulder with skin or fresh pork ham with skin (about 5 lb.) | 1 Tbsp. salt |

Preheat oven to 350°. Rub pork with salt. Roast in oven for 3 1/2 hours. During last hour, occasionally brush pork skin with fat drippings or lard to make skin crisp. Increase heat to 425° and roast for about 30 minutes more. Skin should be hard

(Cont.)

and crisp. Cut into serving pieces and serve with Liver Sauce (see recipe).
Serves 8.

## LECHON SA KAWALI  (Pork Roast in Pan)

| | |
|---|---|
| 2 lb. fresh bacon slab with skin or boneless pork with skin | oil for deep fat frying 3 c. water with 2 Tbsp. vinegar |

Boil pork in water - vinegar for 30 minutes, or until tender. Drain well, cool. Pat dry with paper towels. Fry, uncovered, in at least 3 inches deep hot oil until crisp and golden brown. Transfer meat to strainer to drip excess oil. When cool, slice to bite-size pieces.

Serve with dipping mixture of 1/2 cup vinegar, 1 tablespoon soy sauce, 1/4 teaspoon salt, 1 garlic clove, crushed, and 1 tablespoon thin onion slices.
Serves 6.

## LONGANIZA  (Sausage Philippine)

| | |
|---|---|
| 1/2 c. vinegar | 2 1/2 tsp. salt |
| 1 tsp. pepper | 3 lb. fatty pork (6 c.), coarsely ground or chopped fine |
| 3 Tbsp. sugar | |
| 2 Tbsp. minced garlic | 2 yards pork casing* |
| 1 tsp. paprika | |

Mix first 6 ingredients. Pour over pork and mix well. Let stand for 1 hour or even longer. Insert into pork casing. Form sausage links by tying every 6 inches of the sausage. Dry in a warm oven (120°) for 6 hours, if desired. Otherwise, keep sausage in refrigerator until ready to use. Will keep well for several days. To cook: Boil in 1 inch deep water (covered), until dry. Prick sausages and fry in its own fat until golden brown.

NOTE: If pork casing is not available, cook pork mixture with a little water in a covered pan until water evaporates. Stir while the meat browns.

Achuete coloring (see Glossary) or 1/8 teaspoon red food coloring and 1/4 teaspoon saltpeter may be added, if desired.

*Italian meat stores and other meat stores sell fresh pork casing. In supermarkets Armour has it packed in salt in small cartons.

## MENUDO

2 lb. boneless pork, diced 3/4-inch
1 tsp. salt
3 Tbsp. soy sauce
3 Tbsp. oil
3 garlic cloves, minced
1/2 c. onion, sliced fine
1 c. tomato, sliced
2 c. potato, peeled, diced 1/2 inch
1 sweet green pepper, seeds removed, diced
1/8 tsp. pepper
1/2 tsp. MSG (monosodium glutamate)

Season pork with salt and soy sauce. Set aside.

In hot oil, brown garlic; add onion, saute' a minute. Then add tomato; saute' 3 minutes. Add seasoned pork; saute' uncovered until most of liquid evaporates. Add about 1 cup water; simmer covered for 30 minutes, or until meat is tender. Add potatoes; cook covered for 5 minutes. Add green pepper and monosodium glutamate. Cook covered for 3 minutes. Season to taste with salt and pepper. Only a small amount of thickened liquid should remain in pot.

Serves 5.

This is a popular Tagalog dish.

NOTE: For those who like liver, add about 1 cup of diced pork or beef liver mixed with 2 tablespoons vinegar 10 minutes before adding potatoes.

One cup of drained garbanzos (chick peas) and/or diced carrots may be added with potatoes.

I have a friend who cooks his 'Menudo' U.S. style by simply putting the meat, seasonings and condiments all in a pot, uses 1/2 cup tomato sauce, or catsup, instead of tomatoes, adds a small can of Vienna sausage, sliced, and lets all these simmer covered until meat is done, stirring <u>occasionally</u>; then adds the potatoes and green pepper, cooking them until done. His tasted very good, too!

## PAKSIW LEFTOVER LECHON (Sweet and Sour Stewed Roast Pork)

2 lb. leftover lechon (roast pork), cut into 1 1/2-inch cubes or slices
1/2 c. leftover liver sauce (if available, see recipe)
2 cloves garlic, crushed
3 Tbsp. soy sauce
1/2 tsp. MSG
1/4 tsp. peppercorns
1/2 bay leaf (optional)
1/4 c. vinegar
1/4 c. sugar
1/2 tsp. salt
1/8 tsp. oregano (optional)
1/2 c. water

(Cont.)

Mix all ingredients in a pot. Cover and boil gently for 30 minutes. Taste and correct seasoning.

Serves 6 to 8.

## PORK OR BEEF TORTILLA  (Omelet)

| | |
|---|---|
| 1 lb. ground pork or beef or combination of both | 3 eggs, beaten |
| 1 garlic clove, crushed | 1 Tbsp. minced onion |
| 1 medium-size ripe tomato, sliced | 1 tsp. salt |
| dash of pepper | 1/2 tsp. MSG |
| | 3 Tbsp. vegetable oil |

Brown meat in skillet while stirring. Push meat to one side and saute' garlic, onion and tomatoes. Cook for 3 minutes, then mix in meat. Add salt, pepper and MSG. Pour mixture to beaten eggs. Heat oil in clean skillet. Pour egg mixture and cook over medium heat. Turn over to cook.

Makes 4 servings. Serve with catsup.

NOTE: For raisin lovers, 1/2 cup of raisins may be added after adding tomatoes.

## PORK PAKSIW  (Sweet and Sour Stewed Pork)

| | |
|---|---|
| 3 lb. boneless pork shoulder, cut into 1 1/2-inch cubes or pork hocks | 1 tsp. MSG |
| 1 1/2 tsp. salt | 1 Tbsp. cooking oil |
| 3/4 c. vinegar | 1/4 c. soy sauce |
| 1/2 c. sugar | 3 cloves garlic, crushed |
| 1/2 tsp. peppercorns | 1 bay leaf (optional) |
| | 1 to 1 1/2 c. water |

When buying pork shoulder, ask butcher to bone it. Sprinkle salt over meat, heat oil in pot over high heat and brown pork. Reduce heat and mix in rest of ingredients except the water. Cover pot and simmer for 15 minutes. Add water and let boil for 1 1/2 hours, or until meat is tender. Taste and correct seasoning.

Serves 6.

NOTE: Pig's feet (pata) can be used in place of pork.

## SATE BABI  (Pork Barbecue, Indonesian)

| | |
|---|---|
| 1/4 c. vinegar | 1/2 c. sugar |
| 4 cloves garlic, crushed | 2 tsp. salt |
| 1 tsp. pepper | |

| | |
|---|---|
| 1 tsp. MSG | 2 lb. pork butt, cut into 1-inch |
| 1/4 c. soy sauce | cube or pork chops |

Mix first 7 ingredients in a bowl, marinate pork in mixture for an hour or even overnight. Turn pork occasionally for even marination. Skewer pork pieces in bamboo sticks and charcoal broil or oven broil. Serve with Sate Sauce (see recipe).
Serves 5.

## SINIGANG PORK OR BEEF (Boiled)

| | |
|---|---|
| 1 lb. pork or beef cubes or combination of each | 1/4 lb. green beans |
| | 3 medium tomatoes, sliced |
| 1 medium onion, sliced | 1 tsp. salt |
| 1/4 c. lemon juice | 10 radishes |

In a covered pot simmer meat, onions, tomatoes, lemon juice and salt for an hour or until meat is tender. Add 1 cup of water; simmer, covered, for 5 minutes. Taste and season if needed. Before serving, let dish come to a boil, add vegetables and cook until tender.
Serves 4.
NOTE: Pork chops or beef with bones may be used. Spinach, sliced eggplant, cabbage or okra may also be used for vegetables.

## SAUTEED PORK WITH CUCUMBER

| | |
|---|---|
| 1/2 lb. lean boneless pork | 1 Tbsp. soy sauce |
| 3 Tbsp. vegetable oil | 2 eggs, well beaten with a pinch of salt |
| 3 pieces dried mushrooms, softened, thinly sliced | |
| | 1/2 tsp. salt |
| 1 medium cucumber, unpared, seeds removed, sliced into thin strips | 2 scallion stalks, finely chopped |
| | 1/2 tsp. MSG |

Slice pork into thin strips. Sprinkle salt on pork. Heat oil on high, stir in scallions. Add pork strips and stir-cook for 5 minutes, then add mushrooms and cucumber. Stir-cook 1 minute, add soy sauce and MSG. After a minute add beaten eggs. Stir-cook 2 minutes.
Serves 4.

## SPARERIBS

3 lb. spareribs  
2 Tbsp. sugar  
2 Tbsp. sherry  
3 Tbsp. soy sauce  
1 Tbsp. garlic salt  
2 Tbsp. Hoisin sauce (see Glossary)  
3 Tbsp. catsup  

    Wash and drain spareribs. Mix last 6 ingredients and brush or rub all over spareribs. Let stand 2 hours or even overnight. Brush a small amount of vegetable oil on spareribs before roasting at 325° for 1 hour and 15 minutes.
    Serves 4.

## SWEET AND SOUR PORK

1 lb. pork butt or cutlets, cut into 1-inch cubes  
1/3 c. flour  
1/4 tsp. pepper  
1/2 c. pineapple chunks, drained  
1 whole fresh green pepper, cut into 1-inch squares  
1 fresh carrot, thinly sliced in rounds  
1 Tbsp. soy sauce  
1/4 c. sugar  
2 Tbsp. vinegar  
1 Tbsp. cornstarch dissolved in 2 Tbsp. water  
1 tsp. salt  
3/4 c. vegetable oil for frying  
1/4 c. sweet pickles, drained  
1 c. pineapple syrup (saved from drained pineapple chunks)  
1 tsp. garlic salt  
1 tsp. MSG  

    Combine flour, salt and pepper in a small paper bag. Put 3 pieces of pork at a time in the bag and shake. Fry coated pork in hot oil until golden brown. Drain on paper towel. Remove oil used in frying and return fried pork to clean frying pan. Add pineapple chunks, sweet pickles, green pepper and carrots. In a bowl, mix pineapple syrup, soy sauce, sugar, garlic salt, vinegar and MSG. Taste and season as needed.
    Pour over pork mixture and boil for 2 minutes. Stir in dissolved cornstarch and cook for another 3 minutes.
    Serves 4.
    NOTE: 1/2 cup quartered, fresh, red-ripe tomatoes when included will add a more interesting color combination.

## KARI-KARI

4 pieces pork hocks or 2-3 lb. cut-up fresh oxtail  
2 garlic cloves, crushed  
3 Tbsp. vegetable oil  
3 Tbsp. onion, sliced  
3 Tbsp. bagoong (see Glossary)  
1 small eggplant, cut into serving pieces

1 tsp. MSG  
1/2 lb. fresh green beans  
1/3 c. peanut butter

Boil the pork hocks or oxtail in 5 cups water with 2 teaspoons salt, for 1 hour or until meat is tender. Set aside. Saute' garlic and onion in hot oil, until brown. Spoon out cooked pork hocks or oxtail and saute' with the garlic and onions, stir in bagoong. Saute' for 3 minutes, then add to stock where meat was boiled. Simmer 10 minutes. Add MSG and season to taste. Add eggplant and green beans and cook until tender. Reduce heat to simmer and stir in peanut butter. Mix well and simmer for 5 minutes. Serve hot with sauteed Bagoong Alamang (see recipe).

Makes 4 servings.

NOTE: Kari-Kari may be thickened with 2 to 3 tablespoons of rice flour or all-purpose flour, toasted or browned on a dry pan over medium heat. Make a paste of the toasted flour with the stock and add when adding the peanut butter. For an orange-red color use achuete coloring (see Glossary), if desired.

## TAPA (Dried Meat)

4 cloves garlic, minced  
1/4 c. soy sauce  
1 tsp. MSG  
1/4 c. sugar  
1/4 c. vinegar  
1 tsp. salt  
1 tsp. saltpeter (optional) (see Glossary)  
2 lb. pork butt, thinly sliced (1/8-inch thick) or boneless beef roast, thinly sliced

Thoroughly mix first 7 ingredients in a bowl, marinate meat in mixture for several hours or even several days in the refrigerator. Fry to golden brown, or skewer meat in bamboo sticks or skewers and broil.

Serves 6.

NOTE: "Tapa" can also be made by sprinkling garlic salt generously on each slice of meat. Drying, if desired, may be done in a lukewarm oven (120°) for 6 hours or sun dried. I have seen others spread a piece of aluminum foil over heated radiator and dry the "tapa" right on it!

## TOCINO (Spanish Bacon)

2 lb. pork butt, thinly sliced, 1/8-inch thick  
1 c. sugar  
1 tsp. saltpeter  
1 Tbsp. salt  
3-4 drops red coloring

(Cont.)

Ask meat man to slice pork butt into 1/8-inch thick slices. Mix very well sugar, salt, saltpeter and red coloring. Lightly press both sides of pork slices in this mixture, one slice at a time. Let pork cure in this mixture for at least a day, before frying to a golden brown, on medium heat. Uncooked cured pork can be stored in the refrigerator for several days or a week.

Serves 6.

## ASADO CHICKEN

1/4 c. soy sauce
1 tsp. MSG
4 Tbsp. lemon juice
1/2 c. water

1/2 tsp. salt
3 Tbsp. Worcestershire sauce
2 Tbsp. cornstarch
2 lb. chicken, cut up

Mix first 7 ingredients, then pour on chicken. If time allows let it stand for an hour or so, otherwise proceed to boil gently for about an hour in a covered pot, or until meat is tender. If desired, garnish with fried onion rings.

Serves 4.

NOTE: Above Asado sauce is basic for sliced beef, sliced pork or pork chops, or sliced fish, in place of chicken.

## CHICKEN WITH ASPARAGUS

1 chicken (1 1/2 lb.), whole
  or cut up
salt and pepper to taste
1 tsp. MSG
2 eggs, slightly beaten,
  (optional)
5 c. water with 1 tsp. salt

2 Tbsp. vegetable oil
1 medium onion, finely sliced
1 garlic clove
1 can (14 1/2 oz.) asparagus,
  cut or spears
2 Tbsp. cornstarch dissolved
  in 1/4 c. water

In a covered pot, boil chicken in 5 cups water with 1 teaspoon salt for 30 minutes. Dish out chicken, let cool; bone and slice into small pieces. Save broth.

In hot oil, brown garlic, add onions and cook until transparent. Add chicken broth and asparagus (including liquid) and simmer, covered for 10 minutes. Season to taste with salt, pepper and MSG. Add cornstarch dissolved in water, while stirring. Just before serving, let boil once, remove from heat and stir in slightly beaten egg. Serve hot.

Serves 6.

Can be served as a soup.

## CHICKEN WITH CASHEWS

2 chicken breasts, about 1 lb.
1 garlic clove, crushed
1/2 tsp. minced ginger, fresh
1 small green pepper, seeds removed, cut into thin strips
2 Tbsp. vegetable oil
2 Tbsp. soy sauce
1 small onion, finely sliced
1 tsp. sesame oil
1 c. cashew nuts, roasted

Bone chicken breasts and cut crosswise into thin strips. In hot vegetable oil brown garlic, discard it, then add onions, ginger and green pepper and saute' 1 minute. Add sesame oil, chicken and soy sauce. Saute' 5 minutes on high heat. Remove from heat, stir in cashews and serve hot.
Serves 4.

## CHICKEN BONELESS RELLENO

1 roasting chicken, about 4 lb.
1 Tbsp. soy sauce
2 tsp. salt
2 Tbsp. lemon juice

Stuffing:

1 lb. ground pork
1 c. milk
1 c. seedless raisins
1 c. peas, frozen or canned, drained
2 eggs, beaten
1 c. bread crumbs
1/2 c. sweet relish
1 c. tiny diced carrots
1 tsp. salt
1 tsp. MSG
2 hard-cooked eggs, quartered
1/8 tsp. pepper
1 small onion, minced
1 c. stuffed olives, drained

Debone chicken (see How to Bone a Chicken). Marinate boned chicken in a mixture of salt, soy sauce and lemon juice. Set aside and prepare stuffing.

Meantime, preheat oven to 350°. Mix all ingredients for stuffing, except hard-cooked eggs, until well blended. Close neck opening. Stuff chicken. Arrange hard-cooked egg quarters in stuffing. Sew up rear opening and shape stuffed chicken. Wrap with aluminum foil. Bake in 350° oven for 2 hours. Unwrap, increase heat to 375° and brown chicken a few minutes. Cool and slice as illustrated.

(Cont.)

Serves 12.

NOTE: If one does not have the time and patience to bone chicken, reduce stuffing recipe to half and stuff unboned whole chicken.

## CHICKEN CURRY

1 chicken (2 lb.), cut up
2 garlic cloves, crushed
2-3 tsp. curry powder
1/8 tsp. pepper
2 Tbsp. vegetable oil
1 small onion, sliced

1/3 c. vinegar
1 tsp. salt
1 tsp. MSG
1 green pepper, seeds removed, sliced into strips
1 c. milk or coconut milk

In a covered pot simmer chicken, vinegar, 1 garlic clove, crushed, and salt for 30 minutes or until chicken is tender. Set aside. Heat oil in a separate pan, brown remaining garlic; add onion, cook until transparent. Spoon out cooked chicken, saute' with garlic and onion; add curry, MSG, pepper and green pepper. Cook 2 minutes then transfer to stock where chicken was simmered in. Add milk while stirring and simmer uncovered for 5 minutes.

Serves 5.

## CHICKEN PASTEL

1 chicken (2 1/2 lb.), cut up
3 Tbsp. soy sauce
dash of pepper
1/4 c. butter or margarine
1 Tbsp. cornstarch dissolved in 2 Tbsp. water
1 small can (4 oz.) Vienna sausage, drained, sliced into 3
1 small can (8 1/2 oz.) peas, drained

1 small can (4 oz.) mushrooms, drained
2 hard-cooked eggs, sliced
1 Tbsp. lemon juice
1 tsp. salt
1 tsp. MSG
1/2 c. pepperoni (6 inches long), sliced diagonally
1 ready-made pie crust*

In a covered pot, boil chicken in 1 cup water for 5 minutes. Debone half-cooked chicken and cut meat in large pieces. Discard bones, save broth. Add lemon juice, soy sauce, salt, pepper and MSG to chicken meat and let stand for 10 minutes. Fry pepperoni in butter, then add chicken and fry until brown. Add 1 cup of broth and simmer for 30 minutes or until chicken is tender. Season to taste. Stir in cornstarch solution and cook 2 minutes. Mix in Vienna sausage, mushrooms and peas. Transfer chicken mixture to an ovenproof serving dish. Arrange egg slices on top. Cover dish with pie crust. Press edges and prick crust at several places with a fork. Bake in preheated 425° oven for 15 minutes, until crust is golden brown. Serve hot.

Serves 6.

NOTE: *Frozen ready-made pie crust is available at supermarkets. Instead of deboning chicken, just use chicken with bones cut into serving pieces for easier preparation. Stuffed olives may be added as well.

## CHICKEN TINOLA

1 chicken (about 2 lb.), cut up
2 Tbsp. vegetable oil
1 small onion, sliced
1 tsp. MSG
1 large potato, green papaya or chayote (see Glossary), peeled, quartered
1/2 lb. fresh spinach or 1 pkg. frozen
1 1/2 tsp. salt
2 garlic cloves, crushed
1 tsp. fresh ginger, minced or 1/4 tsp. powdered

Wash and drain chicken. Sprinkle on 1 teaspoon salt. Set aside. In hot oil brown garlic, add onion and ginger, saute' 1 minute. Add chicken, saute' 3 minutes. Add about 4 cups of water, cover and boil 3 minutes or until chicken is tender. Season with MSG and remaining salt. Add potato or substitutes, cook 5 minutes, or until potato is tender. Add spinach, cook 2 minutes. Serve hot with patis (see Glossary).

Serves 4 to 5.

## CHOP SUEY PHILIPPINE

1 chicken (1 1/2 lb.) cut into serving pieces
1 tsp. salt
3 Tbsp. onion, sliced
3 Tbsp. soy sauce
2 c. cabbage, cut into 1-inch squares
2 cloves garlic, crushed
3 Tbsp. vegetable oil
1 c. green beans, diagonally cut
1 pkg. frozen snow pea pods (chitcharo) or 1 c. fresh, (optional)
1 tsp. MSG
1 Tbsp. cornstarch dissolved in 2 Tbsp. water
1 c. carrots, sliced in rounds
1/8 tsp. pepper

Wash and drain chicken, sprinkle on salt. Set aside. Saute' garlic and onion in hot oil. Add chicken and cook covered for 25 minutes, turning occasionally. Add about 1 cup water and soy sauce. Cover and cook 5 minutes or until chicken is cooked. Add green beans and carrots, cook covered for 1 minute, add cabbage and snow pea pods. Add MSG and pepper. Cook covered
(Cont.)

2 to 3 minutes, then add dissolved cornstarch, while stirring frequently until thickened. Vegetables should be crisp.

Serves 6.

NOTE: Other ingredients which may be used in above recipe:
1. Slice pork pieces in combination with chicken.
2. Chicken livers and gizzards in place of chicken.
3. Shelled shrimps in combination with chicken.
4. Sliced Chinese sausage as an added ingredient.
5. Dried mushrooms, softened in water and sliced as an added ingredient.
6. Other vegetables like broccoli, sliced cucumber, cauliflower, etc.

## CHICKEN WITH MUSHROOM SAUCE

2 lb. chicken, cut to serving pieces
1 tsp. onion salt
3 Tbsp. Worcestershire sauce
1 tsp. garlic salt
1 tsp. MSG
1 can (10 1/2 oz.) cream of mushroom soup

Marinate chicken in a mixture of garlic salt, onion salt, MSG and Worcestershire sauce for at least an hour. Simmer, covered, for 35 minutes. Add cream of mushroom soup. Mix well. Continue to simmer, covered, for 10 minutes.

NOTE: Garlic salt and onion salt may be substituted for 1 garlic clove, crushed, 1 medium onion, sliced and 1 teaspoon of salt.

## CHICKEN PESA  (Boiled)

1 whole chicken (3 lb.)
1 inch fresh ginger, crushed or 1 tsp. powdered
1 tsp. whole peppercorns
3 medium potatoes, peeled and quartered
2 scallion, stalks
1 Tbsp. salt
1 tsp. MSG
1 small cabbage, quartered

In a covered pot boil chicken, salt, ginger and peppercorns in 6 to 7 cups water for 45 minutes, or until chicken is tender. Add MSG, potatoes, and cook covered for 5 minutes. Season to taste. Add cabbage and scallions. Cook covered 5 minutes more. Arrange chicken and vegetable on a platter and serve soup in individual cups, if desired.

Serves 4 to 6.

NOTE: Other vegetables like green beans, spinach or Chinese cabbage may be used. Patis (see Glossary) can also be used to season dish.

## FRIED CHICKEN PHILIPPINE

1 chicken, (about 2 1/2 lb.), cut into serving pieces
2 tsp. garlic salt
3 Tbsp. lemon juice
1/4 c. all-purpose flour
1/4 tsp. pepper
1 tsp. MSG
3 Tbsp. sugar
1/4 c. bread crumbs

Drain chicken pieces very well after washing. Using shaker, sprinkle garlic salt on each chicken piece. Add MSG, lemon juice and sugar to chicken. Let stand at least an hour. In a clean paper bag, combine flour, bread crumbs and pepper. Shake chicken, a few pieces at a time, in the bag, coating well. Fry chicken in hot oil (about an inch deep) over medium heat until light brown. Continue to fry, covered, for 20 minutes. Remove cover and fry 7 minutes longer for a crispier crust.
Serves 4.

## FINGER-LICKIN' SOUTHERN FRIED CHICKEN

2-3 lb. chicken, cut into serving pieces
salt and pepper to taste
1/3 tsp. MSG, if desired
flour for dredging, about 3/4 c.

Soak cut-up chicken in salted water, about 4 cups water and 1 tablespoon salt, for several hours or overnight, to remove "malansa" chicken aftertaste. Drain well, pat chicken with paper towels. Sprinkle salt, pepper, and MSG on chicken. Dredge each chicken with flour. Fry on medium hot oil. Use only enough oil, maybe 4 tablespoons, to cover bottom of frying pan, or better still use an electric skillet.
Arrange as many chicken as the pan can hold. Cover and let cook for 10 to 15 minutes, or until oil splatters. Uncover, turn chicken to let other side cook. Cover again, cook for another 10 minutes or until you hear oil splattering.
Chicken should be nicely browned, somewhat crisp and smelling yummy. Transfer to platter lined with paper towels to absorb excess oil. Delicious hot or cold. Perfect for "baons" or picnics. Easy way to fry chicken that is moist and tender inside, crisp on the outside. If gravy is desired, brown about 2 tablespoons flour in the pan of oil used for frying (no need to wash pan, the browned goodies are there). Add about 1 cup milk and 1/2 cup water while stirring constantly over medium heat, until gravy is thick enough for you. Season with salt and pepper. Serve gravy over fried chicken, rice, mashed potato or biscuits.

## ROAST CHICKEN PHILIPPINE

1 whole chicken (about 3 1/2 lb.)
1 tsp. minced fresh ginger or 1 tsp. powdered ginger
1 Tbsp. garlic salt
1 tsp. MSG
2 Tbsp. vegetable oil or margarine

Preheat oven to 350°. Wash chicken and drain very well. Sprinkle garlic salt inside and outside of chicken. Rub ginger and MSG all over chicken. Place chicken on rack, breast side down, in roasting pan. Roast, uncovered, for 45 minutes. Turn chicken, breast side up, brush with oil or margarine and roast another 30 minutes.
Serves 6.

## PATO TIM (Duck in Soy Sauce)

1 whole ready-to-cook duckling (about 4 lb.), fresh or frozen
1 tsp. salt
1/2 c. soy sauce
2 tsp. MSG
2 Tbsp. vegetable oil
1/2 c. abalone, cut (optional)
1/2 c. canned water chestnuts, drained
2 Tbsp. cornstarch
1/4 tsp. pepper
2 Tbsp. patis (see Glossary)
1/3 c. sugar
1 medium onion, finely sliced
1/2 c. dried mushrooms, soaked in water until soft

Thaw frozen duckling completely. Sprinkle salt and pepper inside and outside of duck. Marinate at least 1 hour or overnight if possible, in a mixture of soy sauce, patis, MSG and sugar. Pour some of marinade inside duck. Drain duck and save marinade. In a pot, heat oil until very hot and brown duck all over until it is defatted.
Add onion, cook until transparent, then add about 1 1/2 cups water and the marinade. Cover and boil gently for 45 minutes or until duck is tender. Turn duck occasionally while cooking. Season to taste. Add abalone, mushrooms and water chestnuts. Boil 5 more minutes. Remove about half a cup of sauce, dissolve cornstarch in it and pour back to pot to thicken sauce. Stir 1 minute.
Serves 6.
NOTE: 2 cups pork cut into 1 1/2-inch cubes and 1 chicken cut to serving pieces may be substituted for duckling.

## PEKING DUCK

| | |
|---|---|
| 1 duckling (4-6 lb.), ready-to-cook, fresh or frozen | 2 Tbsp. soy sauce |
| 1 1/2 Tbsp. salt | 1 1/2 Tbsp. sugar |
| | 3 Tbsp. wine, whiskey or sherry |

    With duck at room temperature, wash and drain very well. Pat dry. Rub salt and sugar all over duck inside and out. Pour soy sauce and wine over and inside duck. Let duck marinate for at least 2 hours, turning occasionally.
    Place duck in a roasting rack on a pan and roast uncovered at 375° for 30 minutes, decrease oven temperature to 275° and continue roasting for 1 hour. Increase heat to 400° and roast for 30 minutes more, or until duck is crispy and golden brown. Cut duck to bite-size pieces.
    Serve with Thin Pancakes (see recipe), about a dozen scallions, with green tops removed, and a dipping mixture of 4 tablespoons Hoisin Sauce (see Glossary). On the center of the pancake, each individual places a serving of Peking Duck with a piece of scallion and thinly spreds Hoisin sauce. The pancake is rolled folded on one end and eaten like a sandwich.
    Serves 6.

## THIN PANCAKES FOR PEKING DUCK

| | |
|---|---|
| 2 c. all-purpose flour | 1 c. boiling water |
| 2 Tbsp. sesame oil | |

    Mix flour and boiling water to form a soft round dough. With floured hands knead dough until smooth. Let stand 10 minutes. On a floured surface shape dough into a 12-inch long, 1 1/2-inch diameter roll. Divide roll into 1-inch pieces. Flatten each piece, brush 1 side of each flattened piece with sesame oil. Take 2 oil pieces at a time and stick them together on oiled slides. Roll each stuck piece to a thin 5-inch diameter pancake. Heat ungreased pan over low heat, lay pancake and cook a few minutes until bubbly, turn and cook other side.
    While still warm, carefully pull apart. Cook rest of the pancakes this way. Steam pancakes for 10 minutes, fold each into quarters, then cover with napkin or cloth until ready to serve with Peking Duck (see recipe). These pancakes can be prepared beforehand, kept in freezer and steamed only when ready to use.
    Yields 12 pancakes.

## THAI MEAT SALAD

1 1/2 c. ground turkey, lean beef or pork
3 cloves garlic, crushed
1 Tbsp. red onion, chopped fine
1 tsp. coriander seeds powder
1 tsp. green onion, chopped
2 Tbsp. lemon or lime juice
10 mint leaves
1 tsp. salt
1 tsp. chili powder

In a covered pot cook meat by itself, stirring occasionally for about 10 minutes, or until done. Remove from heat and mix in remaining ingredients.
Serves 4.
NOTE: My new friend Shelmon Bermas, shared this very interesting dish, which can be prepared ahead of time for spices to penetrate. Patis (see Glossary) may be used for seasoning as well.

## PAVO ASADO    (Turkey Roast)

1 whole turkey (10 to 15 lb.), thawed
4 Tbsp. garlic salt
1/2 c. soy sauce
1 c. cooking wine

Stuffing:

1 loaf bread (1 lb.), cut in cubes
2 celery stems, chopped
1 onion, medium, chopped
1/2 tsp. pepper
1 lb. hot dogs, finely chopped
2 c. milk
1/2 c. melted margarine
marinade from turkey

Wash and drain turkey. Rub garlic salt all over and inside turkey. Mix soy sauce and cooking wine. Pour over and inside turkey. Let turkey marinate in this for several hours or overnight, turning occasionally.
Mix stuffing ingredients thoroughly. Close neck opening of turkey and fill turkey with stuffing mixture. Sew or skewer turkey. Roast according to directions included in turkey package.
Serves 16 to 20.

## BOILED CRABS

12 live crabs
1 tsp. salt
1 c. water

When you can, select the heavier crabs (not necessarily the bigger ones), and the female ones (characterized by a rounded flap instead of a pointed one, which folds under body from rear).

Clean crabs very well. Put in a large pot with water and salt. Cover and boil for 5 minutes. When bottom crabs are reddish pink, toss crabs by shaking the covered pan to let top crabs go to bottom of pot.

Lower heat and simmer covered for about 10 minutes. Serve with a dipping mixture of 1/4 cup vinegar, 1/4 teaspoon salt and a clove of crushed garlic. Or dip in lemon butter made by mixing 4 tablespoons of melted butter or margarine with 1 tablespoon lemon juice.

Serves 6.

NOTE: A few fresh lemon slices or 1 tablespoon vinegar boiled with crabs will give a better aroma.

## CRAB RELLENO (Stuffed Crab)

- 3 Tbsp. cooking oil
- 2 Tbsp. onion, minced
- 1 c. potatoes, cut into tiny cubes
- 1 c. crabmeat, cooked or canned
- 1 tsp. MSG
- 1/2 c. seedless raisins, (optional)
- 6 top shells of crabs
- 1 garlic clove, crushed
- 1 medium tomato, minced
- 1/4 c. celery, minced (optional)
- 1 tsp. salt
- 1/8 tsp. pepper
- 2 eggs, beaten
- 3/4 c. cooking oil for frying

In 3 tablespoons hot oil, saute' garlic until brown; add onion and tomato, stir a minute. Add potatoes, celery, crabmeat, salt, MSG, pepper and raisins. Stir for 5 minutes or until potato is cooked. Taste and season if needed. Let cool. Fill cavity of each crab top shell and coat with beaten eggs. Fry and brown in 3/4 cup hot oil. Serve hot with catsup, if desired.

Serves 6.

NOTE: If crab shells are not available, combine stuffing mixture with 4 beaten eggs and fry as omelet.

## BOILED LOBSTER

- 2 (1 to 1 1/2 lb.) live lobsters
- 2 c. water
- 1 tsp. salt

In a large covered pot boil lobsters with salt and water for 5 minutes. Hold down cover if lobsters move it. Reduce heat to low and simmer covered for 15 minutes. Serve hot or cold with a dipping mixture of 1/4 cup vinegar, 1/8 teaspoon salt and a clove of crushed garlic, or lemon butter made by mixing 4 tablespoons melted butter or margarine with 1 tablespoon lemon juice.

Serves 2 to 3.

## LOBSTER CANTONESE

2 fresh lobsters (1 to 1 1/2 lb. each) or 1 large lobster
1 Tbsp. cornstarch
1 Tbsp. sugar
3 Tbsp. cooking oil
2 Tbsp. chopped scallions, save green part for garnishing
1/2 tsp. minced fresh ginger or 1/2 tsp. powdered ginger
1 c. ground raw pork
1/8 tsp. pepper
2 Tbsp. soy sauce
1 tsp. MSG
1 garlic clove, crushed
1/2 tsp. salt
2 slightly beaten eggs

Cut lobster through shell into halves, then cut crosswise into 2-inch pieces, crack the claws and set aside. Mix cornstarch, soy sauce, MSG and 1/4 cup water to a smooth paste, set aside. In hot oil, brown garlic; add scallions, ginger and pork. Season with salt and pepper. Stir and cook 5 minutes, then stir in lobster. Cook, covered, for 10 minutes, then add about 1 cup water. Let boil for 5 minutes. Stir in soy sauce mixture and simmer for 5 minutes. Season to taste. Before removing from heat, stir in eggs and green chopped scallions. Serve hot.
Makes 4 servings.

## BROILED FISH (Inihaw)

1 whole fish (about 2 lb.), cleaned
1/2 tsp. MSG
1 tsp. salt
1 1/2 Tbsp. lemon juice
1/2 c. tomatoes, sliced
1/8 tsp. pepper
2 Tbsp. vegetable oil
1/4 c. onion, sliced
1/4 tsp. salt

With a sharp knife slit fish open from stomach to tail. Sprinkle salt, MSG and lemon juice all over fish. Mix last 5 ingredients and stuff fish. Wrap with aluminum foil. Broil over charcoal or in the oven, 10 to 15 minutes on one side and another 10 to 15 minutes on the other. Fish is done when it flakes.
Serves 5.

## DAING (Marinated Fish)

2 medium-sized fresh or frozen fish, weighing about a lb., dressed or fillet, such as trout, mackerel, bluefish, etc.
1/4 c. vinegar
1 tsp. salt
2 garlic cloves, crushed
1/8 tsp. pepper

Split open fish by using sharp knife close to the bone. Marinate fish in mixture of remaining ingredients for at least an hour, preferably overnight, refrigerated or not. Drain well. Fry to a golden brown.

    Serves 3.

## FISH ORIENTAL

2 lb. salt-water fish, dressed whole (flounder, pompano, perch, bass, etc.)
1 tsp. salt
1 Tbsp. whiskey
1/2 c. vegetable oil
5 dried mushrooms, softened then sliced

1/2 c. canned bamboo shoots, drained, then thinly sliced
1 Tbsp. soy sauce
1 Tbsp. cornstarch
1 tsp. fresh ginger, sliced into thin strips

### Sauce:

3 Tbsp. soy sauce
2 Tbsp. cornstarch

2 Tbsp. brown sugar
3/4 c. water

    Pat dry cleaned whole fish. Score fish forming diamond designs on each side. Rub salt, soy sauce, and whiskey on fish. Let stand for 30 minutes. Pat cornstarch all over fish just before frying. In hot oil fry fish until golden brown on both sides, about 12 minutes total.

    Transfer fish to a dish and set aside. Leave about 3 tablespoons oil in fry pan, heat oil and brown ginger, add scallions, bamboo shoots and mushrooms. Stir-cook 2 minutes. Mix sauce ingredients thoroughly and pour to mushroom mixture, stirring continuously. Add fried fish. Spoon sauce all over fish and cook 3 minutes more. Serve hot with garnishings on fish.

    Serves 4 to 5.

## FISH SINIGANG

1 1/2 c. water
2 Tbsp. onion, sliced
1 tsp. salt
1 fresh fish, about 2 lb., cleaned, cut into serving pieces

1 c. spinach or any green leafy vegetable or green beans, (if desired)
1/3 c. tomatoes, sliced
2 Tbsp. lemon juice
1 tsp. MSG

    Boil first 6 ingredients for 3 minutes. Add fish. Boil 7 minutes. Taste and season if needed. While boiling, add vegetables. Cook 3 minutes more.

    Serves 5.

(Cont.)

NOTE: Any type of fish may be used, even smelts. For Shrimps Sinigang: Use 1 pound of shrimp with shell in place of fish.

For Clams Sinigang: Clean 3 pounds of clams of dirt or sand, and use instead of fish. Reduce water to 3/4 cup and omit lemon juice. Cook until clams are half-opened.

For Squid Sinigang: Substitute fish in recipe for fresh or frozen cleaned squid (whole medium size).

## FISH ESCABECHE (Sweet and Sour Fish)

- 1 whole fish (about 2 lb.), cleaned, or 1 1/2 lb. fish fillets
- 1 1/2 tsp. salt
- 3/4 c. cooking oil for frying
- 2 Tbsp. onion, sliced
- 1 small fresh green pepper, cut into strips and/or 1/2 c. French green beans
- 1 small turnip, cut into strips, (optional)
- 2 Tbsp. lemon juice
- 2 garlic cloves, crushed
- 1 tsp. fresh ginger, cut fine (optional) or 1/2 tsp. powdered ginger
- 1 carrot, cut into strips (optional)

### Sauce:

- 1/4 c. vinegar
- 2 Tbsp. soy sauce
- 1 c. water
- 1 tsp. MSG
- 1/8 tsp. pepper
- 1/4 c. sugar
- 3 Tbsp. catsup
- 2 Tbsp. cornstarch or flour
- 1/2 tsp. salt

Sprinkle salt and lemon juice on fish. Fry until brown. When using fish fillet, shake each fillet in a small paper bag with 1/2 cup flour, then fry. Put on platter.

In 2 tablespoons hot oil, saute' garlic, onion and ginger. Add vegetables. Stir 2 minutes. Mix sauce ingredients in a bowl and pour over vegetable mixture. Stir and cook over medium heat for 5 minutes, or until sauce is thickened. Pour over fish.

Serves 6.

## FISH CARDILLO (Sauteed Fish with Eggs)

- 1 fish (about 2 lb.) whole or sliced into 4 or 1 1/2 lb. fish fillets
- 1 1/2 tsp. salt
- 3/4 c. cooking oil for frying
- 1/4 c. onion, sliced
- 1/2 c. water
- salt and pepper to taste
- 1 1/2 Tbsp. lemon juice
- 2 garlic cloves, crushed
- 3/4 c. ripe tomato, sliced (fresh or canned)
- 1 tsp. MSG
- 2 eggs, slightly beaten

Sprinkle salt and lemon juice on fish. Fry until brown. When using fish fillets, shake each fillet in a small paper bag with 1/2 cup flour, before frying. Set aside.

In 3 tablespoons hot oil, saute' garlic until brown; add onions and tomatoes, stirring until mushy. Add fried fish, water and MSG. Simmer 5 minutes, taste and season with salt and pepper. Pour slightly beaten eggs, simmer a minute.

Serves 5.

NOTE: For Sarciado, reduce water to 1/4 cup. Omit eggs.

## FISH PAKSIW  (Pickled Fish)

2 lb. smelts, dressed  
1/3 c. vinegar  
1/2 tsp. fresh ginger, sliced  
  or 1/4 tsp. powdered  
1 tsp. salt  
1/3 c. water  

Combine all ingredients in a covered pot. Boil 5 minutes, uncover and cook 3 minutes more, or until half of broth has evaporated. Serve hot or cold.

Serves 6.

NOTE: Mackerel, cut into serving pieces, may be used or any other similar fish even bangus (milkfish). Larger pieces of fish require longer cooking time.

## FISH PAKSIW WITH COCONUT MILK

1 lb. smelts, dressed  
1/4 tsp. salt  
3/4 c. thick coconut milk (see How to Extract Fresh Coconut Milk)  
1/4 c. vinegar  
1/2 tsp. turmeric (dilao) for yellow coloring (optional)  

Marinate fish in a mxiture of vinegar, salt and turmeric. Simmer covered for 5 minutes. Add coconut milk, simmer 5 minutes more.

Serves 3.

NOTE: Smelts is substituted for "bia." Omit turmeric and coconut milk for "Fish Pinangat."

## FISH STEAMED ORIENTAL

2 lb. whole sea bass or your favorite salt water fish, cleaned  
1 tsp. salt  
1 tsp. sugar  
1 Tbsp. fresh ginger, minced  
2 Tbsp. cooking oil  

(Cont.)

1 Tbsp. soy sauce
1 Tbsp. wine or cooking
   sherry (optional)

1/2 c. fermented black beans,
   (1 c. if more is desired)

Pat fish dry inside and out with paper towel. With a sharp knife, make diagonal cuts about 1/4-inch deep and 1/2-inch apart all over fish skin, forming diamond shapes. Mix remaining ingredients and rub inside and out of fish. Lay fish on a heatproof dish, steam for 20 minutes or until fish flakes. Serve hot, garnished with parsley, fresh scallions and cherry tomatoes.
Serves 4.
NOTE: Fish may be wrapped in aluminum foil and baked slowly at 325°F. for 20 minutes.

### FISH TINAPA AMERICAN

6 whole (medium-size) fresh
   mullet or milk fish, cleaned,
   but with heads on and
   scales intact preferably

2 tsp. Hickory liquid smoke
   flavoring
1/2 to 3/4 c. soy sauce
1/2 c. cooking oil

Mix liquid smoke and soy sauce. Immerse fish one at a time, turning until fish is seasoned with soy sauce mixture. Transfer fish to a container and pour remaining sauce all over fish. Cover and refrigerate for a day or two, turning fish occasionally. Drain and transfer fish on a baking rack with pan (or charcoal broil). Brush fish with oil.
Bake slowly in 300° to 300°F. oven for 30 minutes; turn fish, brush again with oil, bake another 30 minutes uncovered or until done.
Serve hot or cold with dipping sauce of 1/2 cup vinegar, 2 garlic cloves, crushed, 1/2 cup chopped fresh Coriander (Chinese parsley), 1 cup fresh sliced tomatoes, and chopped onions.
Serves 6.
NOTE: This is Luz Cullen's original recipe. Cooled baked Tinapa may be individually wrapped and frozen a month or two for future use.

### FISH WITH TAHURE OR TAUSI
(Salted Bean Paste or Black Beans)

1 fish (about 2 lb.) whole or
   sliced into 4 or 1 1/2 lb.
   fish fillets
1 1/2 tsp. salt
1/2 c. flour
3/4 c. oil

1/2 c. tomato, sliced
3 Tbsp. tahure or tausi (salted
   bean paste or salted black
   beans - see Glossary), mixed
   with 3 Tbsp. vinegar

| | |
|---|---|
| 3 garlic cloves, minced | 1/2 tsp. MSG (monosodium glutamate) |
| 1 medium onion, sliced | |
| 2 tsp. fresh ginger, sliced fine | 1 small eggplant, cut into bite-size pieces (optional) |

Sprinkle salt on fish. Dredge with flour. Fry fish in hot oil until golden brown. Set aside.

In 3 tablespoons hot oil, saute' garlic until fragrant; add onions, saute' a minute; then add ginger and saute' another minute. Add tomatoes; saute' until mushy. Add salted bean-vinegar mixture; saute' for a minute, then add fried fish and MSG. Add about 2 cups water, eggplant and cook covered for 5 minutes or until eggplant is cooked, while stirring occasionally. Salt to season.

Serves 4.

NOTE: More tahure or tausi may be added, as desired. Unused portion may be stored covered in refrigerator for a week or so. The salted beans, as is, may be eaten with plain hot steamed rice. Very interesting flavor.

**KEKIAM** (Chinese Seafood - Meat Roll)

| | |
|---|---|
| 1 c. raw boneless fish and/or shelled shrimp, coarsely ground | 3 eggs |
| | 1/4 c. green onion, minced |
| 1 c. ground pork | 1/8 tsp. pepper |
| 1 c. flour | 1/2 tsp. MSG |
| 1 c. grated raw carrot | 1 tsp. salt |

Mix all ingredients very well. Shape into a 2-inch diameter log roll and wrap with aluminum foil. Steam or bake in 350° oven for 1 hour or until firm. Let cool. Before serving, remove wrapping and slice diagonally 1/2-inch thick.

Serve warm or cold. If desired, slices may be pan-browned on both sides. Serve with sauce mixture of 2 tablespoons vinegar, 1 tablespoon soy sauce and 2 tablespoons sugar.

Serves about 6.

**TUYO** (Dried Fish)

| | |
|---|---|
| 10 fresh or frozen small fish, such as 5-inch butterfish, spot, perch, etc., dressed | enough salt according to one's taste |

Split open fish, with or without head, by using sharp knife close to the bone. Salt fish all over. For 'not too salty fish' use salt sparingly. Lay fish flat-open on something like an oven rack and sun-dry under full sun 2 to 3 days. Fry to a crispy golden

(Cont.)

brown. Serve with tomato slices or dipping mixture of vinegar and clove of crushed garlic.

Serves 4.

## **RELLENONG BANGUS** (Stuffed Milk Fish)

1 whole bangus (milkfish), about 1 1/4 lb. dressed
1 Tbsp. soy sauce
1/2 tsp. salt
4 Tbsp. vegetable oil
1 medium onion, minced
1/2 c. potatoes, finely diced
1/2 c. frozen peas
1/8 tsp. pepper
1/3 c. raisins (optional)
2 Tbsp. melted butter or margarine
1 Tbsp. lemon juice
1/4 c. water
2 garlic cloves, crushed
2 medium tomatoes, minced
1/2 c. carrots, finely diced
1 tsp. salt
1 tsp. MSG
2 eggs, beaten

Pound body of fish to soften. With a sharp knife, slit back to open, cutting close to the skeletal bone. Remove back bone. Carefully remove fish flesh with a spoon or knife, keeping the skin intact.

Marinate skin (head and tail intact) in soy sauce and lemon juice. Set aside. Simmer fish flesh in 1/2 teaspoon salt and 1/4 cup water for 5 minutes. Cool. Remove bones from fish flesh. Set aside.

In 4 tablespoons hot oil saute' garlic until brown, add onions and tomatoes and cook while stirring until tomatoes are mushy. Add potatoes, carrots and peas. Stir-fry 7 minutes over medium heat or until vegetables are tender. Add cooked fish, salt, pepper, MSG and raisins. Cook 5 minutes more. Let cool. Add beaten eggs to cooked mixture and stuff fish skin. Sew back opening. Brush melted butter or margarine on stuffed fish. Wrap with aluminum foil. Bake in 375° preheated oven for 30 minutes. Unwrap and bake 5 minutes more to brown fish.

Serves 4 or 5.

NOTE: Fresh bluefish or white fish may be substituted for bangus.

## **CAMARON REBOSADO** (Fried Shrimp)

1 lb. large, raw shrimp, with shells
1 tsp. MSG
1/2 c. cornstarch or flour
lash of pepper
1 c. vegetable oil for deep frying
1 tsp. salt
1 egg, large
1 1/2 tsp. baking powder
2-3 Tbsp. water

When shelling shrimps, keep shell at tail intact. Cut a deep slit at the back of each shrimp and devein. Mix salt and MSG. Dip wet finger in salt and MSG mixture and rub between the slits in each shrimp.

In a bowl, beat egg, cornstarch, baking powder and pepper. Mix until smooth. If mixture is too thick add 2-3 tablespoons of water. Coat each shrimp with the mixture, leaving the tail uncoated, and fry in hot oil, a few at a time until golden brown. Drain on paper towel. Serve hot with catsup or Sweet and Sour Sauce (see recipe).

Serves 6.

## PRAWNS IN CRAB FAT

| | |
|---|---|
| 1 lb. jumbo shrimps with heads and tail intact but body shelled, preferably | 3 garlic cloves, crushed fine<br>1 c. canned or frozen crab fat (talangka) |
| 3 Tbsp. cooking oil | |

Clean and prepare shrimps. In hot oil, brown garlic; saute' in shrimps until they become pink, about 5 minutes then stir in crab fat, rinsing with 1/2 cup water and let simmer for another 3 minutes. Season with salt and pepper to taste.

Serves 4.

NOTE: At the famous Tito Rey Restaurant in Daly City, California, this is called "Hinubarang Sugpo Sa Aligue." One of my favorite dishes.

## SHRIMP RELLENO    (Stuffed Shrimps)

| | |
|---|---|
| 10 pieces jumbo shrimps, uncooked (about 1 1/2 lb.) | 1 egg, slightly beaten |
| 1 tsp. salt | 2 eggs, beaten with 4 Tbsp. cornstarch or flour |
| 1/4 c. ground raw pork (increase to 1/2 c., if ham is not used) | oil for deep-fat frying (1-inch deep) |
| 1/4 c. cooked ham, finely chopped | 1 tsp. MSG |
| | 2 Tbsp. scallions, cut fine |
| | 10 strips bacon |
| 1 small carrot, coarsely grated or chopped fine | 2 Tbsp. dried mushrooms, soaked, then cut fine |

When shelling shrimps, keep shell at tail end intact. Cut a deep slit at the back of each shrimp and devein. Mix salt and MSG. Dip wet finger in salt and MSG mixture and rub between the slits in each shrimp.

Mix pork, ham, mushrooms, scallions, carrot and 1 egg. Fill the slit in each shrimp with a tablespoon of this mixture.

(Cont.)

Wrap a strip of bacon around each stuffed shrimp and secure with a toothpick. Dip shrimp one at a time in egg and flour mixture and deep-fat fry to a golden brown over medium heat, about 7 minutes on each side. Serve hot with Sweet and Sour Sauce (see recipe), if desired.

Serves 5.

NOTE: When frying, oil should be just hot (not too hot), so stuffing will be cooked and coating will not brown too soon.

## SQUID ADOBO

2 lb. squid (fresh or frozen)
1 tsp. salt
1/8 tsp. pepper
1 medium onion, finely sliced
1 tsp. MSG
3 garlic cloves, crushed
4 Tbsp. vinegar
3 Tbsp. vegetable oil
1/4 c. water

Pull out cellophane-like backbone from squids, discard, then pull out and discard small jar-like bone from mouth, wash. Slice squids 2/3 inch thick crosswise. Marinate in a mixture of garlic, salt, vinegar and pepper for at least half an hour. Pick out garlic from marinade and brown garlic in hot oil, add onions and cook until transparent. Add squid, stir for 3 minutes, then add water and MSG. Simmer covered for 10 minutes.

Serves 6.

## SQUID BROIL

8 squid, large (about 6 inches long), cleaned, drained
2 Tbsp. oil
2 large fresh tomato, chopped
1 large onion, chopped
1 Tbsp. fresh ginger, chopped
1/4 c. fresh green pepper, seeded and chopped
2 Tbsp. fresh coriander, chopped
1 tsp. sugar
1 tsp. salt
1/2 tsp. MSG
1/4 tsp. pepper

Grease whole squid with oil. Mix remaining ingredients very well and stuff squid. Broil over red-glowing charcoal or broil in oven turning once, for about 6 minutes or until squid is just cooked, otherwise squid will toughen. Garnish with lemon slices.

Serves 6.

NOTE: A sheet of aluminum foil underneath squid will help in clean up. See Squid Adobo recipe for cleaning squid.

## STUFFED SQUIDS

1 1/2 lb. large squids, fresh or frozen (about 10)
4 Tbsp. vegetable oil
1 small onion, minced
1/4 lb. boneless pork, coarsely chopped (about 3/4 c.)
1/2 tsp. salt
1/2 tsp. MSG
1 garlic clove, crushed
1 medium tomato, minced
dash pepper
1 medium carrot, grated or minced

Thaw squids if frozen. Pull out and discard cellophane-like backbone and jaw-like bone on mouth. Wash; set aside. In 2 tablespoons hot oil, brown garlic. Add onions. Cook a minute; stir in tomato and cook until mushy. Add pork; season with salt, pepper and MSG. Stir-cook 5 minutes, or until pork is cooked. Add carrots; remove from fire to cool. Loosely stuff squids with mixture at base of head. Secure opening with a toothpick. Heat 2 tablespoons oil in pan. Pan-fry stuffed squids and let cook, covered, for 5 minutes. Serves 5.

Note: Squid heads may be secured back with toothpick; otherwise, use heads for Squid Adobo (see recipe).

## FIVE COLOR SHRIMP

1 lb. large shrimps, shelled and deveined
1 Tbsp. sherry
1/4 tsp. pepper
1/4 tsp. baking soda
1 medium carrot, pared and diced
1 Tbsp. soy sauce
1 Tbsp. cornstarch dissolved in 1/4 c. chicken broth or water
1/2 tsp. salt
1 Tbsp. cornstarch
1 tsp. fresh ginger, sliced into thin strips
4 medium-size dried mushrooms, softened and diced
1/2 c. canned bamboo shoots, drained and diced
1/2 tsp. sugar
1 c. green peas, frozen
1 egg white
3/4 c. vegetable oil, for frying
1 scallion, finely chopped

Marinate shrimps in next 5 ingredients for 10 minutes. Meanwhile boil peas and carrots in small amount of water for 7 minutes or until vegetables are tender. Drain and set aside. Thoroughly mix egg white and 1 tablespoon cornstarch to shrimps just before frying shrimps.

Heat oil until very hot and stir-fry shrimps (separating them) for 3 minutes or until shrimps turn pink. Remove from heat and transfer shrimps to a dish; set aside. Leave about 3 tablespoons oil in pan; heat until hot, then brown ginger. Stir in scallions, mushrooms, bamboo shoots and soy sauce. Cook 1 minute on high heat. Add cooked

(Cont.)

peas, carrots and shrimps. Mix well. Add dissolved cornstarch and stir-cook 1 minute or until thickened. Serve hot. Serves 4.

NOTE: Shrimps should never be overcooked. Scallops may be used in place of shrimps.

## TEMPURA (Seafood/Vegetable)

Batter:
1 c. all-purpose flour
1/4 tsp. salt
1 Tbsp. cornstarch

1 c. ice cold water
oil for deep fat frying

Gradually add ice cold water to dry ingredients while mixing until smooth. Have a ready tray of cold and fresh, bite-size, pieces of sweet potato slices, green or yellow squash, green onions, snow peas, cauliflower, broccoli, cucumber, eggplant or fresh fish fillet, shelled shrimp, oysters or scallops. Dip tempura ingredients, 1 at a time, into fatter; fry a few at a time in hot oil until crisp and golden. Drain on paper towel. Serve hot with dipping sauce of 1/4 cup soy sauce, 2 Tbsp. water, 1 tsp. sugar, 1/4 tsp. fresh ginger.

NOTE: Children, teenagers and adults love this. Make new batter as needed and keep chilled as the chilled batter hitting the hot oil adds crispiness to tempura.

## MUSSELS (Saute - Tahong)

4 to 5 lb. fresh, cleaned mussels
3 Tbsp. cooking oil
3 garlic cloves, crushed
1 medium onion, minced
1 tsp. fresh ginger, minced (optional)

1/2 c. soy sauce
1/2 c. water
1 Tbsp. sugar
1 Tbsp. cornstarch

In hot oil, saute garlic, onion and ginger for a minute. Add mussels. Cover and cook on medium-high heat 2 minutes; shake covered pot to turn mussels. Mix together soy sauce, water, sugar and cornstarch. Stir mixture into simmering mussels until well mixed. Cover and simmer for 2 more minutes, shaking pot to mix all ingredients. Serves 4 to 6.

NOTE: This is one of my favorite dishes. If desired, 1/4 cup of vinegar or wine may be added while sauteeing.

For baked mussels, put cleaned mussels on cookie sheet in a single layer and bake in preheated, 375°F., oven until mussels open, about 7 minutes. No seasonings needed.

# Main Dishes
## Eggs, Cheese, Pasta and Casseroles

## EGG, CHEESE, PASTA AND CASSEROLE

* To prevent eggs from curdling when they are to be added to hot liquid, add a bit of the hot liquid to the eggs first and letting the temperature equalize. Then they can be added to the remaining liquid with no worries.

* Adding vegetable oil to pasta cooking water before you add the pasta will cut down on sticking.

* When preparing your favorite casserole, double the batch and freeze one for a busy day.

* Egg yolks can be kept for several days in the refrigerator if they are covered with vegetable oil.

* If a casserole dish is lined with several layers of foil and then filled and frozen, the casserole can be lifted out when solid and wrapped for freezing without losing the use of the casserole dish. It will fit right back into the dish when it's time to bake it. This also makes for easier stacking of casseroles in the freezer.

* A dull warm knife works best for slicing cheese.

* Use a fry basket in the pot when cooking pasta. The pasta can be lifted out all at once and rinsed in the same basket.

* Stir eggs while they are boiling to keep the yolks centered. This makes deviled eggs prettier.

* Storing cheese in a tightly covered container with a few sugar cubes will retard mold.

* Hardened cheese can be softened by soaking in buttermilk.

* Bring salted water to a boil, stir in pasta, cover and turn off the heat. Check the pot in ten minutes.

* If grater is brushed with oil before you grate cheese clean up will be a snap!

* Adding vinegar to the water used to cook hard boiled eggs will keep them from 'running' if a shell is cracked.

* Rub shortening around the top of the pot to prevent boil overs.

* Mark hard boiled eggs before they are stored so you won't have to guess the raw eggs from the cooked ones. This can be done with a crayon or by adding food coloring to the cooking water.

* Run cooked spaghetti under HOT water to prevent stickiness.

# EGGS, CHEESE, CASSEROLE

## SALTED EGGS  (Itlog Na Maalat)

6 eggs, duck's or hen's, large     1 1/2 c. salt
2 c. water

   Put eggs in a jar or bowl. Mix water and salt, pour to eggs. Cover. Eggs should be completely immersed. They will float in salty solutions, hence cover to keep eggs down. Let cure 18 to 21 days, test if desired saltiness is reached by boiling an egg for about 7 minutes, until hard-cooked. Cooked salted egg is used as garnishing in siopao and bibingka hot cake (see recipes), and as a salad.
   NOTE: Salt and water solution can be reused.

## ARROZ CALDO

1 (2 lb.) chicken, cut into serving pieces
2 garlic cloves, crushed
1 tsp. fresh ginger, sliced into thin strips or 1/4 tsp. powdered
2 tsp. salt
2 c. rice or 1 c. sweet rice and 1 c. regular rice, washed and drained
1/8 tsp. pepper
2 scallions, finely chopped
2 Tbsp. vegetable oil
1 medium onion, sliced
2 Tbsp. patis (see Glossary)
1 tsp. MSG

   Wash chicken and drain well. Sprinkle on 1 teaspoon salt. Set aside. In hot oil brown garlic, add onion and ginger and saute' until onion is transparent. Add chicken, remaining salt and patis. Cook, covered, for 7 minutes, stirring occasionally. Add rice, stir 2 minutes, then add about 6 cups water. Cover, let come to a rapid boil, lower heat and simmer, covered, 1 hour, stirring occasionally. Season with pepper and MSG, taste. Sprinkle on scallions when serving.
   Serves 8.
   NOTE: In place of chicken, 3 pounds tripe (goto), cut into 1-inch squares or strips, may be used. First simmer tripe in 5 cups water for 1 hour, drain, then saute' with garlic, onion and ginger. Use water where tripe was cooked in cooking rice and tripe.

## ARROZ ALA VALENCIANA

1 chicken, (about 2 lb.), cut to serving pieces
1 lb. boneless pork, cut into 1 1/2-inch cubes
1/4 tsp. pepper
3 garlic cloves, crushed
1 (8 oz.) can tomato sauce
3 c. uncooked rice, washed once and drained
1 tsp. MSG
1/2 c. stuffed green olives
2 tsp. salt
1/3 c. vegetable oil
1/4 c. onions, sliced
1 pepperoni (6 inches long), sliced
2 c. sweet peas, frozen
2 hard-boiled eggs, sliced

    Wash and pat dry chicken and pork. Sprinkle salt and pepper on meats. Heat oil in a large pot (5-quart capacity) and brown meats. Put meats to one side and saute' garlic, onions and tomato sauce. Stir in pepperoni, rice and MSG for 2 minutes. Add about 6 cups of water.
    Cover, let boil rapidly, stir and reduce heat to low. Cover and cook for 20 minutes more, or until rice and peas are soft. Garnish with stuffed green olives and sliced hard-boiled eggs.
    Serves 12 to 15.

## PAELLA

1 1/2 lb. chicken, cut to serving pieces
2 tsp. salt
5 c. water
12-15 fresh clams in shell, washed to remove sand
1 medium onion, finely sliced
1 can (6 oz.) tomato paste
2 c. uncooked rice, washed, drained
3 crabs in shell, boiled, halved (if available)
1/4 c. pimento, sliced into thin strips (optional)
1 lb. boneless pork, cut into 1 1/2-inch cubes
1/2 c. vegetable oil, for frying
2 garlic cloves, crushed
1 lb. large shrimps, shelled and deveined
1 tsp. MSG
1 c. green peas, frozen

    Wash and pat dry chicken and pork, then sprinkle 1 teaspoon salt. Fry meats in a big pot (5-quart capacity) until golden brown. Transfer meats to dish and set aside.
    In another pot, boil 5 cups of water with remaining 1 teaspoon salt. When water is rapidly boiling, add clams. Let it boil once more, then shut off heat. Set aside. Save clam broth. Saute' garlic and onion in hot oil where meats were fried, until garlic is light brown. Add shrimps, fried chicken and pork; saute' 2 minutes. Add tomato paste, MSG and rice. Stir and cook 3 minutes. Add clam broth. Cover, let boil rapidly a minute, stir once, reduce

heat to low and simmer, covered, until mixture is almost dry and rice is almost cooked. Season to taste.

Carefully stir in peas, pimento and clams. Arrange crabs on top. Cover and continue cooking over low heat until rice is cooked (high heat will cause rice to burn).

Serves 10 to 12.

## LUGAO SPECIAL (Porridge)

2 c. cooked rice
1 can cream style corn
2 stalks fresh green onion, chopped
1/2 c. or more shelled shrimp or boneless chicken, diced
5 black whole peppercorns
1 Tbsp. patis (see Glossary)
salt to taste
2 beaten eggs
2 Tbsp. cooking oil
1/4 tsp. MSG

If you have a blender, blend together cooked rice and corn. Set aside. In hot oil saute' green onion, shrimp or chicken, peppercorns, patis and salt until shrimp or chicken is cooked, about 3 minutes. Add MSG, rice-corn mixture and simmer covered for about 10 minutes. Just before serving, stir in beaten eggs.

Serves 4.

NOTE: Ham or ground beef may be used also. Without a blender, use rice-corn as is, but cook longer, for another 10 to 15 minutes. One cup water or broth may be added.

## FRIED RICE

3 c. boiled or steamed plain rice, cold, preferably day old, refrigerated
1 Tbsp. soy sauce
1/2 tsp. Accent or monosodium glutamate
salt and pepper to taste
3 Tbsp. oil
2 garlic cloves, minced
1 c. frozen peas
1/2 c. cooked ham, or leftover roast pork, beef or chicken or bacon, finely sliced or combination of these
2 eggs, slightly beaten, cooked scrambled
3 Tbsp. scallions, finely cut

Mix rice, soy sauce, Accent, salt and pepper. Set aside. In hot oil brown garlic, add peas and meat. Stir-fry a minute or 2. Add rice mixture and stir-cook 5 minutes. Mix in scrambled eggs and scallions. Transfer on platter. Garnish with strips of scrambled eggs and sprinkle more scallions on top. Surround with sprigs of fresh parsley.

Serves 4 to 6.

## BAM-I  (Cebu Noodle Dish)

1 whole chicken, dressed, about 2 lb.
1 lb. pork
3 Tbsp. cooking oil
4 garlic cloves, crushed
1 large onion, finely sliced
1 c. shrimps, shelled
1 tsp. salt
1/4 tsp. pepper
1/2 tsp. MSG

3/4 c. dried black wood ears ('tenga ng daga'), softened in water then sliced
1 (8 oz.) pkg. pancit canton noodles (see Glossary)
2 c. sotanghon noodles, (see Glossary), softened in water
8 c. broth

    In a covered pot, boil chicken and pork in 8 cups water for 30 minutes. Remove meats, cool and slice into small pieces. Save broth. In hot oil saute' garlic and onion, add sliced meats, shrimps, seasonings and black wood ears. Saute' for 5 minutes. Add broth.
    Simmer, covered, for 10 minutes. Taste to preference. Add noodles. Simmer another 10 minutes. Before serving hot, garnish with sliced scallions.
    Serves 10 to 12.
    NOTE: Dried shrimps may be used in place of raw shrimps. Adjust amount of broth for soupier or drier dish.

## PANCIT BIHON  (Rice Sticks)

1 lb. chicken
1/4 c. vegetable oil
1 medium onion, finely sliced
1 Tbsp. patis (optional - see Glossary)
1 c. cabbage, shredded
1/2 c. celery, cut into thin strips
1/2 tsp. salt
1 1/2 c. broth in which chicken and pork were boiled
1 pkg. (1 lb.) rice sticks, soaked in hot water for about 15 minutes, or until soft, then drained

1/3 lb. medium shrimps, shelled, slit into two
1 lb. pork
2 garlic cloves, crushed
2 Tbsp. soy sauce
1 c. green beans, French cut
1 carrot, sliced into thin strips
1 tsp. MSG
1/8 tsp. pepper

    Boil chicken (about half a chicken) and pork in 1 1/2 cups water for 15 minutes. Slice meats in small pieces. Discard bones, save broth. Ready all other ingredients separately on a tray. In hot oil, brown garlic, add onion, saute' until transparent, add meats and stir-cook 5 minutes. Add shrimps, soy sauce and patis, stir-cook 5 minutes.

On high heat add green beans, stir 2 minutes, add cabbage, carrots and celery. Season with MSG, salt and pepper. Add 1 cup broth. Stir-cook 2 minutes, then dish out about a cup for garnishing.

Add rice sticks, cook over low heat for 3 minutes while stirring. If mixture is too dry, moisten with more broth. Transfer to a platter, garnish top with reserved sauteed mixture, and decorate if desired with slices of hard-cooked egg and finely cut scallions. Serve with lemon wedges, and patis or soy sauce.

Serves 10.

NOTE: For Pancit Canton, use pancit canton (fried egg noodles) in place of rice sticks. Pancit canton does not have to be soaked in water. Snow pea pods, sliced Chinese sausages and dried Chinese mushrooms, softened, then sliced, are other ingredients to include.

## PANCIT LUGLUG OR PALABOK

### Garnishings:

1/4 c. vegetable oil
1 garlic bulb, crushed
1 medium onion, finely sliced
2 lb. pork, boneless, sliced into small pieces
1 Tbsp. achuete seeds, rubbed with a pinch of salt, then soaked in 1/4 c. water, (see Glossary)
1 1/2 lb. medium shrimps, shelled, halved lengthwise
1 tsp. salt
1/8 tsp. pepper
3 bean curd cakes (tokwa), diced, fried (see Glossary)
3 hard-cooked eggs, peeled and sliced
1 c. chitcharon (see Glossary), crushed into crumbs
2 scallions, finely sliced
2 lemons, cut into wedges
1/2 lb. medium shrimps with shell, boiled in 1 1/2 c. water, then shelled, save shrimp broth

### Sauce:

3 Tbsp. vegetable oil
2 garlic cloves, crushed
2 c. water or broth
1/2 c. flour
1/2 c. smooth peanut butter
1 tsp. MSG
1 Tbsp. achuete seeds (see Glossary), rubbed with a pinch of salt then soaked in 1 1/2 c. shrimp broth
1 Tbsp. patis (see Glossary)
1/8 tsp. pepper
1/2 tsp. salt

### Pancit:

(Cont.)

1 pkg. (1 lb.) rice sticks (bihon) or Vermicelli or Capellini

Prepare garnishings. In hot oil, brown garlic, leave about a tablespoon in pan, spoon out the rest and save for garnishing. Add onion to pan, cook until transparent, add pork, stir-cook 10 minutes. Strain soaked achuete on pork. Cook, covered, 5 minutes, or until pork is tender. Add shrimps, season with salt and pepper. Stir-cook 7 minutes. Add fried bean curd. Set aside. Ready remaining garnishing ingredients. Set aside.

Make sauce. In hot oil brown garlic, add water or broth and simmer covered 5 minutes. Meanwhile, mix flour and peanut butter, strain over achuete in shrimp broth. Mix to a smooth consistency. Gradually add to simmering garlic-flavored liquid, while stirring continuously. Season with patis, MSG, pepper and salt. Cook over low heat for 5 minutes while stirring or until sauce thickens. Set aside.

Prepare pancit. In rapidly boiling water (about 2 quarts), immerse rice sticks, cook 3 minutes, or until soft. Drain (if vermicelli or capellini is used, cook according to package directions.) Transfer to a large platter. Pour hot sauce all over noodles, liberally garnish with cooked pork mixture, hard-cooked egg slices, brown-fried garlic, chitcharon crumbs, sliced scallions, lemon wedges and shelled shrimps. Serve with patis.

Serves 10.

NOTE: If desired, serve prepared garnishings, sauce and noodles in separate serving dishes, and guests can help themselves in mixing their own Pancit Luglug. Cooked, flaked, smoked fish may be an additional garnishing.

## SOTANGHON (Bean Thread Noodle)

| | |
|---|---|
| 1 chicken (about 2 lb.) | 1 medium onion, sliced |
| 1/2 lb. pkg. (8 oz.) sotanghon (see Glossary) | 4 dried mushrooms, softened, sliced |
| 2 Tbsp. vegetable oil | 1/8 tsp. pepper |
| 2 scallions, finely chopped | 1 Tbsp. patis (see Glossary) |
| 2 tsp. salt | 1 tsp. MSG |
| 2 garlic cloves, crushed | 1 Tbsp. paprika or achuete seeds to color (see Glossary) |

Boil chicken in about 6 to 8 cups water with salt, for 30 minutes, or until chicken is tender. Bone chicken, cut meat into small pieces and set aside. Save broth. Soak sotanghon in hot water until soft, drain and cut to desired lengths. Set aside.

In hot oil, brown garlic; add onions, chicken, patis & mushrooms. Stir-cook 2 minutes. Add broth. When boiling, add sotanghon, MSG, pepper and paprika or achuete coloring. Simmer, covered, for 5

Garnish with scallions just before serving hot.

Serves 6.

NOTE: Above recipe is soup-like. For dry sotanghon, use 2 cups broth only. Chicken cut into serving pieces may be used instead of removing bones. Pork and shrimps may be substituted for chicken as well.

## SPAGHETTI WITH MEAT SAUCE

1 lb. pkg. spaghetti, cooked according to pkg. directions
2 Tbsp. vegetable oil
1 large onion, minced
1 (8 oz.) can tomato sauce
1 tsp. salt
1/8 tsp. pepper
2 garlic cloves, crushed
1 lb. ground beef
1 (6 oz.) can tomato paste
1/2 tsp. MSG

In hot oil, brown garlic, add onions and cook until transparent. Add ground beef and stir-cook for 5 minutes. Skim off extra fat. Add tomato sauce and paste, then season with salt, pepper and MSG. Cook, covered, over low heat and stirring occasionally, 30 to 45 minutes. Mix or pour sauce over cooked spaghetti. Serve with grated Parmesan cheese.

Serves 6.

## LUMPIA MACAO

1 c. ground pork (about 1 1/2 lb.)
1 c. finely chopped shelled shrimps (about 1/2 lb.)
1/2 tsp. salt
1 Tbsp. soy sauce
1/2 c. canned water chestnuts, drained and finely chopped
1/4 c. dried mushrooms, soaked, drained, then finely chopped
3 Tbsp. finely chopped scallions
10 round lumpia wrappers, cut into 20 halves - for square lumpia wrappers, cut into triangular halves (see Glossary)
1/8 tsp. pepper
1/2 tsp. MSG
1 raw egg

Mix well all the ingredients except the lumpia wrappers. In each half lumpia wrapper put a tablespoonful of the mixture and roll into 3 inch long and 1/2 inch diameter lumpia, with both ends of wrapper tucked in and rolled. Deep fry in hot oil until golden brown. Drain on paper towel. Serve with Sweet and Sour Sauce (see recipe).

Serves 6 to 8.

(See illustration on next page.)

(Cont.)

## WRAPPERS FOR LUMPIA FRESH

4 large eggs  
1/4 tsp. salt  
1 c. cornstarch  
2 1/2 c. cold water

    Beat eggs until yolk and white are blended. Beat in cornstarch and salt until well dissolved. Add water and mix thoroughly. Let stand a few minutes to let bubbles disappear. Heat a flat 7-inch bottom-diameter Teflon frying pan on medium heat. (If a non-Teflon is used, grease with oil before each use.) Pour just enough of the egg mixture (about 3 tablespoons) on the heated pan and tilt pan quickly so mixture will coat the pan evenly. Cook a few minutes or until mixture separates from the pan. Cook the rest of the mixture this way, being sure to stir the egg mixture thoroughly before pouring to heated pan. Stack wrapper on plate.

    Yields about 24 wrappers for Lumpia Fresh (see recipe).

    NOTE: Pan temperature should be just right so that the egg mixture will stick and coat the pan. If temperature is too hot, it will cause bubbles and holes. If too cold, mixture will just roll and will not stick. Experiment for the ideal temperature on your stove. This is where practice makes perfect wrappers.

## LUMPIA FRIED (Philippine Egg Roll)

- 3 Tbsp. vegetable oil
- 3 Tbsp. sliced onions
- 1/2 c. shelled shrimps, sliced fine (about 1/4 lb.)
- 1 tsp. salt
- 1/2 lb. green beans, thinly sliced diagonally (French cut)
- 2 c. shredded cabbage
- 1 large sweet potato or yam cut into thin strips or coarsely grated
- 2 Tbsp. soy sauce
- 3 Tbsp. chunk style peanut butter (if desired)
- 12 lumpia wrappers (see Glossary) or wanton wrappers, 6-inch squares
- vegetable oil for deep frying, (3/4-inch deep)
- 2 garlic cloves, crushed
- 1 c. pork, sliced fine (about 1/4 lb.)
- 1/8 tsp. pepper
- 1 tsp. MSG

In 3 tablespoons hot oil, brown garlic; add onions, then pork. Cook 5 minutes on high heat, then add shrimps. Reduce heat, season with salt and pepper. Cook for 5 minutes. Stir in green beans, cook for 1 minute, then add cabbage, sweet potato, soy sauce and MSG. Stir and cook for 2 minutes. Cool.

Wrap by 2 to 3 tablespoons in each wrapper by folding once horizontally, next fold in both ends and roll. Deep fry in hot oil to a golden brown. Drain on paper towel. Serve hot, with a dipping mixture of 1/4 cup vinegar, 1/2 teaspoon salt and a clove of fresh garlic, crushed.

Serves 6.

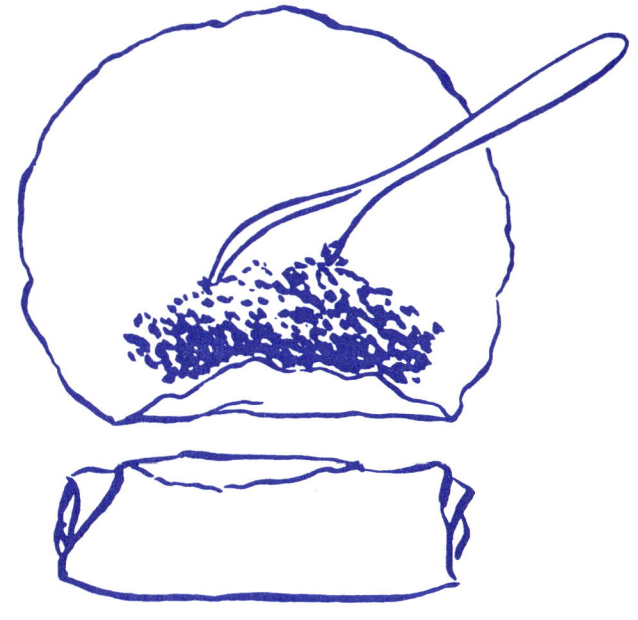

**LUMPIA FRIED**

## LUMPIA FRESH

Use recipe for Lumpia Fried except, cook vegetables a few minutes longer. Wrap with lumpia wrappers (egg roll skin) or Wrappers for Lumpia Fresh (see recipe). Spoon cooked filling on a small lettuce leaf overlapping the lumpia wrapper. Roll, fold 1 end but leave other end open to show the lettuce leaf. Serve as is, with Sauce for Fresh Lumpia (see recipe). A can of "Ubod" (see Glossary) drained and cut into thin strips, added to ingredients in Lumpia Fresh, will be Ubod Lumpia Fresh. Sprinkle a spoonful of ground peanuts sweetened with a little sugar over rolled Lumpia.

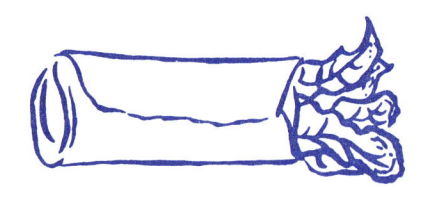

## SAUCE FOR LUMPIA FRESH

3 Tbsp. soy sauce
1/2 c. water
1/8 tsp. pepper
1 tsp. vegetable oil (optional)

4 Tbsp. sugar
1/2 tsp. salt
1 Tbsp. cornstarch

Mix all ingredients very well. Gently boil, while stirring for 5 minutes, or until sauce thickens. If desired, a teaspoon of minced fresh garlic may be sprinkled on top when serving.

Yields about 3/4 cup sauce.

## SIOMAI (Chinese Meat Dumplings)

1/2 c. shelled shrimps, sliced fine (optional)
1 c. ground pork
1 tsp. salt
1/8 tsp. pepper
1/4 c. chopped water chestnuts, canned

1 c. ground beef
1 tsp. MSG
3 Tbsp. chopped scallions
1 or 2 egg yolks (save egg whites)
40 to 50 Wanton wrappers, 3-inch squares (see Glossary)
1 c. oil for frying

Mix first 9 ingredients thoroughly. Place a teaspoonful of the mixture on the center of wanton wrappers, dip finger in the egg white and wet the sides of the wanton wrapper. Fold wrapper diagonally to form a triangle. Press and stick the sides. Deep-fat fry as many as the pan can accommodate and turn to other side when wrapper starts to wilt (a few minutes), then add 1/2 cup of water, cook covered until water evaporates. Spoon out cooked "siomai." Repeat procedure until all stuffed wanton wrappers are cooked. Serve with a dipping mixture of 3 tablespoons soy sauce and 1 1/2 tablespoons lemon juice.

NOTE: Ready-made Wanton wrappers are recommended for use. They are sold in most Chinese or Oriental food stores.

## SIOPAO

### Filling:

1 lb. boneless pork cut into tiny pieces
1 medium onion, diced, if desired
2 Tbsp. vegetable oil

2 tsp. sugar
1 Tbsp. cornstarch dissolved in 2 Tbsp. water
1/4 c. soy sauce

Brown pork in hot oil. Add onions. Cover and cook for 10 minutes until pork is tender. Add sugar, dissolved cornstarch and soy sauce, mixing well over low heat until thickened. Cool and fill in dough.

### Dough:

3 tsp. dry yeast
1 1/2 c. warm water
1/2 c. sugar
4 1/2 c. all-purpose flour

1/2 c. pork lard or Crisco vegetable shortening
waxed paper cut into 24 (2-inch) squares

(Cont.)

In large bowl dissolve yeast in warm water. Add sugar and 2 1/2 cups flour to make a soft sponge. Beat thoroughly with a wooden spoon. Cover, set aside to rise until double in size, about 30 minutes. Add remaining flour, 1/4 cup lard and mix well. Grease surface for kneading flour mixture and knead until smooth.

Divide dough into 24 pieces and form into balls. Flatten each ball with heel of your hand and put filling in the center. Seal edges together forming a pouch, and lay Siopao on waxed paper square with sealed side under. Let rise for 20 minutes. Steam covered for 30 minutes. Serve with Siopao Sauce.

NOTE: Chicken may be used instead of pork. Ready made buttermilk or biscuit dough may be used as Siopao dough. Just grease hands, flatten each biscuit dough, put filling and proceed as above. Cut-up Chinese sausage and/or hard-boiled egg wedge may be added to each filling.

For Siopao Baked, instead of steaming - bake at 350°F. for 20 to 25 minutes, or until light brown.

## SIOPAO SAUCE

1/2 c. water
3 Tbsp. sugar
1 Tbsp. cornstarch
1/2 tsp. MSG

3 Tbsp. soy sauce
pinch of salt
2 tsp. vegetable oil

Mix all ingredients until cornstarch and sugar are dissolved. Gently boil, while stirring for 5 minutes or until sauce thickens.
Yields about 3/4 cup sauce.

## UKOY  (Shrimp Fritters)

1/2 lb. small or medium shrimps with shells
1 c. cornstarch or all-purpose flour
1 tsp. baking powder
1 c. bean sprouts, fresh or canned, drained
2 Tbsp. chopped scallions

vegetable oil for frying, (3/4 inch deep)
2 eggs, well beaten
1 tsp. salt
2/3 c. shrimp broth
1 bean curd, thinly sliced, (optional)

In a covered pot, boil shrimps with 2/3 cup water until shrimps turn pink, 5 minutes. Drain shrimps and split from the back into 2. Save shrimp broth. Set aside.

To well beaten eggs add cornstarch or flour, salt, baking powder and 2/3 cup shrimp broth. Mix until smooth. Add bean sprouts and scallions. Pour about 1/4 cup of the mixture at a time, onto hot oil, gather particles together and lay 4 pieces of shrimps and 2 pieces of sliced bean curd on top. Fry until brown and crispy. Drain on paper towel. Serve with a dipping mixture of 1/4 cup vinegar, 1 garlic clove, crushed, salt and pepper to taste.

Yields about 15 ukoys.

## TAMALE FILIPINO SPECIAL

### Brown Tamale:

2 c. rice powder, browned
3 Tbsp. oil
3 garlic cloves, pounded
1 large onion, diced
1 c. coarsely ground fried
   pork rinds (optional)

3/4 c. crunchy peanut butter
4-5 c. chicken broth
2 tsp. salt
1/2 tsp. pepper
1 tsp. MSG

### White Tamale:

1 c. rice powder (see Glossary)
2 Tbsp. oil
2 garlic cloves, pounded
1 medium onion, diced

2-3 c. chicken broth
1 tsp. salt
1/4 tsp. pepper
1/2 tsp. MSG

Garnishings: Strips or pieces of boiled chicken, boiled pork, Cheddar cheese, cooked ham or hard-cooked egg or combination of two or more of these.

Wrapper: 12 aluminum foil cut into 10 x 12-inch pieces

Brown Tamale: In pan brown rice powder over medium heat while stirring constantly, being careful not to burn rice. Let cool, then blend in half of broth until mixture is smooth. Set aside.

In hot oil brown garlic; add onion, stir 2 minutes, add pork rinds, rice powder mixture, remaining chicken broth, salt, pepper and MSG, stirring constantly over medium-low heat until mixture is the consistency of very thick paste, after about 25 minutes. Correct seasoning while cooking to suit taste. Let cool.

Meanwhile prepare White Tamale basically the same way as Brown Tamale, without browning rice powder and omitting peanut butter and pork rinds. When both tamales are cool, start wrapping.

In the middle of each cut aluminum foil wrapper put about 3 tablespoonfuls of Brown Tamale, shape and flatten to 1 inch thickness; layer 1 1/2 tablespoonfuls of White Tamale over Brown.

(Cont.)

Garnish as desired. Wrap securely. Steam all together even if wrapped tamales are stacked, for 20 minutes.

Yields: 12 tamales.

NOTE: Instead of individually wrapping tamales use glass Pyrex dish (about 8-inch square), spread Brown Tamale first, then layer on White Tamale, garnish top as desired, even sprinkle some Parmesan cheese, bake covered with foil in low oven, 300°F., for 15 minutes. Cut into serving pieces when cool.

Write your extra recipes here:

# Vegetables

# BUYING GUIDE
## Fresh vegetables and fruits

Experience is the best teacher in choosing quality but here are a few pointers on buying some of the fruits and vegetables.

ASPARAGUS—Stalks should be tender and firm, tips should be close and compact. Choose the stalks with very little white—they are more tender. Use asparagus soon—it toughens rapidly.

BEANS, SNAP—Those with small seeds inside the pods are best. Avoid beans with dry-looking pods.

BERRIES—Select plump, solid berries with good color. Avoid stained containers, indicating wet or leaky berries. Berries such as blackberries and raspberries with clinging caps may be underripe. Strawberries without caps may be too ripe.

BROCCOLI, BRUSSELS SPROUTS, AND CAULIFLOWER—Flower clusters on broccoli and cauliflower should be tight and close together. Brussels sprouts should be firm and compact. Smudgy, dirty spots may indicate insects.

CABBAGE AND HEAD LETTUCE—Choose heads heavy for size. Avoid cabbage with worm holes, lettuce with discoloration or soft rot.

CUCUMBERS—Choose long, slender cucumbers for best quality. May be dark or medium green but yellowed ones are undesirable.

MELONS—In cantaloupes, thick close netting on the rind indicates best quality. Cantaloupes are ripe when the stem scar is smooth and space between the netting is yellow or yellow-green. They are best to eat when fully ripe with fruity odor.

Honeydews are ripe when rind has creamy to yellowish color and velvety texture. Immature honeydews are whitish-green.

Ripe watermelons have some yellow color on one side. If melons are white or pale green on one side, they are not ripe.

ORANGES, GRAPEFRUIT, AND LEMONS—Choose those heavy for their size. Smoother, thinner skins usually indicate more juice. Most skin markings do not affect quality. Oranges with a slight greenish tinge may be just as ripe as fully colored ones. Light or greenish-yellow lemons are more tart than deep yellow ones. Avoid citrus fruits showing withered, sunken, or soft areas.

PEAS AND LIMA BEANS—Select pods that are well-filled but not bulging. Avoid dried, spotted, yellowed, or flabby pods.

ROOT VEGETABLES—Should be smooth and firm. Very large carrots may have woody cores, oversized radishes may be pithy, oversized turnips, beets, and parsnips may be woody. Fresh carrot tops usually mean fresh carrots, but condition of leaves on most other root vegetables does not indicate degree of freshness.

SWEET POTATOES—Porto Rico and Nancy Hall varieties—with bronze to rosy skins—are soft and sweet when cooked. Yellow to light-brown ones of the Jersey types are firmer and less moist.

# VEGETABLES

## CABBAGE GUISADO

1/2 lb. boneless pork, cut into small pieces
1/4 lb. medium shrimps, shelled and slit in two
1/2 tsp. salt
1 garlic clove, crushed
1 medium tomato, ripe, finely sliced
1/8 tsp. pepper
1 lb. cabbage, cut into strips of 1-inch squares
2 Tbsp. vegetable oil
1 small onion, finely sliced
1/2 tsp. MSG
1 tsp. patis (optional - see Glossary)

Prepare pork and shrimps. Sprinkle salt. Set aside. In hot oil, lightly brown garlic; add onions, stir-cook until transparent. Add tomatoes and stir-cook for 3 minutes or until mushy. On high heat, add pork pieces, stir-cook 5 minutes or until pork pinkness is gone. Add about 1/4 cup water, cover and cook over medium heat for 10 minutes, or until pork is tender. Add shrimps, MSG, pepper and patis, stir-cook for 5 minutes. Taste and correct seasoning. Add cabbage and cook for 3 minutes. Cabbage should not be over-cooked. Serve hot.
Serves 6.
NOTE: Other vegetables like green beans, French cut; cauliflower; broccoli or other mixed vegetables can be used in place of cabbage.
Ampalaya (Bitter Melon) Guisado: Substitute cabbage in above recipe for a can (21 ounces) of bitter melon, drain and slice into 1/2 inch strips. For fresh, use 1 large, half lengthwise, remove seeds, slice, rub with 1 tablespoon salt, then wash thoroughly.

## CALABASA GUISADO  (Sauteed Winter Squash)

1 1/2 lb. winter squash (Hubbard, Acorn) or young pumpkin, fresh or frozen
1 1/2 tsp. salt
1/4 lb. medium shrimps, shelled and slit into 2
1 garlic clove, crushed
1 medium tomato, sliced
1 Tbsp. patis (optional - see Glossary)
1/2 lb. pork, sliced into small pieces
3 Tbsp. vegetable oil
1 small onion, finely sliced
1 tsp. MSG

Wash and peel fresh squash. Cut into 1-inch chunks. Set aside. Sprinkle 1 teaspoon salt on pork and shrimps. Set aside. In hot
(Cont.)

oil brown garlic; add onions and saute' until transparent, add tomato and cook until mushy, while stirring.

On high heat, add pork and saute' 5 minutes, or until pinkness is gone. Add shrimps, saute' 3 minutes, then add squash and remaining salt. Stir-cook 3 minutes, add about 3 cups water. Cook, covered, over medium heat for 30 minutes or until squash is very soft. Stir occasionally. Season with MSG and patis, taste.

Serves 4 to 5.

### EGGPLANT TORTILLA (Omelet)

| | |
|---|---|
| 1 eggplant, about a pound | 1 c. ground beef or pork |
| 1 garlic clove, crushed | 1 small onion, minced |
| 1 medium tomato, sliced | 1/2 tsp. MSG |
| 1/2 tsp. salt | 1/8 tsp. pepper |
| 2 eggs, large, beaten | 1/4 c. vegetable oil |

Prick eggplant with fork at several places. Keep stump intact all throughout cooking preparation. Roast eggplant over electric stove, gas flame, charcoal or oven broil until it becomes soft and skin partly burnt. Cool, peel. With a fork press and flatten eggplant in beaten egg. Set aside.

Brown meat, push to one side of pan and saute' garlic, onions and tomatoes. Mix meat, season with MSG, salt and pepper. Remove from fire, spread meat mixture over eggplant and press carefully. Let beaten egg coat and bind together eggplant and meat. Heat about 1/4 cup oil in frying pan, fry eggplant mixture. When bottom side is cooked, carefully turn eggplant for other side to cook. Serve hot with catsup.

### MONGO BEAN GUISADO

| | |
|---|---|
| 1 c. dried mongo beans | 4 c. water |
| 1 tsp. salt | 1/2 lb. pork, sliced into small pieces |
| 1/4 lb. medium shrimps, shelled and slit into 2 | 2 garlic cloves, crushed |
| 3 Tbsp. vegetable oil | 2 medium tomatoes, fresh or canned |
| 1 medium onion, finely sliced | 1 tsp. MSG |
| 2 Tbsp. bagoong or patis (see Glossary) | |

Boil mongo beans in 4 cups water for 45 minutes or until mongo beans are soft. Set aside. Sprinkle salt on pork and shrimps. In hot oil, brown garlic; add onions and saute' until transparent. Add tomatoes and cook until mushy. Add pork and saute' for 7 minutes, or until pork pinkness is gone. Add shrimps, bagoong or patis and saute' 5 minutes, then pour to boiled mongo beans.

Cover and simmer mongo bean mixture. Season with MSG and salt to taste, if needed. Simmer, covered, for 10 minutes more.

Serves 6.

## POKEY-POKEY (Sauteed Eggplant)

1 medium-size eggplant, (about 1 lb.)
2 garlic cloves, crushed
1 Tbsp. patis or bagoong (see Glossary)
2 eggs beaten with 1/4 tsp. salt
3 Tbsp. vegetable oil
1 medium onion, finely sliced
1 tsp. MSG
1 medium tomato, finely sliced

With fork, prick eggplant in several places. Roast over gas or electric stove, charcoal or oven broil until eggplant is soft and skin partly burnt. Let cool. Peel off skin. Cut peeled eggplant to pieces. Set aside.

In hot oil saute' garlic until light brown. Add onions and cook while stirring until transparent. Add tomatoes and patis, and stir-cook until tomatoes are mushy. Add eggplant and MSG. Stir-cook for 3 minutes. Stir in beaten eggs and mix well. Cook 2 minutes more.

Serves 4.

## PINAKBET DELUXE

3 Tbsp. bagoong (see Glossary)
1/2 c. sliced tomatoes, fresh or canned
2 garlic cloves, crushed
1 medium eggplant (about 1 lb.), halved lengthwise, sliced 1 inch thick
1 ampalaya (bitter melon), sliced, fresh or canned
1 pkg. frozen okra
1/2 tsp. MSG
1 small pkg. (1 1/2 oz.) fried pork rinds* or 1/2 c. fried pork slices
1/2 c. water
1/4 c. onion, sliced
1 pkg. frozen lima beans
1/2 lb. green beans
2 Tbsp. oil

Mix first 10 ingredients in a pot. Cover and let boil for 15 minutes, with occasional tossing of the covered pot to rotate vegetables, otherwise, stir gently. Add pork rinds and oil. Simmer for another 5 minutes, or until vegetables are cooked.

NOTE: For a simpler pinakbet, omit 1 or 2 vegetables and pork rinds, and adjust seasoning requirements.

*Available at most food stores, snack sections. Brand names: Wise-Bakon Delites, Frito Lay-Baken, etc.

## DINENGDENG  (Vegetable Stew)

2 Tbsp. bagoong (fish sauce, see Glossary)
1 c. water
1 small onion, sliced
1/2 lb. fresh green beans, cleaned
1 small eggplant, cleaned, cut to desired pieces
1 medium tomato, sliced
1 c. cut chitcharon (see recipe) or leftover roast pork or chicken (optional)
1/4 tsp. MSG

In a covered pot simmer bagoong, water, onion, tomato and chitcharon for 10 minutes. Increase to high heat and add vegetables. Cook covered for 5 minutes, or until vegetables are just cooked. Add MSG and salt to taste, if needed. Serve hot immediately.
Serves 4.

## HONEYED SNOW PEAS AND ASPARAGUS

1/2 lb. snow peas, fresh
1 lb. asparagus, fresh
1 tsp. sesame oil
1 tsp. sesame seeds
1 Tbsp. honey
1/4 tsp. fresh ginger, minced

Top and tail snow peas. Peel ends of asparagus with a vegetable peeler, slice asparagus diagonally into 1-inch pieces. Boil, steam or microwave vegetables until tender, refresh with cold water; drain.
In pan, heat sesame oil and seeds until hot, add vegetables, honey and ginger. Stir-fry until heated through.
Serves 4 to 6.
NOTE: Thanks to Shelmon Bermas for this recipe.

## LAING  (Visayan Dish with Coconut Milk)

2 Tbsp. cooking oil
2 garlic cloves, crushed
1 small onion, chopped
1 c. shrimps, shelled
1/2 tsp. salt
1 lb. (4-6 c.) spinach leaves, cleaned
1 c. unsweetened coconut milk

In hot oil, saute' garlic and onions for 2 minutes. Add shrimps and salt. Continue sauteeing for another 3 minutes. Mix in spinach, add coconut milk. On low heat simmer covered for 5 minutes, or until spinach is tender.
Serves 4.
NOTE: Two hot chili peppers (siling la buyo), sliced, may be sauteed with the shrimps. Other tender greens like watercress

may be used. Dried gabi leaves are used in the Philippines. Patis or bagoong (see Glossary), 1 tablespoon may be used in place of salt.

Taro leaves (gabi) are used in the Philippines.

Write your extra recipes here:

**Write your extra recipes here:**

# Breads, Rolls, Pies, Pastries

## BREAD, ROLLS, PIES AND PASTRY

* Place a folded, damp towel under the bowl and it won't slip and slide while mixing.

* When fresh fruit is handy, but you don't have time to bake, just mix the filling as you normally would for pie. Line a pie pan with several layers of foil and place the filling in the pan. Wrap and freeze. When you're ready with a pie crust the filling can be placed in the crust and baked. After filling is frozen solid it can be taken out of the pan so you will be able to use the pan and the fillings will stack neater in the freezer.

* Add ½ teaspoon of sugar to the yeast when stirring it into the water to dissolve. If it foams and bubbles in ten minutes you know the yeast is alive and active.

* Dough can rise with no problem even in a cold kitchen if the bowl is placed on a heating pad set on medium.

* If the oven is turned off just when the meringue is brown, and the door is left slightly open, the pie cools slowly and prevents the meringue from splitting.

* Your bread will be crusty if top and sides are brushed with an egg white that has been beaten with one tablespoon of water.

* A super-fast 'company' pie can be made by using a prepared crust. Add one box of instant pudding mix to prepared whipped topping. Mix well and fill crust. Reserve enough whipped topping to cover pie. Any flavor pudding mix can be used.

* Try substituting ground nuts in a one crust pie. Press pie shell just like you would with a graham cracker crust.

* Use water that has been used to boil potatoes to make bread dough moister.

* If a dull-finish aluminum loaf pan is used it will brown the sides of the bread better.

* Brushing frozen pies with melted butter before baking can eliminate dryness.

* Let baked bread cool on a wire rack so the bottom won't be soggy.

* Dough won't stick to your hands if it is kneaded inside a large plastic bag.

* To get a dull finish on a new pan it can be baked empty in a 350 degree oven.

* If the television is in use, it makes a nice warm spot for dough to rise.

* To thaw, frozen bread loaves, place in clean brown paper and put in 325° oven for 5 - 6 minutes to thaw completely. For thawing rolls allow several more minutes.

## BREAD, ROLLS, PIES, PASTRY

### ENSAIMADA AMERICANA (Sweet Bun)

| | |
|---|---|
| 1/4 c. milk | 1/4 c. warm water, 105°-115°F. |
| 1/4 c. sugar | 1 egg, beaten |
| 1/2 tsp. salt | 2 1/4 c. sifted all-purpose flour |
| 4 Tbsp. butter or margarine | 4 drops yellow food color |
| 1 pkg. (1/4 oz.) Fleischmann's active dry yeast | 1/2 c. melted butter or margarine for greasing |

Combine milk, sugar, salt and butter in small saucepan, heat until butter is melted. Cool to lukewarm. In large bowl dissolve yeast in warm water. Stir in milk mixture. Add beaten egg, 1 1/2 cups flour and yellow food color. Beat with wooden spoon until smooth. Add rest of flour, beating well until dough is smooth and leaves sides of bowl.

With greased hands place dough in greased bowl, cover with towel; let rise undisturbed in warm place (85°F.), free from drafts, until double in bulk, 1 to 1 1/2 hours. Punch down dough. On greased surface roll out dough evenly into 32 x 8-inch rectangle, 1/8-inch thick.

Brush entire surface generously with melted butter. If desired, sprinkle on some raisins and Cheddar cheese bits. Roll up dough from long side, forming a long rope. On greased 8-inch round pan, coil dough rope beginning in center of pan. Brush top generously with melted butter. Cover with towel; let rise in warm place (85°F.), free from drafts, until double in bulk, 1 hour.

In preheated 325°F. oven, bake for 40 minutes. Remove from pan, brush with melted butter while still hot, lightly sprinkle on granulated sugar.

Serves 6.

NOTE: For smaller ensaimada buns, after first rising, divide dough into 10 pieces. Roll out each piece until thin and follow basic procedure as above. Use cookie sheet pan instead of round pan, spacing buns 2 inches apart. Bake for 30 minutes instead.

If kitchen is chilly, let dough rise in an unlighted closed oven, with a large pan of hot water on the rack below, to hasten rising.

### PAN de SAL (Philippine Hard Roll)

| | |
|---|---|
| 2 loaves (2 lb.) frozen bread dough | 1/4 c. shortening like Crisco |
| | 1/2 c. bread crumbs |

(Cont.)

Place frozen bread dough on greased cookie sheet pan, cover with waxed paper and let dough thaw. When soft enough to handle, cut each loaf into 12 oblong shape rolls. Grease each roll with shortening, roll in bread crumbs.

Arrange 2 inches apart on cookie sheet, cover with waxed paper and let rise at room temperature until double its original size, about 3 to 4 hours. Preheat oven to 375°. Remove waxed paper, cover; bake rolls for 15 minutes, or until golden brown. Serve hot.

Yields: 24 rolls.

NOTE: Ready-made frozen white bread dough or French bread dough is available at almost any grocery. Read suggestions for speedy dough rising and other recipe ideas printed on package.

### PAN de SAL (From Scratch)

3 1/2 to 4 1/2 c. all-purpose flour
2 pkg. active dry yeast
1/2 c. sugar
1 1/2 tsp. salt

1 c. warm water (120°F.)
2 Tbsp. vegetable oil
1 egg
1 1/2 c. bread crumbs

Combine 1 cup flour, yeast, sugar and salt in a large mixing bowl. Stir in water, oil and egg; beat until smooth, about 3 minutes on high speed of electric mixer. Gradually stir in more flour to make a soft dough.

Turn dough onto a floured surface; knead until smooth and elastic, 3 to 5 minutes. Cover with bowl or pan and let rest about 20 minutes. Divide into 18 equal pieces, shaping each piece into smooth oval. Roll in bread crumbs and place on a greased baking sheet, an inch apart. Let rise until double in bulk, about 15 minutes.

Bake at 400°F., for 15 to 20 minutes. For a crisper crust, place in a shallow pan of hot water on lowest oven rack during baking.

Yields: 1 1/2 dozen.

### BUCHI-BUCHI (Fried Sweet Rice Ball)

1/2 c. mongo beans, raw
2 c. water
1/2 c. sugar
3 c. sweet rice flour or 1 lb. box of Mochiko sweet rice flour

1 1/2 c. water
oil for deep fat frying

Slowly boil mongo with 2 cups water in a covered pot until mongo is soft and mushy; throughly mix in sugar and cook over low heat while stirring and mashing mixture until it is paste-like. Cool.

In another bowl mix rice flour with 1 1/2 cups water, forming a dough ball. Take about a whole egg size amount of dough at a time and, with hands, shape each ball into a 4-inch flat circle. Put a tablespoon of mongo mixture in the center, bring edges together to fully cover mongo filling, forming a round pouch, oblong or flat patty (whichever shape one desires).

In hot, 1-inch deep, frying oil, fry filled pouches until golden brown. Drain on paper towel. Watch out for unexpected popping while frying as hot oil may splatter on hands and face. Serve warm. Good as snack.

Makes about 20.

## HOPIA

### Filling:

| | |
|---|---|
| 1 c. peeled, split mung beans | 1 1/2 c. sugar |
| 3 c. water | 2 Tbsp. margarine |

### Pastry:

| | |
|---|---|
| 1 c. boiling water | 3/4 c. lard or shortening, like Crisco |
| 3 c. all-purpose flour | |

Prepare filling by simmering in a covered pot, beans, water and sugar until beans are very soft, about 45 minutes. Watch that pot doesn't boil over. During last 15 minutes, stir frequently, mashing beans. Add margarine when mixture is thick and paste-like. Cool. Shape into 2-inch diameter patties. Set aside.

Pastry: In boiling water mix 1 1/2 cups flour. Stir into a dough ball. Set aside, cool. Mix lard with remaining 1 1/2 cups flour until well blended. Knead together with flour-water dough. Flour hands if dough is sticky.

Divide into 20 pieces. Using your hands flatten each piece into a 3-inch diameter round, 1/8-inch thick. Place filling pattie in the middle of each round pastry, bring pastry edges together covering patties. Smooth out surface. Place 'hopia' in greased cookie sheet, bake at 350°F. for 10 minutes, turn 'hopia,' bake another 10 minutes.

Yields: 20 hopia.

NOTE: Peeled, split mung beans can be purchased at Oriental stores. Red kidney beans or black beans sold in health stores can also be used. Soften in water, soaked overnight.

## MASTER MIX

What is Master Mix? It is an all-purpose baking mix you can make up ahead of time and store in quantity. It can be used in recipes calling for a commercial biscuit mix and adapted to other recipes. <u>Master Mix saves time and money.</u> Excellent for Puto (see recipe), pancakes, biscuits, cookies, breads, muffins and cakes.

This mix made at home is cheaper than a commercial mix. It already contains milk. It gives a tender produce because of the fat content. Check recipes on box of "Bisquick."

<u>12 Cups of Master Mix:</u>

8 c. unsifted all-purpose flour, don't shake or pack
1/3 c. double-acting baking powder
1 Tbsp. salt

2 Tbsp. sugar
2 c. non-fat dry milk
1 2/3 c. lard (or 2 c. shortening like Crisco)

Sift dry ingredients together until well mixed. Cut lard into flour mixture until lard is so finely blended you can't tell it from the flour. Store in covered container or plastic bag. May be stored at room temperature for 6 weeks if shortening is used. Refrigerate if lard is used. Omit baking powder and salt if self-rising flour is used.

### <u>PUTO</u>  (Steamed Rice Cake)

2 c. Bisquick mix or Master Mix (see recipe)
1 c. sugar

1 c. milk
2 eggs

Mix all ingredients to a smooth consistency. Pour to muffin pans, 2/3 full. Steam in large, well covered pan with about 3 inches deep water for 15 minutes, or until inserted toothpick comes out clean. Add more water as needed during steaming period. Loosen and remove puto from muffin pans. Serve with Dinugguan (see recipe) or with Salabat (see recipe).

Yields 4 dozen tiny puto or 2 dozen regular-size muffin puto.

For colored Puto - divide batter to 3 bowls. Add few drops of green food color to one bowl; yellow to another, and red to the third bowl to produce a pink color. Pour to muffin pans and steam.

## PUTO BULACAN (Steamed Rice Cake)

| | |
|---|---|
| 2 c. rice flour | 1 c. Bisquick mix |
| 1 pkg. dry yeast | 2 c. warm water |
| 1 c. sugar | 1/4 tsp. anise seeds (optional) |

Follow above procedure for Puto.

## PUTO CHINESE (Spongy Steamed Rice Cake)

| | |
|---|---|
| 3 c. rice flour, from long grain rice | 3 c. water |
| | 2 tsp. yeast |
| 1 1/2 c. sugar | 2 Tbsp. warm water |

Mix rice flour, sugar and 3 cups water until smooth. In separate cup mix yeast and warm water and let stand 10 minutes. On medium-low heat cook rice flour mixture, while stirring constantly until thickened, about 20 minutes. Pour hot batter to a sieve into a large bowl then mix in dissolved yeast. Let stand for 6 to 8 hours, until bubbles appear. Pour into suitable pan lined with cheesecloth or plastic wrap. Cover and steam for 25 minutes, or until inserted toothpick comes out clean. Cool. Cut into diamond shapes.
   Serves 6 to 8.

## MARUYA (Banana Fritters)

| | |
|---|---|
| 1 c. flour | 1 c. milk |
| 3 Tbsp. sugar | 2 ripe cooking bananas (plantain), sliced slanting |
| 1 tsp. baking powder | |

Mix first 4 ingredients until smooth. Blend in sliced bananas. Drop by spoonfuls into deep hot oil and fry until golden brown. Drain on paper towel.
   Makes 20 fritters.
   NOTE: A cup of grated sweet potato or 1 large sweet potato sliced thinly may be used in place of banana for Kamote fritters.

## PILIPIT (Twists)

| | |
|---|---|
| 1 lb. box Mochiko sweet rice flour (see Glossary) | 1 egg |
| | 1/2 tsp. baking powder |
| 1 c. dry flake or fresh shredded coconut | 1 tsp. grated fresh lemon rind |
| | 1 1/4 c. water |

   Mix all ingredients and knead. On rice-floured surface roll
(Cont.)

into a long, thin rope 1/3-inch diameter and cut into 6-inch lengths. Twist each cut strip together like a rope, starting with ends. Deep-fat fry until golden brown. Transfer fried twists to a deep bowl.

Meanwhile, boil for 3 minutes mixture of 1 cup sugar, 1/2 teaspoon baking soda and 1/4 cup water. While boiling pour over bowl of fried twists mixing to sugar-coat twists.

Makes about 50 crystallized twists.

NOTE: When dough is not twisted, but rather a straight rod, it is called "bitsu-bitsu," when it is shaped into flattened balls the size of a penny, I think my Grandmother called them "cascaroons." Powdered sugar may be used to coat fried twists, instead of crystallized sugar.

## TURON  (Wrapped Bananas)

6 pieces Fillo (Phyllo) dough sheets
1 c. melted butter or margarine
1 c. corn flakes, crushed

6 bananas, medium ripe, sliced into 4 lengthwise
1 c. sweet preserved jackfruit (langka)

Cut each Fillo sheet into 2 crosswise. Cover unused Fillo with damp towel while working. Brush sheet generously with melted butter, sprinkle a tablespoon of corn flake crumbs, lay 2 slices of banana on long edge, top with 4 pieces of jackfruit strips, wrap and fold securely like an egg roll. Brush outside with melted butter. Arrange on ungreased cookie sheet and bake in preheated 350°F. oven for 30 to 40 minutes, until golden brown.

Makes 12.

NOTE: Dr. Amor Barongan shared this recipe. The unbaked turon can be frozen, ready to bake, unthawed when needed. Wrap properly for freezer. Fillo dough is in a box in freezer section of supermarkets.

Carmen Quiogue uses lumpia wrapper (egg roll skin) and fries each to a golden brown. She prefers using ripe plantain bananas.

## TINUDOK OR CARIOCA

1 c. sweet rice flour, (see Glossary)
1/2 c. coconut, grated, packaged or fresh

1/4 c. water
1 c. vegetable oil for deep fat frying

### Syrup:

1/2 c. sugar

1/2 c. water

bamboo skewers (optional)

    Mix first 3 ingredients to a soft dough, form into 1-inch diameter elongated balls. Deep fat fry in hot oil, a few at a time, until golden brown. Drain on paper towel.
    While frying watch out as they sometimes splatter with a popping sound. Cover pot. Make syrup by boiling sugar and water for 5 minutes, or until syrup thickens, while stirring occasionally. Drop fried balls, one at a time, until coated. Transfer coated ball to a dish. Skewer 2 or 3 balls on each bamboo stick, if desired.
    Yields about 20 balls.
    NOTE: If syrup is not desired, add 2 tablespoons sugar to sweet rice flour before mixing.
    "Tinudok" is an Ilocano term for pierce.

## SUMAN SA IBUS

2 c. sweet rice grains,
  (see Glossary)
3 c. water
1/2 tsp. salt

1 c. coconut milk
aluminum foil cut into
  20 (6-inch) squares

    In a pot mix rice, water and salt. Cover and let boil slowly until rice is partially cooked, about 20 minutes. Remove from heat. Stir in coconut milk, mixing well. Cool. Spoon rice mixture in the middle of each aluminum foil square. Roll to the shape of a 1-inch diameter tube; fold ends securely so liquid will not enter.
    In covered pot, boil wrapped suman in enough water for about 20 minutes, or until rice is soft. Serve with Latik (see recipe) or sugar for dipping. Unwrap to eat.
    Yields: 20.
    NOTE: For Suman Sa Lihya, add 1 1/2 teaspoons lye water (see Glossary) when adding coconut milk.

## WHEAT GERM YELLOW SQUASH BREAD

    Beat 3 eggs to blend. Add 1 cup corn oil, 1 cup granulated sugar, 1 cup brown sugar and 3 teaspoons maple flavoring. Continue beating until thick and foamy. Stir in 2 cups coarsely shredded yellow squash (washed but not peeled).
    Combine 1 1/2 cups whole wheat flour, 1 cup enriched white flour, 1/2 cup wheat germ, 2 teaspoons soda, 2 teaspoons salt, 1/2 tsp. baking powder and 1 cup chopped English walnuts. Stir gently into squash mixture just until blended. Turn into 3 oiled and floured 7 1/2 x 3 1/2-inch loaf pans (or use 2 (9 x 5-inch)
                                                     (Cont.)

loaf pans.)

Sprinkle 1/3 cup sesame seeds evenly over top. Bake in preheated 350° oven for 1 hour. Cool in pans for 10 minutes. Turn out and wrap. Loaves freeze well. Serve plain or spread with cream cheese.

NOTE: As one of the judges at the Times-World News Inc., annual Favorite Reader's Recipe Contest, 1976, the above was first prize winner, recipe of Mrs. Ida Eller.

## BUKO PIE (Young Coconut Pie)

1 (16 oz.) pkg. frozen "buko" (soft coconut meat)
2 1/2 c. coconut milk, sweetened
1/2 c. cornstarch
9-inch unbaked pie shell, (frozen, ready to bake)

Mix first 3 ingredients in a pot and cook on medium heat while stirring constantly until mixture thickens and becomes paste-like. Pour into unbaked pie shell and bake in preheated 425° oven for 30 minutes, or until crust is light golden brown. Serve warm or chilled.

Serves 6 to 8.

NOTE: If desired, bake pie shell separately for about 10 minutes, add cooked filling and ready to serve.

## EMPANADITAS (Pastry Tarts)

1/2 c. milk
1 1/2 tsp. lemon juice
1/2 c. butter or margarine
1 egg yolk (save egg white)
2 c. all-purpose flour, sifted

Combine milk and lemon juice until milk curdles. Cream butter and yolk until light and fluffy. Sift flour onto creamed butter mixture, alternating with sour milk, while mixing. Gather into a ball, wrap with waxed paper and chill for about 1 1/2 hours. On a lightly floured surface, roll out chilled dough to 1/8-inch thick and cut into 3-inch rounds using cookie cutter or jar rim. Put a teaspoonful of filling on center and fold dough to half-moon shape. Seal edges with egg white and press down with fork tines.

Bake on greased sheet at 350°F. in preheated oven for 15 to 20 minutes, or until light brown.

### Filling:

1 c. chopped almonds or cashews
1/2 c. honey
1/4 c. sugar
2 Tbsp. butter

Combine all ingredients in saucepan and cook slowly until sugar is dissolved.

NOTE: Dough may be shaped into little boats and filled. Or, spread filling on rolled uncut dough, roll like in jelly roll to 1 1/2 inch diameter and cut into 1/2-inch pieces or coins.

Write your extra recipes here:

Write your extra recipes here:

# Cakes, Cookies, Icings

# CAKES, ICINGS AND COOKIES

* Adding a pinch of baking powder to powdered sugar icing wil help it stay moist and not crack.

* Your frosting will look more professional if you first frost with a thin layer and let it set. Then apply a second coat of frosting.

* An easy way to form drop cookies is to drop them onto the cookie sheet and then press them with the bottom of a water glass that has been dipped in sugar.

* To preserve the creamy texture of frozen cheesecake, thaw in refrigerator for 12 hours.

* Dipping the cookie cutter in slightly warm salad oil will give you a much cleaner cut.

* A quick frosting can be made by adding a bit of chocolate syrup to prepared whipped topping.

* If powdered sugar is sprinkled on top of each layer before filling or frosting, this will keep the filling from soaking through the cake.

* Spaghetti is great with cake! While waiting for icing to set, a few sticks of dry spaghetti will hold the layers in place. Also, a piece of raw spaghetti works well to light birthday candles.

* To cut down on cholesterol, substitute two egg whites stiffly beaten for each whole egg called for.

* Icings won't become grainy if a pinch of salt is added to the sugar.

* Use cocoa to dust baking tins so cookies and cakes won't have a floury look.

* Trace the bottom of the baking pan onto wax paper and cut it out. Now this can be placed in the bottom of the pan and the sides greased and floured like normal. When the cake is done it can be inverted and the paper taken off while still warm with no sticking.

* For a thinner, crispier rolled cookie try rolling the dough directly onto a greased and floured cookie sheet. Cut the cookies out then pick up the scrap dough.

* If eggs are beaten and added slowly to batter it won't make the batter too stiff.

* Cookies will stay moist in the jar if a slice of bread is placed in the jar.

* Two tablespoons of salad oil added to cake mix keeps the mix moist, less crumbly.

* Adding a pinch of salt to chocolate dishes will enhance the flavor.

## CAKES, COOKIES, AND ICINGS

### MAMON (Sponge Cake)

| | |
|---|---|
| 1 c. sifted all-purpose flour | 3 eggs, large |
| 1 tsp. baking powder | 1 c. sugar |
| 1/4 tsp. salt | 1 tsp. vanilla extract |
| 1/2 c. warm milk | 1/4 tsp. anise seeds (optional) |

Sift flour with baking powder and salt; set aside. In a large bowl, beat eggs at high speed until thick and lemon-colored. Add sugar gradually, beating well after each addition, until well blended.

At low speed, blend in flour mixture just until smooth, then add warm milk, vanilla and anise until just blended. Pour batter immediately into 24 ungreased or paper-lined 2 1/2-inch cupcake cups, or fluted pans or springform pan. Bake in 350° preheated oven for 15 minutes for cupcakes, and 25 minutes for cake pans, or until toothpick inserted in center comes out clean. Remove from oven and brush top of cake with melted butter, sprinkle on a little sugar, while cake is still hot. When cool, remove from pans.

NOTE: The above recipe is an excellent substitute for "Torta Cebu."

### MACAPUNO PASTRY (Sweet Preserved Coconut) or LANGKA PASTRY

| | |
|---|---|
| 1 sheet Pepperidge Farm puff pastry | 1 c. langka preserve (jackfruit) |
| 1 c. macapuno preserve (sweet preserved coconut) | 1/2 c. melted butter or margarine |

Spread out puff pastry sheet on floured board. Brush with melted butter. Arrange macapuno and langka on center row of pastry sheet. Wrap or roll like huge egg roll (lumpia). Place on ungreased cookie sheet, brush outside with melted butter. Bake in preheated 350°F. oven for 35 to 40 minutes. Cool before slicing.

Serves 6.

NOTE: This is Dr. Amor Barongan's recipe. Bananas or apples sprinkled with cinnamon and brown sugar can also be used for filling. Puff pastry in a box is found in the frozen section of supermarkets.

## M.D.'S CAKE

This is such a delicious cake. Sift together:

| | |
|---|---|
| 3 c. all-purpose flour | 1 tsp. soda |
| 2 c. granulated sugar | 1 tsp. cinnamon |
| 1 tsp. salt | |

Add:

| | |
|---|---|
| 1 1/2 c. vegetable oil | 1 (8 1/4 oz.) can undrained |
| 1 1/2 tsp. vanilla | crushed pineapple |
| 3 eggs | |

Mix well, but do not beat with electric mixer. Fold in 2 cups finely diced bananas and 1 cup chopped pecans or black walnuts. Batter will be thick. Pour into well greased and floured 10-inch tube pan. Bake in 350° preheated oven for 1 hour or until toothpick inserted comes out clean.

### Cream Cheese Frosting:

Cream 1 (8 ounce) package softened cream cheese and 1 stick (1/4 pound) margarine. Add 1 (1 pound) box confectioner's sugar and 1 teaspoon vanilla. Beat until smooth.

### Brandy Sauce (if desired):

In saucepan, beat 3 egg yolks, slightly. Add:

| | |
|---|---|
| 1 c. sugar | 1 1/2 c. milk |
| 1 tsp. vanilla | |

Blend well. Cook over low heat, stirring until mixture boils. Blend 1 tablespoon cornstarch with 1/4 cup water; stir into hot mixture. Cook, stirring until thickened. Remove from heat and stir in 3 tablespoons brandy. Serve warm or chilled.

## SANS RIVAL (Cake Without a Rival)

### Icing:

| | |
|---|---|
| 6 egg yolks | 1/2 c. light corn syrup (Karo) |
| 1/2 lb. butter or margarine | |

### Wafers:

6 egg whites, from large
  eggs
3/4 c. sugar
1 tsp. vanilla

1/2 lb. (1 1/2 c.) roasted cashew
  nuts, preferably unsalted,
  finely chopped manually or
  by blender

    Beat egg yolk until light and lemon-colored. Heat corn syrup over low heat until bubbly for 2 minutes. Immediately pour syrup in thin streams to egg yolk while beating. Chill to cool. Cream butter or margarine. Beat in cooled egg yolk mixture. Set aside in a cool place.
    Preheat oven to 325°. Line 3 (12 x 18-inch) cookie sheets with waxed paper. Liberally grease and flour waxed paper-lined pans. Set aside.
    Beat egg whites until soft peaks form when beater is slowly raised. Gradually beat in sugar, 3 tablespoons at a time, beating well after each addition. At high speed, beat until stiff peaks form when beater is slowly raised. Fold in 1 cup of finely chopped cashews (save 1/2 cup for garnishing) and vanilla, using rubber spatula, until blended into egg whites. Spread evenly on prepared cookie sheets, 1/4-inch thick.
    Bake at 325° for 20 minutes, or until golden brown. Immediately cut wafer in the center, loosen and transfer to a clean, flat surface lined with waxed paper, and quickly but carefully peel off waxed paper used in baking. Cooled wafers are crisp and fragile. Spread icing thinly on top of each wafer (total of six 12 x 9-inch cut wafers) and arrange layer by layer. Ice top layer and sprinkle with remaining 1/2 cup finely chopped cashew nuts. Freeze. Cover cake when icing has hardened.
    Serves 12.

## STRAWBERRY SHORTCAKE

4 c. ready to eat strawberries,
  fresh or frozen
1/2 c. sugar, enough to sweeten
  strawberries
2 1/3 c. "Bisquick" buttermilk
  baking mix or Master Mix,
  (see recipe)

3 Tbsp. sugar
1/2 c. milk
3 Tbsp. butter or margarine,
  melted and cooled slightly
1 c. heavy cream, whipped or
  plain

    Heat oven to 450°. Grease square pan, 8 x 8 x 2-inch. Set aside.
    Mix strawberries and enough sugar to sweeten according to one's taste. When using fresh strawberries, crush fruit slightly with sugar. Set aside. Mix Bisquick, 3 tablespoons sugar, melted butter or margarine, and milk until a soft dough is formed. Transfer
(Cont.)

dough into pan. Bake about 15 minutes. While warm, cut shortcake into 6 pieces. Split, spread with butter or margarine, then fill and top with sweetened strawberries. Serve warm with heavy cream.

Serves 6.

## FOOD FOR THE GODS

6 eggs, large
1 1/2 c. sugar
1 1/2 c. shelled walnuts, coarsely chopped
3/4 c. graham cracker crumbs
1/2 lb. dates, pitted, coarsely chopped
1 1/2 tsp. baking powder

Preheat oven to 350°F. Line pan (6-inch square x 1 1/2-inch or 9-inch round layer) with waxed paper and grease.

Separate egg whites from egg yolks. In a large bowl beat egg whites until soft peaks form. Gradually beat in 1/2 cup of sugar and continue beating until stiff. Set aside.

In another bowl beat egg yolks until lemon-colored. Beat in 1 cup sugar gradually. Set aside. Mix walnuts, crumbs, dates and baking powder. Fold into egg yolk mixture until well blended. Next fold egg yolk-walnut mixture into beaten egg whites. Pour into prepared pan. Bake at 350°F. for 30 minutes, or until inserted toothpick comes out clean.

Serves 6.

## CHEESECAKE

1 (8 oz.) pkg. cream cheese, softened at room temperature
1/2 c. sugar
3 eggs
2 tsp. vanilla
*1 ready-made graham cracker pie crust in aluminum pie pan
1/2 c. sour cream
1 Tbsp. sugar
1 1/2 tsp. vanilla
drained cherries, fruit cocktail, or sliced peaches for garnishing

Beat soft cream cheese and sugar until smooth. Beat in eggs, one at a time, beating well after each addition. Blend in 2 teaspoons vanilla. Pour to graham cracker pie crust and bake at 300°F. in preheated oven for 1 hour or until inserted toothpick comes out clean. Cool for 5 minutes, then top with a mixture of sour cream, sugar and vanilla. Return to 325°F. oven and bake 5 minutes more. Cool. Decorate top with well drained cherries, fruit cocktail or sliced peaches. Chill.

Serves 8.

*Trademark - Johnston Ready Crust Graham Cracker.

## COCOROONS

1 c. egg whites, from large
  eggs about 8
2 c. sugar
1 tsp. vanilla

4 c. flaked or shredded coconut,
  packaged, about 10 to 12 oz.
3 c. corn flakes, slightly
  crushed

    Preheat oven to 325°F. Beat egg whites until soft peaks form. Beat in sugar 3 tablespoons at a time, beating well after each addition. Continue to beat until stiff peaks form. Add vanilla. Fold in coconut and corn flakes until well blended. Drop by teaspoonfuls onto well greased cookie sheet. Bake at 325° to 350°F. for 15 to 20 minutes, or until golden brown. Cool and store in tightly-covered dry container.
    Yields about 3 dozen.

## SILVANAS

### Butter Icing:

1 c. sugar
1/4 c. water
6 egg yolks, beaten until
  lemon-colored

1 c. butter

    Over medium heat cook sugar and water until light brown and syrupy, <u>without stirring</u>, about 7 minutes. Pour boiling syrup in a thin steam over beaten egg yolks while continuing to beat until mixture is hard and fluffy. Cool. Cream butter and beat in cooled egg yolk mixture.

### Meringue:

6 egg whites, (no trace
  of egg yolk whatsoever)
1 c. sugar
6 Tbsp. flour, sifted

1 c. unsalted cashew nuts,
  finely ground
1 c. cake crumbs

    Line a cookie sheet with waxed paper, grease well then dust with flour. Set aside.
    Beat egg whites until stiff. Add sugar gradually beating well after each addition. Fold in flour and ground cashew nuts. Using a tablespoon, drop meringue on prepared cookie sheet, shaping oval uniformly size cookies, about 20. Bake in preheated 250°F. oven for 20 minutes, or until light brown. Cool. Spread butter icing all over cookie meringue, then roll in cake crumbs. Chill.
                                                                              (Cont.)

Makes about 20 silvanas.

NOTE: Other butter icing recipes can be used, and if so egg yolks can be used for Leche Flan (see recipe).

## FLAN TOPPED CHIFFON CAKE

### Topping:

In a baking pan, 9 x 13-inch rectangular or 12-inch square, mix 1 cup sugar and 1/2 cup water. Heat over medium heat, stirring constantly until syrup turns brown and tilt pan to coat an inch on the sides and cover bottom of pan. Remove from heat and set aside.

Make flan.

### Flan:

8 egg yolks
4 egg whites (save remaining 4 egg whites for cake)
1 (14 oz.) can condensed milk
1 (14 1/2 oz.) can evaporated milk, undiluted
1 tsp. grated fresh lemon, lime or orange rind
1 tsp. vanilla

Mix all ingredients until well mixed and pour into syrup-coated pan. Set this pan on a larger pan with about 1 inch deep water and bake in 350° oven for 30 minutes. While this is baking, mix Chiffon Cake.

### Chiffon Cake:

2 1/4 c. sifted cake flour
1 1/2 c. sugar
1 Tbsp. baking powder
6 egg yolks
1/2 c. cooking oil
1 tsp. grated fresh lemon, lime or orange rind
2/3 c. milk
2 tsp. vanilla
10 egg whites, including 4 egg whites from Flan
1/2 tsp. cream of tartar

In a large mixing bowl, sift together flour, sugar and baking powder. Make a well; add yolks, oil, grated rind, milk and vanilla. Beat until smooth, scraping sides of bowl.

In a separate large bowl, free from grease or yolk, beat egg whites and cream of tartar until soft peaks form. Gently fold in with up and down cutting motion using a rubber spatula, egg-flour batter until well blended.

Pour mixture over cooked Flan. Again rest cake pan in a larger pan with about 1 inch deep water; bake in 350°F. for 30 minutes, or until toothpick inserted comes out clean. Cool. Loosen edges and invert on a serving platter.

Serves 16.

NOTE: Sweet preserved macapuno or langha (see Glossary) may be added to Flan.

Write your extra recipes here:

**Write your extra recipes here:**

# Desserts

# Helpful Hints For The Kitchen

An excellent thickener for soups is a little oatmeal. It will add flavor and richness to almost any soup.

Give mashed potatoes a beautiful whipped cream look by adding hot milk to them before you start mashing.

Don't add sugar to stewed fruits until they have boiled for 10 minutes. They need less sugar then.

Add a teaspoon of lemon juice to each quart of water used to cook rice. The grains will stay white and separated.

Potatoes will take on a golden taste and appearance if sprinkled lightly with flour before frying.

Lettuce won't "rust" in the refrigerator if it is wraped in paper toweling.

Remember that every time you open the oven door the temperature drops about 25 degrees.

The coldest part of any refrigerator is the top back shelf.

Never freeze more than four pounds of fresh food per cubic foot of freezer capacity at one time.

For highest refrigerator efficiency, air should circulate around each container.

If sweet cream is just starting to sour, restore the sweetness with a pinch of baking soda.

Dripping faucets can be quieted by tying a string to it that reaches into the sink. The water will slide down the string quietly.

Try loosening rusty screws by putting a drop or two of ammonia on it.

Keeping a piece of charcoal in the tool drawer will keep the moisture out preventing rust.

Rusty bolts can usually be loosened by pouring club soda on them.

# DESSERTS

## MAJA BLANCA  (White Pudding)

2 c. coconut milk
1 c. undiluted evaporated milk
1/2 c. sugar
1/2 c. cornstarch
1 lb. can corn, cream style, drained

    Mix all ingredients in a pot and cook over low heat while stirring frequently until thick, pour into a 6 or 7-cup capacity serving dish, greased.
    Serves 6, warm or chilled.

## PUTO SECO  (Butter cookies)

2 sticks (1/2 lb.) butter, softened at room temperature
1 box (1 lb.) cornstarch
3 eggs, slightly beaten
1 tsp. cream of tartar
1 c. sugar
1 tsp. baking powder

    Mix all ingredients thoroughly in a bowl. Shape into 1-inch balls. Bake in cookie sheet lined with waxed paper, about 1 inch apart, in preheated 375° oven for 12 minutes, or until light brown. Let cool.
    Yields: about 5 to 6 dozen.

## EASY BIBINGKA  (Rice Cake)

1 box Mochiko sweet rice flour (1 lb.)
3 eggs
2 c. milk or coconut milk
1 c. sugar
1/4 c. (1 stick) margarine or butter, melted
about 1 c. dehydrated coconut flakes (optional)
about 1/2 c. grated Parmesan cheese (optional)
2 tsp. vanilla

    In a large bowl, mix all ingredients except coconut flakes and cheese, until smooth. Pour into greased 8-inch square x 2-inch pan or similar size pan. Sprinkle coconut flakes and Parmesan cheese evenly on top. Bake in preheated 350° oven for 40 minutes, or until toothpick inserted comes out clean. Let cool.
    Serves 8.
    NOTE: Undiluted evaporated milk flavored with 1 teaspoon coconut flavoring (omit vanilla) may be used as milk.

## BIBINGKA

1 fresh coconut
1 1/2 c. white sugar or brown sugar, firmly packed
1 c. thick coconut milk mixed with 6 c. warm water
4 c. sweet rice flour (see Glossary)
1/4 c. brown or white sugar
2 c. rice flour (see Glossary)

Preheat oven to 300°.
Grate coconut (see How to Extract Fresh Coconut Milk). Add 1 cup water to grated coconut and extract about a cup of thick coconut milk. Mix thick coconut milk with 1/4 cup sugar. Set aside. Add 5 cups water to grated coconut. Gradually add glutinous rice flour and sweet rice flour to grated coconut and mix until blended.

Add sugar and mix thoroughly. Pour to a pan (8 x 12 x 2-inch) lined with aluminum foil and greased with margarine. Bake at 300° for 1 1/2 hours, or until inserted toothpick comes out clean. Pour thick coconut milk mixture evenly on cooked bibingka. Return to oven and broil a few minutes until top is browned. Cool, cut to diamond shapes.
Serves about 16.

## BIBINGKA CASSAVA

4 c. coarsely grated cassava, (yucca - see Glossary)
2 c. coconut milk (see How to Extract Coconut Milk)
2 Tbsp. melted butter or margarine
3 eggs, slightly beaten
1 c. thick coconut milk
1 c. sugar
1 c. coarsely grated Cheddar cheese
1 c. brown sugar

Mix very well grated cassava, 2 cups coconut milk, melted butter or margarine, sugar and eggs. Pour to aluminum foil-lined pan, 11 x 8 x 2-inch. Bake at 325° for 40 minutes. Sprinkle grated cheese on top.

Continue to bake for 10 minutes, or until inserted toothpick comes out clean. Meanwhile, simmer thick coconut milk and brown sugar until thick and syrupy. Top cooked bibingka with syrup. Set oven to broil and brown top to bibingka in 5 minutes.
Serves 10 to 12.

## BIBINGKANG KANIN

2 c. sweet rice grains, washed once
2 c. coconut milk
1 c. brown sugar
3 1/2 to 4 c. water with pinch of salt

**Topping:**

1/2 c. brown sugar

3/4 c. thick coconut milk (see How to Extract Fresh Coconut Milk)

    In a covered pot bring rice and water with salt to a boil, stir; lower heat to low and simmer, covered, for 30 minutes, or until rice is soft. (Similar to boiling regular rice. Cook in electric rice cooker if available.)
    Mix 2 cups coconut milk and 1 cup brown sugar thoroughly. Pour to hot, cooked rice and mix well. Transfer to an aluminum foil-lined pan, 6 inch squares x 1 1/2-inch. Pat firmly, and bake at 300° for 45 minutes. Mix topping mixture and pour evenly on baked bibingka. Broil in oven until topping is brown and bubbly but not burned.
    Serves 6.

## BIBINGKA HOT CAKE

1 1/2 c. Aunt Jemima pancake mix or Master Mix (see recipe)
3/4 c. coconut milk
1 Tbsp. melted margarine or vegetable oil

several thin strips of white Cheddar or Mozzarella cheese, about 1/4 c.
1/4 c. sugar
1 egg

    Preheat oven to 375°. Line pan, (6 inch square x 1 1/2-inch or 8-inch round layer) with waxed paper. Set aside. Place pancake mix, sugar, coconut milk, egg and melted margarine or vegetable oil in a bowl. Stir until mixture is fairly smooth. Pour to prepared pan.
    Arrange cheese strips on top. Bake in preheated oven for 15 minutes, or until inserted toothpick comes out clean. Brush top with melted margarine. Serve hot with grated fresh coconut.
    Serves 6.
    NOTE: If griddle pan is used, pour mixture onto hot, lightly greased griddle, to desired size and thickness. When tops are covered with bubbles and edges look cooked, arrange cheese strips on top, turn only once and cook other side.

## "BRAZO" EGG WHITE ROLL

6 egg yolks, from large eggs
1/4 lb. butter
4 tsp. melted margarine or butter for greasing
6 egg whites, from large eggs

1 can (14 oz.) condensed milk
1/2 c. sugar
1 tsp. vanilla
1 tsp. cream of tartar
1 tsp. vanilla     (Cont.)

Mix egg yolks and condensed milk; cook on top of a double boiler. Stir while cooking until thick or paste-like. Add butter and 1 teaspoon vanilla; mix well. Let cool. Prepare a 12 x 18-inch cookie pan by lining it with waxed paper heavily greased with melted margarine or butter.

Preheat oven to 400°.

Beat egg whites and cream of tartar until soft peaks form when beater is raised. Gradually beat in 1/2 cup sugar, 2 tablespoons at a time, beating well after each addition. Continue beating until stiff peaks form.

Beat in 1 teaspoon vanilla. Spread evenly in prepared pan. Bake at 400° for 10 minutes, or until lightly brown. Invert hot meringue onto another 12 x 18-inch heavily greased waxed paper. Gently but quickly peel off waxed paper used in baking. Spread egg yolk mixture on meringue. Starting with long edge, roll meringue, seam side down. Use greased waxed paper to cover roll and chill at least 1 hour before serving.

To serve, slice diagonally with serrated knife.
Serves 12.

## CHAMPORADO (Chocolate Rice)

1 c. sweet rice (malagkit)  6 c. water
1 c. sugar  5 Tbsp. cocoa
1/4 tsp. salt

Wash rice and drain. Boil gently in a covered pot with 6 cups water for 15 minutes, or until rice is partially cooked. Mix sugar, cocoa and salt and add to partially-cooked rice. Simmer, covered, for 15 minutes more, stirring occasionally. Serve with milk.
Serves 6.

## CHAMPORADO DELUXE

3 c. leftover plain cooked rice  1/2 c. sugar mixed with
2 c. milk  1/2 c. Hershey cocoa
  1/2 c. peanut butter

Re-cook rice in 1 1/2 cups water, covered, for 10 minutes, or until very soft. Mix in remaining ingredients, stirring constantly over medium heat so mixture will not burn. Cook for another 10 minutes. Correct sweetness. Serve hot with flaked smoked fish, if desired.

Serves 4 to 6.

NOTE: This recipe is one of Manong Sergio Donato's specialties.

## CONDENSED MILK CUSTARD

1 can (15 oz.) condensed milk        6 pineapple slices, canned,
                                                             drained and chilled

Boil unopened can of condensed milk in enough water to completely immerse can. Boil covered for 2 hours. Let can cool. Open both ends of can and push out jellified condensed milk. Slice crosswise into 6 slices. Top each drained pineapple slice with a slice of cooked condensed milk.
Serves 6.

## DILA-DILA

2 lb. yucca (kamoteng kahoy,        2 1/2 c. grated fresh coconut
   2 pieces)                                         1/2 c. sugar

Boil yucca in enough water to cover, until soft. Peel skin with knife. Grate or mash. Form into patties. Generously sprinkle grated coconut and a little sugar to sweeten before eating.
Makes 20 patties, or dila-dila (literal translation tongues). Eaten as snack or dessert.

## GINATAAN

1 fresh coconut
1 c. flour or sweet rice flour,
   mixed with 1/2 c. water,
   shaped into 1/2-inch diameter
   balls
2 c. sugar
2 c. sweet potato or yam,
   peeled and diced

2 c. yautia (gabi), peeled and
   diced (see Glossary)
1/2 c. tapioca pearls
2 c. ripe plantain banana,
   peeled and diced (see Glossary)
10 to 12 c. water

Grate coconut. Add 1 cup hot water to greated coconut and extract coconut milk (see How to Extract Fresh Coconut Milk). Set aside coconut milk from first extraction. Do about 3 or 4 more extractions, adding more water to make about a total of 10 cups of watery coconut milk.
In a covered pot, simmer the watery coconut milk, drop flour dough ball, cover and stir occasionally. Cook for 25 minutes, or until balls float on top. Add sugar, bananas, sweet potato, yautia and tapioca pearls and simmer, covered, for 20 minutes or until yautia is soft. Stir occasionally while simmering. Add the first extracted coconut milk before removing from fire or use it as topping when serving.

(Cont.)

Serves 12 to 15.

NOTE: 1/2 cup of sweet preserved nangka (Jackfruit) may be added a few minutes before cooking is completed. If desired, flour dough balls and tapioca pearls can be omitted.

## HALO HALO (Mixings)

| | |
|---|---|
| 1 c. cooked custard or gelatine, diced | 1 c. red kidney beans, cooked in syrup |
| 1 c. canned whole kernel corn | 1 c. ripe plantain banana, cooked in syrup, diced (see recipe) |
| crushed ice, about a quart | |
| 2 c. milk | sugar to taste, if desired |

In 6 tall glasses, equally portion custard of gelatin, red kidney beans, corn and banana. Fill glasses with crushed ice. Pour about 1/3 cup milk on top of crushed ice. Serve with long stem teaspoons. Mixing will be done by individuals and sugar added according to one's taste.

Serves 6.

NOTE: A whole variety of fruit (fresh, frozen or canned) can be used. A small amount of sweet preserved macapuno*, Kaong*, or nangka*, can be added; even garbanzos (chick peas), cooked in syrup. A scoop of ice cream on top of the crushed ice and a red cherry makes it beautiful. Ten ice cubes, crushed and 1 cup of milk blenderized will make "snow" which can be used in place of the above crushed ice and milk.

*See Glossary.

## KUTSINTA

| | |
|---|---|
| 1 c. all-purpose flour or Wondra flour | 1/2 c. white sugar |
| | 1/2 c. brown sugar |
| 2 c. water | 1 tsp. lye water (see Glossary) |

Mix all ingredients to a smooth consistency. Pour to muffin pans, 3/4 full. Steam in a large, well covered pan with 2 inches deep water for 25 minutes, or until inserted toothpick comes out clean. Add more water as needed in pan during steaming period. Loosen and remove kutsinta from pans. Serve with fresh grated coconut.

Yields 20 tiny kutsinta or 10 large.

## LECHE FLAN AMERICAN

1 (8 oz.) pkg. cream cheese, softened
1 (14 oz.) can condensed milk

1 (14 1/2 oz.) can evaporated milk
3 eggs, slightly beaten

Syrup:

1/2 c. sugar

1/2 c. water

    Blend all ingredients thoroughly except syrup. Set aside. Make syrup by melting sugar in pan over medium heat. When melted, add 1/2 cup water. Stir and boil until syrup is thick. Pour to mold pan (4-cup capacity) and tilt mold pan to coat sides and bottom.
    Pour in milk mixture. Bake at 350°F. on a pan of water for 45 minutes or until inserted toothpick comes out clean. Cool a little. Loosen sides with knife and invert mold to a platter.
    Makes 6 servings.
    NOTE: See other Leche Flan recipe. Leche Flan is one of the more popular Philippine desserts.

## PALITAO

3 c. sweet rice flour (see Glossary)
1 fresh coconut, grated (see How to Extract Fresh Coconut Milk)

1 1/2 c. water
3/4 c. sugar
1/2 c. sesame seeds, toasted, (optional)

    In a bowl, mix sweet rice flour and water to a smooth dough. With floured hands, shape dough into flat, elongated patties 3 x 2 x 1/4-inch. Drop patties, a few at a time, in 3-inch deep boiling water. Boil uncovered for 5 minutes, or until patties float on top. Scoop patties with a perforated ladle, so as to drain water. Coat each cooked patty with freshly grated coconut. Sprinkle sugar mixed with toasted sesame seeds, when serving.
    Yields about 40.

## LECHE FLAN (Custard)

1 can (14 oz.) condensed milk
8 egg yolks

1/4 tsp. lemon, lime or orange rind (optional) or 1 tsp. vanilla
1 can (14 1/2 oz.) evaporated milk

(Cont.)

Syrup:

1/2 c. sugar          1/2 c. water

Blend first 4 ingredients. Set aside. Make syrup by melting sugar in pan over medium heat. When melted add 1/2 cup water. Stir and boil until syrup is thick. Pour to mold pan (4-cup capacity) and tilt mold pan to coat sides and bottom with syrup. Pour egg-milk mixture. Bake at 350° on a pan of water for 45 minutes or until inserted toothpick comes out clean. If steam cooking is desired, cover mold pan with aluminum foil and steam over simmering water for 45 minutes. Cool a little bit. Loosen sides with knife and invert mold to a platter.

Makes 6 servings.

NOTE: Prepared syrups like pancake syrup, may be used instead of making one's syrup.

## **GULAMAN ALMOND**   (Gelatin Almond)

2 Tbsp. unflavored gelatin, like Knox
1 c. cold water
1/2 c. sugar
1/2 c. evaporated milk, undiluted

1/2 tsp. almond extract
1 can (11 oz.) Mandarin oranges, fruit cocktail, pineapple or other canned fruits

Sprinkle gelatin over cold water in saucepan. Place over low heat, stir constantly until gelatin dissolves when water gets hot. Remove from heat and stir in sugar and evaporated milk, until sugar dissolves. Mix in almond extract.

Pour into dish or 4 individual dessert dishes. Chill until firm, about 45 minutes. Cut into diamond shapes, if desired. Pour syrup from fruit and decorate fruit on top.

NOTE: This is so easy to make for snack or light dessert after a heavy meal.

## LUBI-LUBI OR NILU PAK (Mashed Bananas with Coconut)

3 cooking bananas, plantain/ saba, half-ripe
1 c. fresh grated coconut
3/4 c. brown sugar
1 tsp. vanilla

Cut unpeeled bananas into 2 if too long then boil covered in about 4 cups water for 30 minutes. Cool. Remove peel, slice thinly and blend in food processor with coconut, sugar and vanilla until smooth and mushy. If too dry add about 1/4 cup hot water.

Makes about 4 cups.

NOTE: In the Philippines country side, this delicacy is made from half-ripe "saba" bananas pounded in a primitive large cement mortar and life-size wood pestle. I beheld 'lubi-lubi' making only once in my lifetime as a teenager invited to a teenage party. It was a unique sight.

## SAPIN-SAPIN (Layers)

2 c. rice flour (Mochiko)
2 c. coconut milk
2 c. sugar
red food color, 6 drops
purple food color, 6 drops red and 3 drops blue
yellow food color, 4 drops
1 c. toasted grated coconut

Mix rice flour, coconut milk and sugar until smooth. Divide into 3 portions. Add and mix red color to one, purple color to another and yellow to the third.

Line a cake pan (8-inch round) with cheesecloth or aluminum foil and pour in red mixture, cover with another foil and steam, covered, for 20 minutes or until firm.

Pour in purple mixture and repeat process, then pour in yellow mixture and repeat process. Cool. Slide or invert to a serving platter. Slice and serve with toasted coconut.

Serves 10 to 12.

## SAPIN SAPIN PUDDING

| | |
|---|---|
| 2 c. coconut milk | 1 tsp. vanilla |
| 1 can (14 1/2 oz.) undiluted evaporated milk | red food color, 4 drops |
| | purple food color, 4 drops red mixed with 2 drops blue |
| 1/2 c. sugar | |
| 1/2 c. cornstarch | yellow food color, 3 drops |
| 1 Tbsp. Knox unflavored gelatine dissolved in 1 c. boiling water | 1 c. toasted grated coconut, (optional) |

In a pot mix coconut milk, evaporated milk, sugar and cornstarch until smooth. Cook over low heat while stirring constantly until mixture thickens, about 10 minutes, then add dissolved gelatine, cook and mix well for another 2 minutes. Correct sweetness. While mixture is still hot divide into 3 equal portions. Add red color to one blending well; purple color to the second, and yellow color to the third.

Keep purple and yellow mixtures at warm temperature. Pour red mixture to a glass pie dish, smoothen surface. Chill in freezer until set, about 7 minutes. Pour purple mixture over red, repeat chill process then pour yellow mixture over purple. Refrigerate until firm. Sprinkle on toasted grated coconut.

Serves 6.

## TAHO (Bean Curd in Syrup)

| | |
|---|---|
| 1 c. soy bean powder or flour | 4 Tbsp. lemon juice |
| 4 c. water | 2 c. brown sugar syrup |
| 1 envelope (1 Tbsp.) Knox unflavored gelatine | |

Mix soy bean powder and water and let stand 1 hour or overnight at room temperature, occasionally stirring mixture. Bring to a boil, while stirring constantly. Reduce heat and simmer 8 minutes.

Stir in gelatine until dissolved and not lumpy. Remove from heat; add lemon juice, all at once, while stirring. Transfer to a serving bowl and chill in refrigerator until set.

To serve: Slice off thin layers from the top. Pour enough hot syrup to cover. Boiled tapioca pearls may be added.

Serves 8.

I make my own syrup by dissolving 1 cup brown sugar in 1 cup water and letting mixture boil for 5 minutes. Taho is good for snack or as a dessert.

Soft bean curd, ready-made, is now available at supermarkets. Microwave until warm. (Cont.)

NOTE: I found the soy bean powder at our local Revco Drug Store. The trademark is Fearn Natural Soya Powder in an 11 ounce box manufactured by Fearn Soya Foods, Melrose Park, Illinois 60160.

Pancake syrup may be used instead.

## TUPIG  (Sweet Rice Bars)

| | |
|---|---|
| 1 lb. Mochiko sweet rice flour (see Glossary) | 1 c. coconut pieces or tidbits, fresh or dried |
| 2 c. coconut milk | 10 aluminum foil wrappers, cut into 6 x 12-inches |
| 1 c. dark brown sugar, firmly packed* | |

*White sugar may be used by those who want a "White Tupig." Personally, I prefer the brown kind.

Mix all ingredients with spatula until well blended. This will produce a very thick batter. Place about 1/2 cup of batter in the middle of a cut aluminum foil; fold wide edges together several times, shaping into an 8-inch long, 2-inch wide, 1/2-inch deep bar; seal both ends by folding unfilled portions several times to prevent batter leakage.

Place on ungreased baking pan and bake at 350°F. in preheated oven for 45 minutes, or when inserted toothpick comes out clean. Remove from oven and let cool.

Yields: 10 yummy, chewy sweet rice cake bars.

NOTE: This is a popular Ilocano delicacy served during the Christmas season; as traditional as the American fruit cake.

## ICE CREAM MANGO

| | |
|---|---|
| 4 c. whole milk | 2 eggs, slightly beaten |
| 4 Tbsp. cornstarch | 1 c. ripe mango, mashed or blended |
| 1 1/2 c. sugar | |

Using a double boiler heat milk until very hot, not boiling. Remove about 1/4 cup hot milk and mix with cornstarch to a smooth paste, then pour to hot milk while stirring continuously until mixture becomes thick like condensed milk. Add sugar and beaten eggs, stirring while cooking for another 2 to 4 minutes. Stir in mashed mango, taste to desired sweetness and cool. Freeze until firm.

Serves 8.

NOTE: For Macapuno Ice Cream, use about 2 cups preserved macapuno, instead of mango, adjust sugar amount to individual taste. For Langha Ice Cream, use about 1 cup shredded langha

(Cont.)

preserves. Adjust sugar.

Try atis, guayabano, and ube using the powdered package. Experiment.

Write your extra recipes here:

# Candy, Jelly Jam, Preserves

# Candy & Frosting Chart

| | |
|---|---|
| 230 degrees - 234 degrees | Thread |
| 234 degrees - 240 degrees | Soft Ball |
| 244 degrees - 248 degrees | Firm Ball |
| 250 degrees - 266 degrees | Hard Ball |
| 270 degrees - 290 degrees | Soft Crack |
| 300 degrees - 310 degrees | Hard Crack |

## Birthdays

Monday's child is fair of face,
Tuesday's child is full of grace,
Wednesday's child is loving and giving,
Thursday's child works hard for a living,
Friday's child is full of woe,
Saturday's child has far to go,
But the child that is born on the Sabbath day
Is brave and bonny, and good and gay.

## PERPETUAL CALENDAR
### SHOWING THE DAY OF THE WEEK FOR ANY DATE BETWEEN 1700 AND 2499

### Table of Dominical Letters

| Year of the Century (*Denote Leap-Years) | | | | Centuries | | | |
|---|---|---|---|---|---|---|---|
| | | | | 1700, 2100 | 1800, 2200 | 1900, 2300 | 2000, 2400 |
| 0 | *28 | *56 | *84 | C | E | G | A |
| 1 | 29 | 57 | 85 | B | D | F | G |
| 2 | 30 | 58 | 86 | A | C | E | F |
| 3 | 31 | 59 | 87 | G | B | D | E |
| *4 | *32 | *60 | *88 | E | G | B | C |
| 5 | 33 | 61 | 89 | D | F | A | B |
| 6 | 34 | 62 | 90 | C | E | G | A |
| 7 | 35 | 63 | 91 | B | D | F | G |
| *8 | *36 | *64 | *92 | G | B | D | E |
| 9 | 37 | 65 | 93 | F | A | C | D |
| 10 | 38 | 66 | 94 | E | G | B | C |
| 11 | 39 | 67 | 95 | D | F | A | B |
| *12 | *40 | *68 | *96 | B | D | F | G |
| 13 | 41 | 69 | 97 | A | C | E | F |
| 14 | 42 | 70 | 98 | G | B | D | E |
| 15 | 43 | 71 | 99 | F | A | C | D |
| *16 | *44 | *72 | | D | F | A | B |
| 17 | 45 | 73 | | C | E | G | A |
| 18 | 46 | 74 | | B | D | F | G |
| 19 | 47 | 75 | | A | C | E | F |
| *20 | *48 | *76 | | F | A | C | D |
| 21 | 49 | 77 | | E | G | B | C |
| 22 | 50 | 78 | | D | F | A | B |
| 23 | 51 | 79 | | C | E | G | A |
| *24 | *52 | *80 | | A | C | E | F |
| 25 | 53 | 81 | | G | B | D | E |
| 26 | 54 | 82 | | F | A | C | D |
| 27 | 55 | 83 | | E | G | B | C |

### Month / Dominical Letter

| Month | | | | | | Dominical Letter | | | | | | |
|---|---|---|---|---|---|---|---|---|---|---|---|---|
| January, October | | | | | | A | B | C | D | E | F | G |
| Feb., Mar., Nov. | | | | | | D | E | F | G | A | B | C |
| *Jan.*, Apr., July | | | | | | G | A | B | C | D | E | F |
| May | | | | | | B | C | D | E | F | G | A |
| June | | | | | | E | F | G | A | B | C | D |
| *February*, August | | | | | | C | D | E | F | G | A | B |
| Sept., Dec. | | | | | | F | G | A | B | C | D | E |
| 1 | 8 | 15 | 22 | 29 | | Su | Sa | F | Th | W | Tu | M |
| 2 | 9 | 16 | 23 | 30 | | M | Su | Sa | F | Th | W | Tu |
| 3 | 10 | 17 | 24 | 31 | | Tu | M | Su | Sa | F | Th | W |
| 4 | 11 | 18 | 25 | | | W | Tu | M | Su | Sa | F | Th |
| 5 | 12 | 19 | 26 | | | Th | W | Tu | M | Su | Sa | F |
| 6 | 13 | 20 | 27 | | | F | Th | W | Tu | M | Su | Sa |
| 7 | 14 | 21 | 28 | | | Sa | F | Th | W | Tu | M | Su |

### EXPLANATION

Find first the *Year of the Century* and in line with that figure at the right, in the proper column under the heading *Centuries*, will be found the Dominical Letter of the year. Then in the table headed *Dominical Letter* and in line with the proper *Month* find the letter previously determined. Run down this column until you are in line with the proper Day of the Month and at the intersection you will find the Day of the Week.

In Leap-Years the Dominical Letters for January and February will be found in the lines where these months are printed in *italics*.

### EXAMPLES

On what day of the week did January 5, 1891, fall? For 1891 the Dominical Letter is "D." After finding this letter opposite January in the upper right hand table, and running down that column until you are opposite 5 (the day of the month), you will find Monday. For *January* 1, 1876, the Dominical Letter is "A." Under "A," and in line with 1 is Saturday.

# CANDY, JELLY, JAM AND PRESERVES

## POLVORON

2 c. all-purpose flour
1 1/2 c. powdered milk
1/2 lb. butter or margarine, melted

3/4 c. sugar
1 tsp. vanilla (optional)

On medium heat, cook flour on pan while continuously stirring until light brown. Remove from heat. Cool. Add sugar, powdered milk and vanilla. Mix very well. Pour melted butter or margarine over mixture and mix well. Mold with Polvoron molder or chocolate moder. Wrap molded polvoron in tissue wrapping paper. Yields about 35 (1-inch diameter, 1/2-inch thick) molded round 1-2. An improvised Polvoron molder from a small cake decorator tube with the pusher plugged to move 1/2 inch deep only.

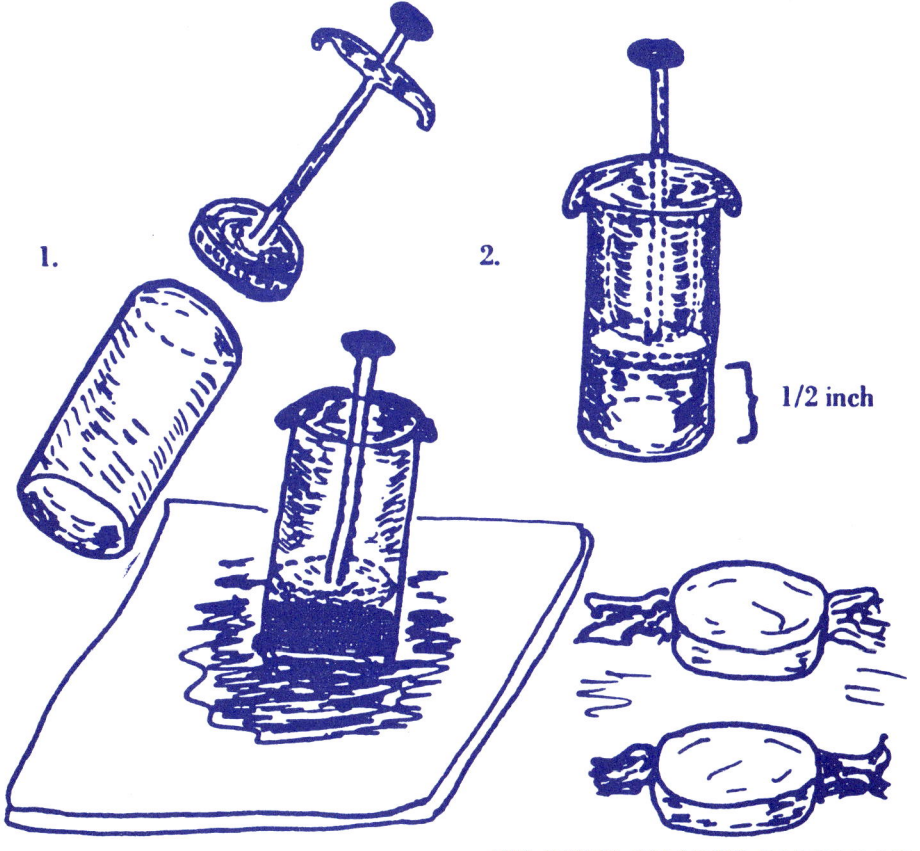

1.

2.

1/2 inch

**MOLDING POLVORON**

**WRAPPED MOLDED POLVORON**

## YEMA (Candy)

| | |
|---|---|
| 10 egg yolks | 1 can (14 oz.) condensed milk |

Syrup:

| | |
|---|---|
| 1 c. sugar | 1/2 c. water |

    Mix egg yolks and condensed milk; cook on top of a double boiler. Stir while cooking until thick enough to shape into balls. Chill to cool. Grease hands with butter or margarine and shape cooled egg yolk mixture into 3/4-inch diameter balls. Dissolve sugar in water. Cook, over medium heat, stirring occasionally until a small amount in cold water forms a ball. Quickly coat the balls one at a time. With a fork dish out the coated ball. Reheat syrup if it hardens. Cool coated balls without touching each other. Wrap in cellophane.
    Yields: about 30 balls.
    NOTE: Balls may be rolled in confectoner's powdered sugar instead of coating with syrup.

## ESPASOL (Sweet Rice Chewies)

| | |
|---|---|
| 1 box (1 lb.) sweet rice flour, Mochiko (see Glossary) | 2 c. sugar<br>1 c. coconut milk |

    Measure 1 cup of sweet rice flour, mix thoroughly with 1 cup water. Cook over medium heat while stirring constantly until thick, about 20 minutes. Set aside. In another pot, boil sugar and coconut milk until thick and syrupy, about 15 minutes, stirring occasionally. Meanwhile brown remaining sweet rice flour (about 2 1/2 cups) on medium-high heat, turning constantly, being careful not to burn sweet rice flour. Set aside. Mix boiled sweet rice flour with coconut milk syrup; gradually add in browned rice flour, reserving 1/2 cup, until mixture is dry enough to roll.

Sprinkle some browned rice on clean surface; roll mixture to 1/2-inch thick. Sprinkle more bronwed rice to prevent from sticking. Cut to desired shapes of bite-size pieces. Wrap with tissue paper, if desired.

    Yields: 2 dozen 2 x 1-inch bars.

    NOTE: Bits of fresh coconut may be added to mixture. Will keep 2 weeks in refrigerator.

### ESPASOL SPECIAL REODICA'S

| | |
|---|---|
| 1 box (1 lb.) Mochiko sweet rice flour | 1 c. coconut milk |
| 1 can (12 oz.) evaporated milk, undiluted | 1 jar (12 oz.) macapuno (sweet young coconut preserve) |
| | 1 c. sugar |

    Brown rice flour in pan on medium heat while frequently mixing for even browning. Sift to remove lumps if any. Reserve 1/2 cup for dusting. Simmer evaporated milk, coconut milk, sugar and macapuno while stirring constantly for 10 to 15 minutes. Add browned rice flour to hot milk mixture and mix very well. Remove from heat.

    Divide into 3 portions, shape each into a 1 1/2-inch diameter long and dust with reserved 1/2 cup browned rice flour. Slice into 1/2-inch thick slices and serve. For freezing or storage, wrap each log with aluminum foil. Will freeze well. Thaw in microwave when ready to use, after removing foil.

    Serves 12.

### LATIK (Coconut Creme Syrup)

| | |
|---|---|
| 1 c. thick coconut milk (see How to Extract Fresh Coconut Milk) | 1/2 c. sugar, white or brown |

    Mix coconut milk and sugar until sugar is dissolved. Boil uncovered for 20 minutes or until thickened, while stirring occasionally. Good as a sauce for rice desserts or snacks.

    Yields about 1 cup.

    NOTE: A tablespoon of cornstarch dissolved in 2 tablespoons water, stirred into simmering syrup, will shorten cooking time to 10 minutes.

## BANANA IN SYRUP

2 medium-ripe plantain      1 c. sugar
  bananas                            1 c. water

    Peel bananas, slice or dice. Set aside. Mix sugar and water, boil for 5 minutes. Add bananas and let simmer, uncovered, for 5 to 8 minutes. Serves 3. May be served as is or with milk or in Halo-Halo (see recipe).

    NOTE: For Sweet Potato (Kamote) in syrup, use sweet potatoes in place of bananas. Cook longer or until soft.


Write your extra recipes here:

# Beverages and Miscellaneous

# For Pensive Moments

A word of advice - do not give it.

Love thy enemies - it will drive them nuts.

To share with a friend is to see twice the beauty.

The recipe that is not shared with others will soon be forgotten, but when it is shared, it will be enjoyed by future generations.

There is nothing wrong with the younger generations that twenty years will not cure.

The flower that follows the sun, does so even on cloudy days.

A loose tongue often gets into a tight place.

One mother can care for five children, but five children cannot care for one mother.

A neighbor asked a small boy if his family said prayers before the meals. "No," he replied, "We don't have to. My mother is a good cook".

People who expect the worst, usually find it.

Even a mosquito does not get a slap on the back until he starts working.

Always do right - this will gratify some people and astonish the rest.

Happiness is like potato salad - when you share it with others, it is a picnic.

Remember when health foods were whatever your mother said to eat - or else?

Be careful how you live - you may be the only Bible some people read.

I can keep a secret, but those I tell it to never can.

Delicious food that melts in your mouth also sticks to your hips.

The most difficult meal for the average housewife is to get dinner out.

Even worse than a storm or a riot is a bunch of kids who are suddenly quiet.

One should never question his wife's judgement - after all, she married him.

Good judgement comes from experience. Experience comes from bad judgement.

It takes a clever man to know how to agree with his wife in such a way that she will change her mind.

## BEVERAGES AND MISCELLANEOUS

### CANTALOUPE DRINK

1 ripe cantaloupe  
6 c. cold water (partly ice cubes)  
1/2 c. sugar, more or less  
1 fresh lemon  
fresh mint leaves (optional)

Wash cantaloupe, cut in half and scoop seeds to bowl of cold water, mix and strain. Save water and discard seeds. Dissolve sugar in cantaloupe flavored water. Set aside. Scrape cantaloupe into strands, near but not next to rind. A special scraping instrument is used, if you don't have one, scrape thinly with spoon or use a ball scooper. Mix scraped cantaloupe, sweetened water and juice of fresh lemon. Pour into tall glasses and serve well chilled. Decorate with sprig of fresh mint leaves.
Serves 6 to 8.

### GREEN MANGO JUICE

1 green mango (unripe)  
3 c. water, cold  
4 Tbsp. sugar

Thinly peel mango. Slice fine, put in blender with 1 cup water, sugar and liquefy. Add remaining water. Sweeten according to taste.
Serves 3.
NOTE: To make juice more sour in taste add 2 tablespoons concentrated limeade or lime juice.

### SAGO DRINK  (Tapioca or Palmstarch Pearls)

1/2 c. uncooked sago pearls  
12 c. water  
pancake syrup or sugar to sweeten  
vanilla or lemon extract to flavor

In 6 cups boiling water, add sago and cook while stirring frequently for 40 minutes or when sago becomes transparent. Remove from heat, strain and run cold water over sago to wash away sticky liquid.
Transfer drained sago to a container, add 6 cups cold water. If desired, flavor with 1/2 teaspoon vanilla or 1/8 teaspoon lemon extract or 1/2 teaspoon fresh lemon rind. Serve well chilled on dessert dishes or tall glasses.

(Cont.)

Serves 6.

NOTE: Cooked Knox unflavored gelatine cut into cubes, about 1 cup, or a 15 ounce can of chilled lychees in syrup may be added to sago drink. A refreshing drink anytime, especially during the summer.

## SALABAT DRINK

| | |
|---|---|
| 1 inch fresh ginger root, peeled and crushed | 4 c. water<br>4 Tbsp. sugar, brown or white |

In a covered pot boil ingredients together for 5 minutes. Remove ginger and serve hot as beverage.
Serves 4.

## CHESTNUTS (Castanias)

1 lb. chesnuts, (about 2 1/2 c.)   2 tsp. vegetable oil
1/3 c. water

Wash chestnuts. In covered pot or pan boil chestnuts, water and oil for 15 to 20 minutes or until water has evaporated. Stir occasionally. Cook uncovered for 5 minutes more on medium heat. Cool and serve.

NOTE: Another way to cook is to put washed chestnuts in a cookie sheet pan on a single layer. Bake at 325°F. for 25 to 30 minutes. Test one for doneness.

## CASTA-NIOG (Chestnut - Coconut)

1 fresh coconut in shell, mature

Wash coconut. Crack open. Save coconut water as a refreshing drink, if desired. Pry coconut meat with brown rind intact, out of shell, preferably in large pieces. Charcoal or oven grill until spotty browned on both sides, 4 minutes total time. Serve hot or cold. Taste like roasted chestnuts.

## SUBSTITUTES FOR PHILIPPINE ITEMS

Achuete coloring - paprika.
Bia Fish - smelts, jumbo size or small whiting.
Bihon (rice sticks) - "Capellini," an extra, extra thin spaghetti or "Vermicelli," extra thin spaghetti.
Bangus (milkfish) - blue fish, fresh or white fish, fresh.
Chorizo de Bilbao - pepperoni, least hot brand.
Coconut milk, fresh, thick, 1 cup - a) 4-5 tablespoons "coconut cream," solidified, dissolved in 1 cup hot water or milk.
   b) 1 cup top layer of canned "cream of coconut" liquid, obtained by letting "cream of coconut" stand, undisturbed.
   c) 1 cup medium cream with 1 teaspoon "coconut flavoring."
Coconut milk, fresh, thin, 1 cup - a) 2 tablespoons "coconut cream," solidified, dissolved in 1 cup hot water or milk.
   b) 1 cup canned "cream of coconut," liquid.
   c) 1 cup whole milk with 1 teaspoon "coconut flavoring."
Cornstarch, 1 tablespoon - flour, 2 tablespoons for thickening or coating purposes.
Gabi - yautia, sold at local supermarkets or Spanish food stores.
Garlic, fresh - garlic salt, garlic powder or dried minced garlic.
Ginger, fresh - powdered or dried ginger.
Kamoteng Kahoy - yucca, sold at local supermarkets or Spanish food stores.
Kangkong (swamp cabbage) - watercress, land cress, spinach.
Lemon juice, fresh - reconstituted lemon juice.
Kalamansi - lemon.
Miki, fresh or dried - package dried egg noodles in size desired, abundant in local food stores.
Onion, fresh - onion salt, onion powder or dried minced onion.
Papaya, green, grated for pickles - sauerkraut.
Patis - Maggi seasoning by Nestle's Food or Knorr Foods.
Pechay - Chinese cabbage sold at local supermarkets.
Pinipig, fine - wheat germ.
Sampaloc (tamarind), in cooking - lemon juice.
Singkamas - purple top turnip when used in cooking.
Saging, Saba - Plantain banana sold at local supermarkets and Puerto Rican food stores.
Sugar, white granulated - brown sugar.
Tinapa (bangus) - smoked white fish sold at Jewish delicatessens.
Vienna Sausage - frankfurter.
Ube ice cream - Black raspberry ice cream (lavender color).

## HOW TO EXTRACT FRESH COCONUT MILK

Fresh coconut milk is the best to use.

Select a heavy fresh coconut. Crack and split coconut in half. Grate with coconut grater. For electric blender grating, remove coconut meat from shell and slice coconut meat into small pieces. Blend 3/4 cup sliced coconut and 1/2 cup water at a time, for several seconds. One coconut yields about 5 cups grated coconut.

First extraction – add about 3/4 cup water to grated coconut. Hand-press several times. Transfer to a clean cloth. Twist or secure cloth in such a way that no grated coconut escapes. Squeeze out liquid. This first extraction yields almost a cup of rich, creamy coconut milk.

Second extraction – to pressed grated coconut add about a cup of water. Proceed as for first extraction. Yields 1 cup of thinner coconut milk than first extraction.

Repeat above procedure until a milkish liquid can still be extracted. Total extracted coconut milk from one coconut is about 2 2/3 cups.

Solidified coconut cream in pint jars, can be purchased at Spanish, Philippine and other Asian food stores.

Two tablespoons coconut cream in 1 cup hot water – yields a thin coconut milk.

Four tablespoons coconut cream in 1 cup hot water – yields a thick coconut milk almost equivalent to first extraction.

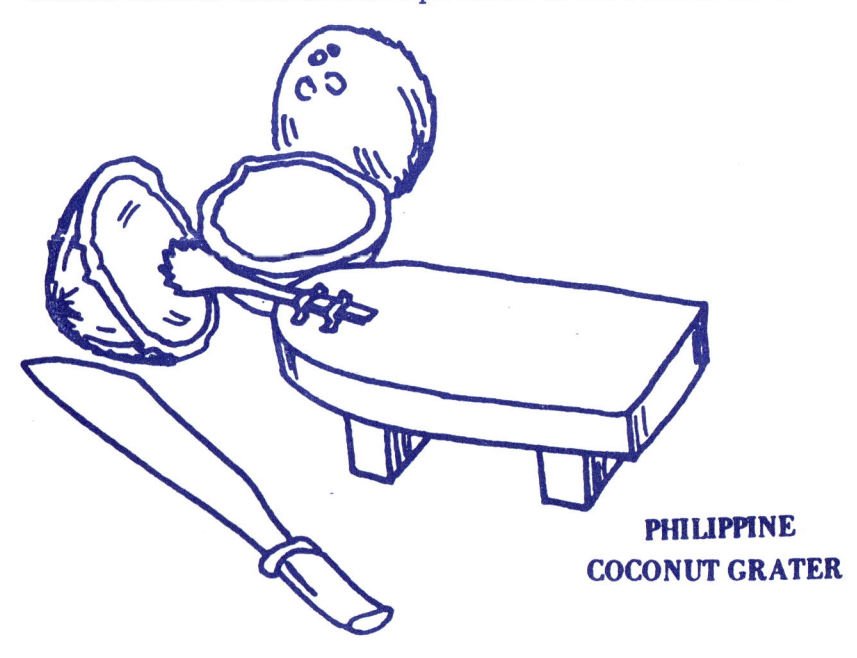

**PHILIPPINE COCONUT GRATER**

## HOW TO BONE A CHICKEN

Select a plump roasting chicken. Wash chicken and drain. With a small sharp knife, cut around chicken neck, being careful not to cut through skin at any time. Always work knife close to bones, separating meat from bone. Disjoint wing bone from back bone. Scrape meat from wing bone and take out wing bone. Leave wing-end bone intact. Next, knife around back and breast bone while pressing down chicken meat; go on to thigh and leg bone, disjoint and take out thigh and leg bone.

Chicken skin should be in one piece without cuts or holes, except in neck and rear opening. Proceed to stuff, see recipe for Chicken Boneless Relleno.

## HOW TO COOK A HUSBAND (OR SPOUSE)

"A good many husbands are utterly spoiled by mismanagement. Some women keep them constantly in hot water; others let them freeze by their carelessness and indifference. Some keep them in a stew by irritating ways and words. Others roast them; some keep them in a pickle all their lives. It cannot be supposed that any husband will be tender and good managed in this way, but they are really delicious when properly treated. In selecting your husband, you should not be guided by the silvery appearance, as in buying mackerel, nor by the golden tint, as if you wanted salmon. Be sure and select him yourself, as tastes differ. Don't go to the market for him, as the best are always brought to your door. It is far better to have none unless you know how to cook him. A preserving kettle of finest porcelain is best, but if you have nothing but an earthenware pipkin, it will do, with care. See that the linen in which you wrap him is nicely washed and mended, with the required number of buttons and strings nicely sewed on. Tie him in the kettle by a strong silk cord called comfort, as the one called duty is apt to be weak and they are apt to fly out of the kettle and be burned and crusty on the edges, since like crabs and lobsters, you have to cook them alive. Make a clear, steady fire out of love, neatness and cheerfulness. Set him as near this as seems to agree with him. If he sputters and fizzles, do not be anxious; some husbands do this till they are quite done. Add a little sugar in the form of what confectioners call kisses, but no vinegar or pepper on any account; a little spice improves them, but it must be used with judgment. Do not stick any sharp instruments into him to see if he is becoming tender. Stir him gently; watch the while, lest he lie too flat and too close to the kettle, and so becomes useless. You cannot fail to know when he is done. If thus treated you will find him very digestible,

(Cont.)

agreeing nicely with you and the children, and he will keep as long as you want, unless you become careless and set him in too cold a place."

(Quoted from the "Moravian Cook Book" published in 1910 by the Home Mission Society of the Moravian Church, Lancaster, Pa. with the kind permission of The Reverend Vernon Graf.)

Write your extra recipes here:

## PHILIPPINE MENUS

### I

**MONDAY**
- Fruit Juice
- Chop Suey Philippine
- Enriched Rice
- Ice Cream
- Beverage

**TUESDAY**
- Vegetable Soup
- Beef Steak
- Enriched Rice
- Fresh Fruit
- Beverage

**WEDNESDAY**
- Sinigang Pork
- Enriched Rice
- Leche Flan
- Beverage

**THURSDAY**
- Pancit Bijon
- Lettuce-Tomato Salad
- Enriched Rice
- Jello
- Beverage

**FRIDAY**
- Crab Relleno or Omelet
- Guisado (Sauteed Green Beans
- Enriched Rice
- Chilled Canned Peaches
- Beverage

**SATURDAY**
- Kari-Kari with Bangoong
- Enriched Rice
- Fruit Salad
- Beverage

### II

**MONDAY**
- Meat Loaf
- Mixed Vegetables
- Enriched Rice
- Banana
- Beverage

**TUESDAY**
- Easy Barbecue Pork Chop
- Mongo Guisado
- Enriched Rice
- Frozen Strawberries with Ice cream
- Beverage

**WEDNESDAY**
- Chicken Curry
- Carrot and Raisin Salad
- Enriched Rice
- Fresh Fruit
- Beverage

**THURSDAY**
- Broth
- Eggplant Tortilla (omelet)
- Enriched Rice
- Chilled Canned Fruit Cocktail
- Beverage

**FRIDAY**
- Camaron Rebosado
- Pinakbet
- Enriched Rice
- Condensed Milk Custard
- Beverage

**SATURDAY**
- Roast Chicken
- Guisado (Sauteed) Cabbage
- Enriched Rice
- Ice Cream
- Beverage

SUNDAY
  Afritada Pork and Chicken
  Spinach Salad
  Enriched Rice
  Polvoron
  Beverage

SUNDAY
  Misua Soup
  Fried Lumpia
  Enriched Rice
  Cheesecake

## PARTY MENU SUGGESTIONS

### I

| | | |
|---|---|---|
| Olives | Fruit Juice Punch | Pickles |
| Potato Chips | Onion Dip | Cocktail Crackers |
| | Pancit Canton | |
| | Lechon | |
| | Liver Sauce | |
| | Chicken Salad | |
| | Tossed Green Salad | |
| | French Dressing | |
| | Enriched Rice | |
| | Sans Rival | |

### II

| | | |
|---|---|---|
| Celery Hearts | Fried Shrimp Flavored Chips (Kropec) | |
| | Carrot Sticks | Cucumber Slices |
| | Cream Cheese Dip | |
| | Lumpia Macao | |
| | Paella | |
| | Beef Tongue Estofado | |
| | Chop Suey Vegetables | |
| | Enriched Rice | |
| | Ginataan | |

### III

Cocktail Nuts
Pig Ears Kilawin
Fried Pork Rinds (Chitcharon)
Pancit Luglug
Fish Escabeche
Chicken Pastel
Lettuce-Tomato-Cucumber Salad
Enriched Rice
Fruit Salad

# ILLUSTRATIONS

1. **Ingredients**

2. **Cutting Methods**

WATER
CHESTNUTS

DRIED
MUSHROOMS

FRESH GINGER

(PLANTAIN)
COOKING BANANA

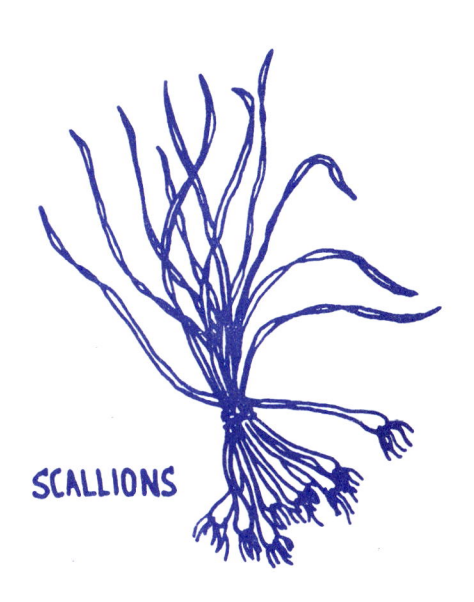

SCALLIONS

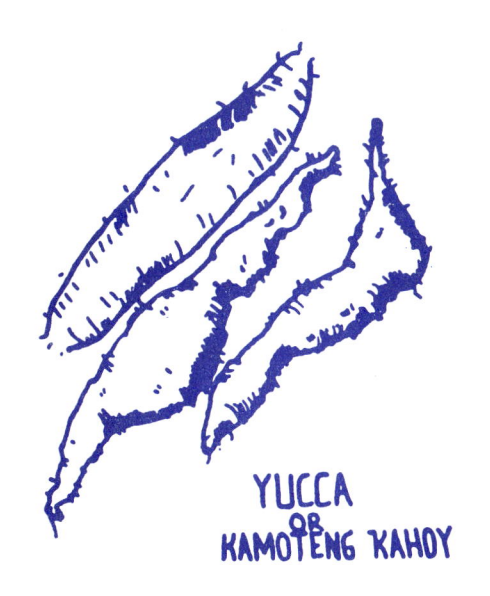

YUCCA
OR
KAMOTENG KAHOY

BAGOONG

**SOYBEAN CAKE OR CURD (TOKWA)**

**VARIOUS NOODLES, PACKAGED**

**Canton noodles** - Fried Egg noodles for Pancit Canton
**Bijon** - Rice sticks for Pancit
**Miswa (or Misua)** - Thread-like noodle for Soups

To Slice Slanting or Diagonally

Cubes (cut into 1" to 1½" square side)

To Dice

Thin Strips

Chop

Minced
(Finer-than chop.)

MEAT SLICED IN SMALL PIECES OR FINELY SLICED

SHELLED WHOLE SHRIMP

SHRIMP SLIT

SHRIMP SLIT INTO 2

GARLIC BULB

GARLIC CLOVE (2)

GARLIC CLOVE CRUSHED or POUNDED

# GLOSSARY

Arroz – rice.

Arroz Caldo (pospas) – rice soup.

Achara – pickle made with green papaya usually.

Achuete or Achiote – anatto seeds used for a reddish-orange coloring in dishes. A tablespoon of the seeds is rubbed with half a teaspoon of salt until color is produced. Add about half a cup of water, strain over dish and cook. May be substituted for saffron.

Adobo – a dish cooked with vinegar and garlic, with or without soy sauce. Popular Philippine dish is chicken-pork adobo.

Agar-Agar – gulaman. A gelatin derived from a red seaweed. Originated from Japan, marketed in slender sticks or blocks, or powder form. Knox unflavored gelatin is a good substitute.

Almondigas – meat balls.

Ampalaya – a bitter Philippine melon. May be bought fresh or canned in most Oriental food stores, labeled as "Bitter Melon" or "Bitter Cucumber."

Angkak – red-colored rice grains used to lend color to fermented fish preparations.

Anis mascado – nutmeg.

Apahap fish – sea bass.

Asado – in Philippines, a dish of meat or fish browned in a little oil and cooked with a brown sauce.

Baby corn – "tiny" corns bigger than thumb-size, usually canned and obtained from Oriental food stores.

Bacalao – dried codfish.

Bagoong – salted and fermented sea food, i.e., fish bagoong, shrimp, oyster or clam.

Bagoong Sauce – anchovy sauce. A reddish-brown liquid from fish bagoong, sold in bottles usually.

Banana blossoms or flowers – clusters of match-like flowers found inside a banana pod. Dried banana blossoms are sold in most Oriental food stores.

Bangus – milkfish, very popular in the Philippines. Has a delicate flavor but very bony.

Batter – a mixture of flour and liquid with or without other ingredients, of pouring consistency.

Bay leaf – laurel leaf used as an herb.

Bean sprouts – togue. Sprouted mongo beans.

Bibingka – Philippine rice-coconut milk pudding or cake baked usually in a banana leaf.

Bico – coconut-rice pudding.

Calabasa – pumpkin. The different types of winter squash can be used as "calabasa" in Philippine cooking.

Caldereta - a Philippine stew of goat's meat or lamb, usually.

Cardillo - a dish of fried fish, sauteed with sauce and beaten egg.

Cassava - kamoteng kahoy. Some food stores label it "yucca" or "Manioc." The root of a tropical plant.

Chayote - pear-shaped squash, which is greenish-yellow and firm.

Cheesecloth - a thin, cotton cloth with a loose weave. May be used for straining or for wrapping foods to be steamed.

Chinese cabbage - a type of flat-stemmed cabbage with light green leaves.

Chinese parsley (kinchay) - an aromatic, pungent parsley. Interchanged with coriander leaves.

Chitcharon or sitsaron - crispy fried pork rind or skin. Sold in cellophane packages as "Wise Bakon Delites," "Frito Lay Baken," etc.

Chop - cut into fine pieces.

Coconut milk - liquid extracted from grated coconut meat, diluted with water.

Cold fat - other names are leaf lard or omentum. Used for wrapping food stuffs to be cooked, like embutido.

Cube - cut into 1 or 1 1/2-inch square sides.

Daing - a fish, slit flat, seasoned with salt and dried. May be fried or broiled.

Deep-fat fry - cooking in enough hot oil to cover food being fried.

Dice - cut into small (1/2-inch) cubes.

Dinuguan - a chocolate-colored meat dish cooked in pig's or chicken blood.

Dried mushrooms, Chinese - brown mushrooms which give interesting color and flavor to a dish. First, they are soaked in cold or hot water until soft, then sliced or used whole before cooking. Sold in most Oriental stores and some supermarkets.

Embutido - ground meat roll, usually made with ground pork.

Empanada - small pastries filled with meat, either fried or baked.

Escabeche - sweet and sour fish dish.

Estofado - spicy stew or casserole.

Fold in - method of mixing, usually into egg whites, with a down-and-up (under-and-over) motion until ingredients are thoroughly mixed. Purpose is to keep the air already incorporated into the beaten egg whites.

Gabi - an edible tropical root. Labeled as "yautia" in food stores.

Garlic clove, crushed - a segment of the garlic bulb, pounded until mushy. Fresh garlic can be crushed by using a garlic press, mortar and pestle, meat pounder or pressed with the back of a spoon.

Goto - tripe (stomach). Beef tripe is popularly used.

Guisado - a dish using a basis of sauteed garlic, onion, pork and shrimps - (see saute').

Gulaman – see agar-agar.

Halo-halo – a medley of sweet fruits or preserves, top with crushed ice and milk.

Hibi – dried shelled shrimps.

Hoisin Sauce – a Chinese sauce which is thick, dark and spicy. Sold in cans at Chinese food stores. Used in cooking and as dip.

Kamoteng kahoy – see cassava.

Kangkong – swamp cabbage. Watercress, land cress or spinach are good substitutes.

Kaong – palm nut preserved. Sold in jars at Philippine and Chinese food stores.

Kilawin – dish of roasted goat cooked rare, or raw fish, or any other raw food, highly seasoned with onions, garlic and vinegar.

Knead – to mix and press dough hard usually with the heels of the hands, to make dough elastic.

Kropec – a shrimp flavored chip, fried to a crispy texture. Sold at most Oriental food stores as "Shrimp Flavored Chips," cooked or uncooked.

Langka or nangka – jack fruit. Sold as sweet preserves at Philippine and Chinese food stores.

Lapu-lapu fish – grouper, member of sea bass family.

Latik – coconut creme syrup made by boiling thick and rich coconut milk with sugar. May be purchased in jars from Philippine and some Chinese food stores.

Lumpia – Philippine egg roll wrap in lumpia wrappers, either fresh or fried.

Lumpia wrappers – egg roll skin. A round or square white tissue-like starch wrapper usually about 8 inches in diameter, sold in Chinese and Philippine food stores.

Luya – ginger root used fresh, dried or in powder form.

Lye water – lihiya, potassium carbonate solution sold in bottles at Chinese or Oriental food stores.

Makapuno – member of the coconut family having a very soft coconut meat. Sold as a sweet preserves at Philippine and Chinese stores.

Malagkit – glutinous or sticky rice. In powdered form, purchased in Oriental food stores as "Sweet Rice Flour." Malagkit grains are basically the same as "Sweet Rice" grains.

Marinade – seasoned liquid in which meat and other foods are soaked in.

Marinate – to soak in a seasoned liquid, to give more flavor to food, and sometimes to tenderize the meat.

Miki – fresh or dried wheat-egg noodle. May be substituted for egg noodles found in American food stores.

Mince – cut up or chop into minute pieces.

Misua thread-like wheat noodle, dried; Philippine water noodle.

Mongo – mung beans, greenish in color, bigger than rice grains.

Morcon – stuffed meat roll.

MSG – abbreviation for monosodium glutamate. A white, crystal powder used to bring out the flavor in foods. Common Philippine name is "Vetsin." A teaspoon or less of MSG in a dish is sufficient. Common American name is "Accent."

Nangka – "Jackfruit."

Oyster Sauce – a Chinese sauce made of salted oysters in soy.

Paksiw – a dish flavored with vinegar and garlic in broth, with or without sugar for a mildly sweet and sour taste.

Pancit – a Philippine sauteed dish made with noodles.

Pancit bihon – Philippine sauteed dish made with rice sticks or noodles.

Patani – fresh or frozen lima beans.

Patis – amber-colored liquid extract from salted and fermented seafood usually fish. When recipe calls for 1 tablespoon patis, about 1/4 teaspoon salt may be substituted, but without the flavor of patis.

Patola – a green Philippine squash with curvy lengthwise indentions. Zucchini or green summer squash may be substituted.

Pechay – a dark green Chinese cabbage sold at Oriental food stores as "bark choy" or "bok choy."

Pinipig – a type of immature rice, greenish, roasted and pounded until flat. Eaten with milk and sugar.

Pimiento – sweet red pepper eaten raw, canned or pickled.

Pipi-an – chicken and pork cooked with peanut sauce.

Plantain Banana – cooking banana. A good substitute for "saging na saba." Sold in supermarkets and Spanish-Latin stores.

Relleno – any stuffed dish.

Rice flour or Rice Powder – regular rice grains in powder form. Not as sticky as sweet rice flour or "malagkit."

Rice sticks – bihon. Fine, dried rice noodles usually sold in 1 pound packages at Chinese and other Oriental food stores.

Rice water – obtained from the first and second washings of rice, before rice is to be cooked.

Saltpeter – salitre. May be obtained in crystalline powder from druggists under the chemical name of potassium nitrate. Used for curing meat. Small quantities add a red color to meat, but an excess toughens it.

Sarciado – a dish of fried fish sauteed with sauce.

Saute' Guisa – to fry quickly in a small amount of fat, with continuous stirring. Sauteeing is a principal method of cooking Philippine dishes. In a small amount of hot oil, fresh crushed garlic is lightly browned, then sliced onions added and cooked while stirring until transparent. Sliced fresh tomatoes are stirred in next and cooked until mushy. Meat, then shrimps (if called for) are stirred in until meat pinkness is gone, before water or broth is added. A delicious aroma is produced while sauteeing and this is one indication of proper sauteeing.

Score - to make shallow cuts on the surface for decorative purposes or to prevent curling up.

Scallion - green or spring onion (sibuyas na mura). In Philippine cooking broth the green and white parts are used.

Shrimp Juice - liquid in which shrimp or raw shrimp shells are boiled in. In the Philippines, it is obtained by pounding raw shrimp heads and tails, adding water and straining the liquid. Used for flavoring.

Simmer - cooking below the boiling point. Boil gently over low heat.

Singkamas or Sinkamas - yam bean. Purple top turnip may be used as a substitute in cooking.

Sinigang - a dish boiled in ample water usually seasoned with tomatoes, onions and lemon juice.

Skewer - a long wooden or metal pin used to hold meat together while cooking; or used to pierce foods to be barbecued.

Sotanghon - sometimes called "bean threads" or "cellophane noodles." Fine transparent dried noodles made from mongo bean starch. Comes packaged in ounce sizes and sold at most Oriental food stores.

Steam - cooking in a covered utensil with enough water to produce steam while boiling.

Stock - liquid where meat, fish or vegetables are cooked in. Sometimes interchanged for broth.

Sweet Rice Flour - usually a Japanese brand "Mochiko" sweet rice flour (powdered 'malagkit'). Sticky when cooked as in rice cake or rice pudding.

Tahure - bean curd cheese obtained by fermenting bean curd in Chinese rice wine. Purchased in Chinese food stores, canned bearing name "Wet Bean Curd."

Tapa - meat slices cured usually with salt and/or vinegar.

Tausi - black soy beans salted and fermented.

Tinapa - smoked dried fish.

Tinola - a garlic flavored chicken soup.

Tokwa - fresh soybean curd or cake. Usually sold in 3-inch square cakes at most Oriental food stores.

Tuyo - dried salted fish.

Ube - Philippine purple yam.

Ubod - heart of palm. May be obtained canned from Latin food stores and some Oriental food stores. Used in lumpia fresh or sauteed.

Ukoy - usually a thin fried batter with shrimps, bean sprouts or bean curd.

Upo - a Philippine gourd. Substitute would be Chinese squash or Canadian squash.

Wanton Wrapper - egg roll wrapper. Sold in most Chinese stores in 6-inch or 3-inch square packages.

Water Chestnut - apulid. Sold fresh or canned. Opened can of water chestnut should be drained and transferred in a jar of fresh cold water and kept covered in the refrigerator for as long as 2 weeks. Water should be changed every other day.

Write your extra recipes here:

# INDEX OF RECIPES

## I. APPETIZERS, PICKLES, RELISH

| | |
|---|---:|
| Achara (Pickles) | 9 |
| Bagoong Alamang Guisado (Sauteed Salted Shrimp Fry) | 10 |
| Burong Isda (Fermented Fish) | 10 |
| Burong Kanin (Fermented Rice) | 10 |
| Chitcharon Chicken | 11 |
| Dilis Crisps (Anchovy Crisps) | 11 |
| Fried Bean Curd (Tokwa) | 11 |
| Fried Squid Strips or Rings | 12 |
| Kilawin (Pig Ears) | 12 |
| Kimchi (Oriental Pickled Cabbage) | 9 |
| Pata | 12 |
| Pinsec (See Pancit Molo, Note) | 13 |
| Relish Philippine | 10 |

## II. SOUPS, SALADS, DRESSINGS, SAUCES

| | |
|---|---:|
| Chicken with Misua Soup | 14 |
| Egg Drop Soup | 15 |
| Egg Noodle Soup | 15 |
| Hot and Sour Soup | 16 |
| Mami Chicken Soup (Chinese Style) | 14 |
| Misua Soup (Thread-like Noodle Soup) | 14 |
| Pancit Molo (Philippine Wanton Soup) | 13 |
| Vegetable Soup | 15 |
| Basic Philippine Marinade for Salads | 16 |
| Bean Salad Deluxe | 16 |
| Bean Sprouts (Togue) Salad | 17 |
| Burong Mustasa (Salt-preserved Mustard Greens) | 18 |
| Camote Tops Salad (Sweet Potato Green Buds) | 18 |
| Chicken Salad | 19 |
| Cucumber Salad with Peanuts | 19 |
| Fruit Salad | 19 |
| Mango Salad | 21 |
| Salted Egg Salad (See Salted Eggs) | 69 |
| Fresh Spinach Salad | 20 |
| Spinach Salad | 20 |
| Sotanghon Salad | 21 |

| | |
|---|---|
| Barbecue Sauce | 22 |
| Sweet and Sour Sauce | 22 |
| Liver Sauce | 22 |
| Sate Sauce | 23 |

## III. BEEF RECIPES

| | |
|---|---|
| Asado Beef (See Asado Chicken, Note) | 48 |
| Beef Oriental | 25 |
| Beef Sinigang (See Sinigang Pork or Beef) | 45 |
| Beef Steak Philippine | 25 |
| Beef Tongue Estofado | 26 |
| Beef Tortilla (See Pork or Beef Tortilla) | 44 |
| Calderetta | 26 |
| Callos (Beef Tripe) | 27 |
| Charcoal Broiled Steak | 27 |
| Empanada (Meat Turnover) | 28 |
| Goto Arroz Caldo (See Arroz Caldo, Note) | 69 |
| Meat Loaf | 30 |
| Mechado | 29 |
| Morcon (Beef Roll) | 30 |
| Picadillo (Boiled Ground Beef) | 32 |
| Pinapaitan (Bitter-Flavored Meat) | 31 |
| Pochero | 31 |
| Spicy Beef with Green Pepper | 32 |
| Tapa Beef (See Tapa Pork) | 47 |

## IV. PORK RECIPES

| | |
|---|---|
| Adobo | 33 |
| Afritada Pork and Chicken | 33 |
| Asado Pork (See Asado Chicken, Note) | 48 |
| Batchoy | 34 |
| Bicol Hot Express | 34 |
| Binagoongan | 35 |
| Burong Babi (Cured Pork, Pampangga-Style) | 35 |
| Chinese Sausage | 35 |
| Chitcharon | 36 |
| Chorizo de Bilbao (Spanish Sausage) | 35 |
| Dinuguan | 37 |
| Easy Barbecue Pork Chops | 37 |
| Embutido | 37 |

| | |
|---|---:|
| Fried Pork Slices | 38 |
| Guisado (Basis for Sauteed Dishes) | 38 |
| Ham Smoked Pork Shoulder | 39 |
| Higado | 39 |
| Humba (Pork in Brown Sauce) | 40 |
| Kari-Kari | 46 |
| Kekiam (See Kekiam Seafood/Pork Roll) | 63 |
| Kilawin (Pig Ears) | 12 |
| Lechon (Pork Roast) | 41 |
| Lechon de Leche (Suckling Pig Roast | 40 |
|     Liver Sauce | 22 |
| Lechon Sa Kawali (Pork Roast in Pan) | 42 |
| Longaniza (Sausage Philippine) | 42 |
| Menudo | 43 |
| Paksiw Leftover Lechon | 43 |
| Pata | 12 |
| Pata Paksiw (See Pork Paksiw, Note) | 44 |
| Pork and Chicken Tim (See Pato Tim, Note) | 54 |
| Pork Chop Barbecue (See Barbecue Sauce Recipe) | 22 |
| Pork or Beef Tortilla (Omelet) | 44 |
| Pork Paksiw | 44 |
| Sate Babi (Pork Barbecue Indonesian) | 44 |
|     Sate Sauce | 23 |
| Sauteed Pork with Cucumber | 45 |
| Sinigang Pork or Beef (Boiled) | 45 |
| Spareribs | 46 |
| Spicy Pork with Green Peppers | |
|     (See Spicy Beef with 7 Green Peppers) | 32 |
| Sweet and Sour Pork | 46 |
| Tapa (Dried Meat) | 47 |
| Tocino (Spanish Bacon) | 47 |

## V. POULTRY RECIPES

| | |
|---|---:|
| Adobo Chicken (See Adobo, Note) | 33 |
| Asado Chicken | 48 |
| Chicken Arroz Caldo (See Arroz Caldo) | 69 |
| Chicken with Asparagus | 48 |
| Chicken Barbecue (See Barbecue Sauce Recipe) | 22 |
| Chicken Boneless Relleno | 49 |
| Chicken with Cashews | 49 |
| Chicken Chitcharon | 11 |
| Chicken Curry | 50 |

| | |
|---|---|
| Chicken Empanada | 28 |
| Chicken Pastel | 50 |
| Chicken Salad | 19 |
| Chop Suey Philippine | 51 |
| Chicken with Misua Soup | 14 |
| Chicken with Mushroom Sauce | 52 |
| Chicken Pesa (Boiled) | 52 |
| Chicken Relleno | |
|     (See Chicken Boneless Relleno, Note) | 49 |
| Chicken Tinola | 51 |
| Finger-Lickin' Southern Fried Chicken | 53 |
| Fried Chicken Philippine | 53 |
| Roast Chicken Philippine | 54 |
| Pato Tim (Duck in Soy Sauce) | 54 |
| Peking Duck | 55 |
|     Thin Pancakes for Peking Duck | 55 |
| Pavo Asado (Turkey Roast) | 56 |
| Spicy Chicken with Green Pepper | |
|     (See Spicy Beef with Green Pepper, Note) | 32 |
| Thai Meat Salad | 56 |

## VI. FISH AND SEAFOOD RECIPES

| | |
|---|---|
| Asado Fish (See Asado Chicken, Note) | 48 |
| Bagoong Alamang Guisado | |
|     (Sauteed Salted Shrimp Fry) | 10 |
| Boiled Crabs | 56 |
| Boiled Lobster | 57 |
| Broiled Fish (Inihaw) | 58 |
| Camaron Rebosado (Fried Shrimp) | 64 |
| Clams Sinigang (See Fish Sinigang, Note) | 59 |
| Crab Omelet (See Crab Relleno, Note) | 57 |
| Crab Relleno | 57 |
| Daing (Marinated Fish) | 58 |
| Dilis Crisps (Anchovy) | 11 |
| Fish Cardillo (Sauteed Fish with Eggs) | 60 |
| Fish Sarciado (See Fish Cardillo, Note) | 60 |
| Fish Escabeche (Sweet and Sour Fish) | 60 |
| Fish Oriental | 59 |
| Fish Steamed Oriental | 61 |
| Fish Paksiw (Pickled Fish) | 61 |
| Fish Paksiw with Coconut Milk | 61 |
| Fish Pinangat | |
|     (See Fish Paksiw with Coconut Milk, Note) | 61 |

| | |
|---|---|
| Fish Sinigang | 59 |
| Fish Tinapa American (Smoked) | 62 |
| Fish with Tahure or Tausi | |
|    (Salted Bean Paste or Black Beans) | 62 |
| Five Color Shrimp | 67 |
| Five Color Scallops (See Five Color Shrimp, Note) | 67 |
| Fried Squid Strips/Rings | 12 |
| Lobster Cantonese | 58 |
| Mussels Saute | 68 |
| Mussels Baked (See Mussels Saute) | 68 |
| Prawns in Crab Fat (Aligue) | 65 |
| Rellenong Bangus (Stuffed Milk Fish) | 64 |
| Shrimp Relleno (Stuffed Shrimp) | 65 |
| Shrimp Sinigang (See Fish Sinigang, Note) | 59 |
| Squid Adobo | 66 |
| Squid Broil | 66 |
| Squid Sinigang (See Fish Sinigang, Note) | 58 |
| Stuffed Squid | 67 |
| Tuyo (Dried Fish) | 63 |
| Tempura Seafood/Vegetable | 68 |
| Tahong (See Mussels Saute) | 68 |

## VII. RICE, NOODLE (PANCIT), EGG ROLL (LUMPIA) RECIPES

| | |
|---|---|
| Arroz Caldo (Pospas) | 69 |
| Arroz Ala Valenciana | 70 |
| Bam-i (Cebu Noodle Dish) | 72 |
| Egg Noodle Soup | 15 |
| Fermented Rice (See Burong Isada/Kanin) | 10 |
| Fried Rice | 71 |
| Lugao Special (Porridge) | 71 |
| Lumpia Fried (Philippine Egg Roll) | 77 |
| Lumpia Fresh | 78 |
|     Ubod Lumpia Fresh (See Lumpia Fresh) | 78 |
|       Wrappers for Lumpia Fresh | 76 |
|       Sauce for Lumpia Fresh | 78 |
| Lumpia Macao | 75 |
| Misua Soup (Thread-like Noodle Soup) | 14 |
| Pancit Bihon (Rice Sticks) | 72 |
| Pancit Canton (See Pancit Bihon, Note) | 72 |
| Pancit Luglug or Palabok | 73 |
| Pancit Molo (Philippine Wanton Soup) | 13 |
| Paella | 70 |
| Pinsec (See Pancit Molo, Note) | 13 |

| | |
|---|---:|
| Sotanghon (Bean Thread Noodle) | 74 |
| Sotanghon Salad | 21 |
| Spaghetti with Meat Sauce | 75 |
| Tamale Filipino Special | 81 |

## VIII. VEGETABLE RECIPES

| | |
|---|---:|
| Achara (Pickles) | 9 |
| Ampalaya Guisado (See Cabbage Guisado, Note) | 83 |
| Bean Sprouts (Togue Salad) | 17 |
| Broccoli Guisado (See Cabbage Guisado, Note) | 83 |
| Cabbage Guisado | 93 |
| Cauliflower Guisado (See Cabbage Guisado, Note) | 93 |
| Calabasa Guisado (Sauteed Winter Squash) | 93 |
| Chop Suey Philippine | 51 |
| Dinengdeng | 86 |
| Eggplant Relleno (See Eggplant Tortilla, Note) | 84 |
| Eggplant Tortilla (Omelet) | 84 |
| Green Beans Guisado (See Cabbage Guisado, Note) | 83 |
| Honeyed Snow Peas and Asparagus | 86 |
| Laing (Visayan Dish with Coconut Milk) | 86 |
| Mongo Bean Guisado | 84 |
| Pinakbet Deluxe | 85 |
| Pokey-Pokey (Sauteed Eggplant) | 85 |
| Relish Philippine | 10 |
| Spinach Salad | 20 |
| Fresh Spinach Salad | 20 |
| Tempura Vegetables (See Tempura Seafood) | 68 |

## IX. BEVERAGES AND MISCELLANEOUS RECIPES

| | |
|---|---:|
| Cantaloupe Drink | 123 |
| Green Mango Juice | 123 |
| Sago Drink | 123 |
| Salabat Drink | 124 |
| Chestnuts (Castanias) | 124 |
| Casta-Niog (Chestnut-Coconut) | 124 |
| Hopia | 91 |
| Master Mix (All Purpose Baking or Biscuit Mix) | 92 |
| Pan de Sal | 89 |
| Pan de Sal From Scratch | 90 |
| Salted Eggs (Itlog na Maalot) | 69 |

| | |
|---|---|
| Siomai (Chinese Meat Dumplings) | 79 |
| Siopao (Steamed Meat Bun) | 79 |
| Siopao Baked (See Siopao, Note) | 79 |
|     Siopao Sauce | 80 |
| Ukoy (Shrimp Fritters) | 80 |

## X. DESSERTS, MERIENDA (SNACKS), BIBINGKA (RICE CAKES), AND SWEETS

| | |
|---|---|
| Banana in Syrup | 122 |
| Bibingka (Rice Cake) | 108 |
| Bibingka Cassava | 108 |
| Bibingka Hot Cake | 109 |
| Bibingka Kanin | 108 |
| Bitsu-Bitsu (See Pilipit Recipe, Note) | 93 |
| "Brazo" Egg White Roll | 109 |
| Buchi-Buchi (Fried Sweet Rice Ball) | 90 |
| Buko Pie (Young Coconut Pie) | 96 |
| Cascaroon (See Pilipit Recipe, Note) | 93 |
| Champorado (Chocolate Rice) | 110 |
| Champorado Deluxe | 110 |
| Cheesecake | 102 |
| Cocoroons | 103 |
| Condensed Milk Custard | 111 |
| Dila-Dila | 111 |
| Easy Bibingka | 107 |
| Empanaditas (Pastry Tarts) | 96 |
| Ensaimada Americana | 89 |
| Espasol (Sweet Rice Chewies) | 120 |
| Espasol Special Reodica's | 121 |
| Flan Topped Chiffon Cake | 104 |
| Food for the Gods | 102 |
| Fruit Salad | 19 |
| Ginataan | 111 |
| Gulaman Almond | 114 |
| Halo-Halo (Mixings) | 112 |
| Ice Cream, Mongo, Macapuno, Langka, Atis, Guayabano, Ube | 117 |
| Kamote (Sweet Potato) Fritters (See Maruya, Note) | 93 |
| Kutsinta | 112 |
| Langka (Jackfruit) Pastry (See Macapuno Pastry) | 99 |
| Latik (Coconut Creme Syrup) | 121 |
| Leche Flan (Custard) | 113 |
| Leche Flan American | 113 |

| | |
|---|---|
| Lubi-Lubi (Mashed Banana with Coconut) | 115 |
| Macapuno (Soft Coconut) Pastry | 99 |
| Maja Blanca (White Pudding) | 107 |
| Mamon (Sponge Cake) | 99 |
| Maruya (Banana Fritters) | 93 |
| M.D.'s Cake with Cream Cheese Frosting | 100 |
| Nilupak (Pounded or Mashed Banana) | |
| (See Lubi-Lubi Recipe) | 115 |
| Palitao | 113 |
| Pilipit (Twists) | 93 |
| Polvoron (Powdered Candy) | 119 |
| Puto (Steamed Rice Cake) | 92 |
| Puto Bulacan | 93 |
| Puto Chinese (Spongy Steamed Rice Cake) | 93 |
| Puto Seco (Butter Cookies) | 107 |
| Sans Rival (Cake without Rival) | 100 |
| Sapin-Sapin (Layers) | 115 |
| Sapin-Sapin Pudding | 116 |
| Silvanas with Butter Icing | 103 |
| Strawberry Shortcake | 101 |
| Suman Sa Ibus | 95 |
| Suman Sa Lihya (See Suman Sa Ibus, Note) | 95 |
| Sweet Potato in Syrup (See Banana in Syrup, Note) | 122 |
| Taho (Bean Curd in Syrup) | 116 |
| Tinudok or Carioca | 94 |
| Torta Cebu (See Mamon, Note) | 99 |
| Tupig (Sweet Rice Bars) | 117 |
| Turon (Wrapped Bananas) | 94 |
| Wheat Germ Yellow Squash Bread | 95 |
| Yema Candy | 20 |

## XI. HOW TO'S

| | |
|---|---|
| How to use a 1200-1500 Calorie Controlled Diet | 8a |
| How to Extract Fresh Coconut Milk | 126 |
| How to Bone a Chicken | 127 |
| How to Select Crabs (See Boiled Crabs Recipe) | 56 |
| How to Clean Fresh Beef Tongue | |
| (See Beef Tongue Estofado Recipe) | 26 |
| How to Saute (See "Guisado" Recipe and Glossary) | 83 |
| How to Clean Squid (See Squid Adobo Recipe) | 66 |
| How to Make Substitutions for Philippine Items | 125 |
| How to Cook Chestnuts (See Chestnuts Recipe) | 124 |
| How to Sprout Mongo Beans | 17 |
| How to Cook a Husband (or Spouse?) | 127 |

## ABOUT THE AUTHOR

Marilyn Ranada Donato came to the United States for postgraduate training in Dietetics at Grasslands Hospital, Valhalla, New York, in 1962. She was Staff Dietitian at Yale-New Haven Hospital, New Haven, Connecticut from 1963-1968. Various work experiences include therapeutic, clinic, teaching, administration and consultation at Sinai Hospital, Detroit, Michigan; Hospital Career Development Program in Boston City Hospital, Boston, Massachusetts; Catawba Hospital in Virginia, with Hospital Dietetics-Interstate United. Her current professional work involves an independent private practice in Nutrition and Dietetics; Nutrition lecturer at Virginia Western Community College Nursing and Dental Hygiene Programs; consulting dietitian at nursing homes and hospitals renal consulting dietitian; and food editor for several Philippine-American newspapers.

Active and involved in several community, civic, religious and professional organizations, Marilyn was selected an Outstanding Young Woman of America in 1973. She was president-elect and president of Southwest Virginia Dietetic Association in 1974-1976; president of the Board of Directors of Catholic Family and Children's Service of S.W. Va., Inc. 1980-81, and president, YWCA, Roanoke, Va., 1990; vice president of the National Conference of Christians and Jews, Roanoke Chaper, 1993; president-elect and president of the Roanoke Academy of Medicine Alliance, 1994-1996.

In 1982 Marilyn received an award as an outstanding woman of Southwest Virginia sponsored by the Roanoke Times and World News. And in 1992 the Daughters of the American Revolution General James Breckinridge Chapter awarded their Americanism Medal Award to Marilyn. Likewise, the Virginia Skyline Girl Scout Council selected Marilyn as their 1992 Women of Distinction awardee.

Marilyn was born in Laoag City, Philippines, the eldest daughter of Judge Santiago Ranada and Mary Javier Ranada. She is married to Antonio T. Donato, M.D., a thoracic surgeon. The Donatos are blessed with six children: Mary Anne, Bernadette, Pauline, Jude, Grace and James.

Marilyn considers this book the first of its kind published in America, a work of art in sharing one's culture and "secrets" so that others may taste and enjoy.

Dr. and Mrs. Florencio A. Hipona

**Notes:**

# BOOKORDER

I hope that you enjoy this cookbook and wish to order more copies to share with friends or give as gifts.

## Philippine Cooking in America

3707 Alton Road, S.W.

### Roanoke, Virginia 24014

Telephone: 1-540- 345-2033

FAX: 1-540-344-3872

Please rush me!

_____ copies at $19.95 a copy.

**SAVE!** Order two for $38.00

Please Print:

Total amount enclosed $. _____

Name: _____

Address: _____

City _____ State _____ Zip _____

---

## Philippine Cooking in America

3707 Alton Road, S.W.

### Roanoke, Virginia 24014

Telephone: 1-540- 345-2033

FAX: 1-540-344-3872

Please rush me!

_____ copies at $19.95 a copy.

**SAVE!** Order two for $38.00

Please Print:

Total amount enclosed $. _____

Name: _____

Address: _____

City _____ State _____ Zip _____